AMERICAN PEWTER

COVERED SUGAR BOWL BY G. RICHARDSON AND THE BOTTOM OF THE SAME BOWL WITH
RICHARDSON'S MARKS

AMERICAN PEWTER

BY

John ARRett

J. B. KERFOOT

*With Illustrations from Photographs by the Author
of Specimens in his own Collection*

CROWN PUBLISHERS
NEW YORK

Republished by Gale Research Company, Book Tower, Detroit, 1976

**Library of Congress
Cataloging in Publication Data**

Kerfoot, John Barrett, 1865-1927.
   American pewter.

   Reprint of the 1942 ed. published by Crown Publishers,
New York.
   Includes index.
   1. Pewter--United States. 2. Pewter--Collectors
and collecting. I. Title.
NK8412.K4   1976   739'.533'0973   75-29215
ISBN 0-8103-4147-6

TO
MY WIFE
ANNIE HAIGHT KERFOOT
WHO
EVEN AFTER LIVING THROUGH THE MAKING
OF A BOOK ABOUT IT
STILL LOVES
PEWTER
THIS VOLUME IS LOVINGLY
DEDICATED

CONTENTS

A REFERENCE LIST OF THE ILLUSTRATIONS

AMERICAN PEWTER

.·.

CHAPTER I

COLLECTING, COLLECTIBLES, AND COLLECTIBILITY

IF it weren't for the jackdaw, the pack-rat, and several other feathered and
furred creatures with strong collectors' instincts, one might be tempted
(in the introduction to a collectors' manual) to refer to Man as "The
Collecting Animal."

Manifestly, however, he is only one of them.

But this fact does not really detract from the interest or the significance
of his habit. Rather, it furnishes it with an evolutionary background and
identifies it as a human superstructure raised upon the foundation of an
instinct.

In other words, that which, in the squirrel, is an inherited mechanism of self-
intrenchment, has become, in the collector, a subtle technique of self-express-
ion, self-emphasis, and self-extension.

The squirrel is as safe as his hoard.

The collector is as famous as his collection.

Of course it is unlikely that either of them looks at the matter exactly from
this angle. The squirrel probably does not fancy himself as a far-sighted chap
and a good provider. Few collectors say to themselves, "Go to! Let us make
for ourselves a name collecting birds' eggs — or Botticellis." Both of them
collect, no doubt, just because they like it.

But the fact remains that the squirrel collects only nuts — and only such
nuts as will keep (and keep him) through the winter; and that the collector
collects only — but what *is* the common denominator of collectibility that
runs through the whole gamut of collectibles, from birds' eggs to Botticellis?

Come to think of it, no one of the many collectors' manuals I have had dealings with has ever paused to inquire.

Most collectors, I imagine, at some stage of their careers, have tried to collect the uncollectible; or at the very least have devoted themselves for a time to matter of low collectibility.

I recall undertaking, when a boy in Chicago, to make a collection of specimens of wood from all the vessels that sailed the Great Lakes.

The idea, I think, grew out of a paper-cutter I had seen which was said to have been made from a piece of the frigate *Constitution*.

At any rate, the pursuit, for a time, proved most exciting. I communicated the fever to a small band of enthusiasts. We haunted the waterfront; outwitted watchmen; boarded lumber schooners and grain boats; marked our trophies for identification; met to swap yarns and compare possessions.

We even had a real collectors' tempest in a teapot over the question as to whether, in the case of steel boats, a piece, say, of kindling from the cook's galley should be admitted as a legitimate "specimen."

But we soon found that there was no distinction in "collecting" those boats that came regularly to port. And the boats that came only semi-occasionally soon became indistinguishable except as names. A *Mary Ann* of Mackinac was just as good as, but no better than, a *Susan Jane* of Sheboygan. The affair degenerated into a mere race for numbers. And, as far as we could see, the numbers were endless.

We took up postage stamps.

Here, then, is the determinative factor of collectibility — the numbers must never be endless.

Any series, to be a collectible series, must be closed at both ends. Any field, to lend itself to the collector's uses, must be entirely fenced in. And if the closed series is so long, or the fenced field so large, that the boundaries are invisible to the naked eye; then it must needs be divided up into manageable subdivisions, based either on natural lines of cleavage or on lines of arbitrary demarcation.

For collecting is a game, and competition is the soul of it. And competition is only possible under compression. And you can't maintain compression in the open air.

That is why only First Editions of living authors are of interest to collectors.

It also explains the fact that the paintings of prominent artists jump in price when they die.

And it is not the least of the reasons why, from the beginning of history onward, "antiques" have been so dear to the collector's heart. For while the Dictionary tells us that an antique is "a specimen of antique art, especially Roman or Greek," the Dictionary is talking in its sleep. An "antique" may be *any specimen of human handicraft that belongs to a closed series.*

For it is not positively, but only relatively, that the oldness of an "antique" takes on importance in the eyes of a collector.

Thus among collectors of American glass you will find those who specialize in early "snake-skin" Sandwich looking with disdain upon those who collect late Sandwich hen dishes. And you will find collectors of Stiegel being supercilious about collectors of any Sandwich whatever. And if you could present to a collector of Factory Wistarburg one of the first dozen pieces blown at that pioneer institution in 1739, he would probably lose his mind. Yet few collectors of American glass would look upon an excavated Roman tear bottle as anything but a curiosity.

So that it is not generally, throughout the whole field of human handicraft, that relative oldness counts; but only locally, between different subdivisions of one series, or between different classes of one subdivision. And even here it is not really for itself that this relative earliness is valued; but rather as a symbol of that increasing rarity that usually accompanies it. For Rarity is the ultimate flower of that root that we have called the closed series. Rarity is compression made manifest. Rarity — near to hand if possible, but far-sought-out if must be — is the very oxygen of the collector's atmosphere.

All this is delightfully illustrated in the history of English pewter collecting — a history, by the way, that only covers the last thirty years.

In England, as in America, the making of pewterware on the old lines continued well into the first quarter of the nineteenth century. And it throws a strong light on the rapidity with which changes have come in the modern world and upon the completeness with which the discarded is forgotten in it, to note that when, in 1887, the entertainment committee of a small society of English artists, wished to stage a discussion on the subject of pewter, Mr. H. J. L. J. Massée was appointed a sub-committee of one to arrange the matter "because he was the only member present who owned a piece of pewter."

This meeting — which he conducted alone because he could find no pewter-lovers to help him — bore late but excellent fruit in the shape of Mr. Massee's pioneer treatise on "Pewter Plate," published in 1904, and in the pioneer exhibition of pewter arranged by him at Clifford's Inn Hall in London the same year; from which twin events may be dated the public interest in English pewter.

Here, then, was an interest (primarily esthetic, but rich in patriotic association and antiquarian allure) sprung up in a handicraft that had for generations been knit into the most intimate and habitual doings of the nation. And here was a growing body of young, enthusiastic student-collectors vying with each other in exploring the new field and in making reports on their investigations. If you knew nothing of the ways of collectors and of the character of their handbooks, you would imagine that the result of these conditions would be a catalogued survey of the whole field. You would expect to be able, in almost any treatise on the subject, to find such information as would enable you to identify, classify, and locate in the development of the handicraft any specimen that had come into your hands as a beginning collector.

But instead of this, you would probably find both your author's text and his illustrations given over to excavated Elizabethan dishes, earth-eaten and crumbling; to miniature eucharistic vessels buried in the tombs of medieval Abbots and recovered one does not inquire how; to Cromwellian salts, Charles II tankards, and Tappit Hens. You would find the fourteenth century spoken of with awe; the fifteenth with bated breath; the sixteenth and seventeenth with respect, and the eighteenth with tolerance. But if the nineteenth was mentioned at all, it would be in the sort of whisper with which one refers to a relative who has been convicted of forgery or suspected of stealing sheep.

Perhaps, then, puzzled at finding no mention of your treasure trove in this expert's volume, you would take another look at your specimen of pewter to try to find what ailed it. And, seeing that it did, as you had thought, have dignity of form, beauty of line, textural quality, and an exquisite soft brilliance, you would ask yourself, "Why is *this* beyond the pale? Why is *it* relegated to that category of cats and dogs that this author evidently has in mind when he says that 'nowadays it is hard to find anything in pewter worthy of a collector's notice'?"

The answer could be captured in a word. But perhaps if we approach it somewhat warily from behind we shall stand a better chance of taking its true meaning alive.

The art of the pewterer is, as we shall see presently, a very old one. It was practiced in England at least as early as the twelfth century. But at that time, and for centuries afterward, England, and indeed the whole European world, was too desperately poor for pewterware to be a common possession. It was not until after the Restoration that it came, even among the very rich, into daily household use. And the eighteenth century was well under way before the average wealth of England permitted the substitution of pewter for wood in the houses of the moderately situated.

But then, for the better part of a hundred years, all England more or less ate off of pewter, drank out of it, and used it for half the adjuncts and utensils of ordinary living.

So that when, in the eighteen-nineties, our new collectors began to canvass their virgin field, the trenchers and chargers and vessels, dating, say, from 1730 to 1810, soon proved to be too common to be collectible. The vessels of the Great Lakes themselves were not more impossible. And so, like entombed miners, forced to push back into half-forgotten galleries and abandoned levels in search of oxygen to breathe, these pioneers in pewter were forced back and back into forgotten centuries and abandoned customs until they found the rarity that they could not live without and remain collectors.

And this needful attribute of rarity was what your unlisted piece of pewter lacked. It was not beauty, or decorative value, or fine craftsmanship, or sentimental association with the past, that it fell short in. And, indeed, you will note that our author (whether he fully sensed the distinction or not) did not say that it was hard to find pewter worthy of the attention of a lover of beauty, or of an appreciator of fine craftsmanship, or of a student of past customs. He said, "worthy of a collector's notice." And from the point of view of a collector, although an object has all these things, and has not rarity, it is nothing.

Yet beauty and craftsmanship; historic interest; racial, national, and regional association; — these things are by no means indifferent to the collector. So far, indeed, is this from being true that, either singly or in some one of their many combinations, they are the very things that usually determine the character of his collecting.

Thus, sooner or later, the collector who is sensitive to beauty will be found collecting some closed series where art has been active. And sooner or later the collector who loves fine workmanship will be found specializing in some finished phase of craft development and skill.

And in such cases a collector seldom acknowledgedly, or even consciously, gives to mere rarity the precedence over these other values. On the contrary, it is these other qualities that he is conscious of desiring in the objects of his search. It is in terms of these other attributes that he thinks of his treasures. And it is for these other excellences that he praises them. But since the game — the collector's game — that he is playing with them can be played only when rarity coexists with these other traits, he is always in danger of confusing the nature of the stimuli to which he is reacting, and is often found misnaming the emotions with which he responds to them. Like the doctor who speaks of a "beautiful case," the collector is only too prone to translate the thrills that he gets from rarity into terms of esthetic feeling.

Yet this is, on the whole, a good sign. For the journey from perfect squirrel to perfect collector — from being a connoisseur in nuts to being an amateur of beauty — is a long one, the early stages of which have little to do with esthetics. Rarity is a demonstrable fact. The sensing of beauty is a personal adventure. When we make the misstep of confusing the two, we are already beginning to walk alone.

And we seldom, as beginning collectors, attempt to walk alone. We then generally have our wants predetermined for us. We collect, as it were, on the dotted line. The ordinary stamp album, with its indicative blanks and its fore-ordained groupings, is the classic example. Here we find not only personal choice and responsibility reduced to a minimum, but we get competition as nearly chemically pure as it is practicable to supply it.

A small boy's game? Yes, but a large boy's game, also. For the boy is father to the man; and many men are the living image of their father!

"Have you a ninety cent 1869?"

"Have you the ninety, 1869, inverted?"

"Have you a twenty cent St. Louis?"

"Have you a two cent British Guiana?"

These are, respectively, questions that office boys, stock brokers, millionaires, and emperors ask each other with, respectively, identical interest and excitement. The dotted line is there in all of them. But the degrees of rarity have been graded to suit the increasing developments of purse and of perseverance.

Collectors are thus seen to fall, theoretically, into two groups. First, the group whose symbol is the stamp album. The group who like their competition "straight." The group whose dream is to fill all the blank spaces — or to fill more of them than the other fellow. And, second, the group to whom competition is the sauce, not the meat. The group in whose activities personal taste and personal choice must be at least reasonably free to state and restate themselves. The group whose ideal achievement and satisfaction lie, not in the competitive solving of a picture puzzle, but in the competitive creation of a picture.

In practice, of course, the two groups actually merge by indistinguishable gradations, and there is something of both types in almost all of us who are collectors. He is a hard-boiled competitionist, indeed, who does not invest the rarity possessed by a rival and lacked by himself with some more sublimated form of attractiveness than just the ability to equalize the score between them. And he would be an esthete too Simon pure for this world whose joy in a beautiful possession would not be dashed by seeing two hundred duplicates of his treasure in a Woolworth show window.

Two urges, then, meet in every collector — that of competitive rivalry and that of personal taste; the desire to beat the other fellow, and the desire to follow one's own inclination. And inside of the boundaries set by his financial resources, every collector's activities are largely conditioned by the clash of these two forces. If both of them are weak, he may begin and end by seeking simply what his immediate competitors already possess. If both are strong in him, he may completely turn the tables and make the collectibles of his own discovery and choosing the goal and envy of his competitors. But, in any case, his collection will be expressive of the man.

It follows, of course, that any closed series or group of collectibles will rank high or low in collectibility according as it is capable of appealing to many or few of these collectors' susceptibilities. And we shall find, I think, that American pewter appeals to almost all of them.

American pewter is late. But America itself is late and so are all its collectibles. The statement in that form is meaningless. The significant fact is that American pewter has been neglected — has even, on occasion, been thrust disdainfully aside — because it has been classed with the uncollectible English pewter of the same period. Examined anew as an American handicraft — a closed series in itself — the whole case is altered.

To begin with, there is no American pewter — not even the latest and most negligible — that is not rare enough to be collectible. Here the lover of fine line, of pure form, or beautiful texture, does not have to deny his taste for the sake of his competitive enjoyment. He can give free rein to all of these collectors' impulses at once. The lover of craftsmanship cannot go wrong, competitively, while following his own bent here. Nor the student of our national past and of our social development. Nor the sentimental patriot, hunting eagles. Even the catalogue fan can be happy.

For whereas there have been thousands of pewterers in England, so that their individual work never has been, and never conceivably will be, collected as such; the entire list of known American pewterers runs to only a few over two hundred names, with less than half of these represented by surviving specimens of their work. The ideal collection of American pewter would, therefore, probably consist of chosen specimens showing, not only all types of the ware made here, but each of the marks of each of the makers whose work survives. It would be a small collection, but —

There is one variety of collector to which we have made no reference. Perhaps one might call the type the *Hors Concours* collector, or the secret competer. At any rate, these collectors are typified in my own mind by the Chinese gentleman of the old school who, with a broad jade ring over the joint of each thumb to show that he did not have to work, used to walk abroad with some exquisite amber or crystal treasure sewed inside the crown of his hat — walked sedately down the street, internally enraptured to be hiding so much beauty from the unsuspecting passers-by.

To the secret competers of America, I suggest that they serve a dinner to their philistine friends on pewter plates, the unseen bottoms of which bear the touches of Frederick and Francis Bassett, Henry and William Will.

CHAPTER II

THE WHAT, WHEN, AND WHERE OF PEWTER

NICE old ladies who keep antique shops in the Latin Quarter in Paris tell you that French pewter is superior to English pewter "because it contains more silver."

Nice young ladies in America point to a bright piece in your collection and say that they suppose "there is more silver in that piece."

The wisest reply to make to the old ladies of the Latin Quarter is "Oui, Madame." It is usually sufficient to tell the young ladies in America that it isn't more silver, but more "elbow grease" that has made the bright specimen brighter. But it is well for the pewter collector both to know that silver is never intentionally added to the ingredients of pewter and to understand why.

Pewter is an alloy of which the chief factor is tin.

The other metals added to tin (either singly or in varying combinations) to make different forms of this alloy were copper, lead, antimony, and bismuth. Zinc has figured in most modern alloys of this category, but seems to have been little used in early times.

Copper, antimony, and bismuth were used to toughen, harden, and temper the tin. Lead was used to cheapen it as well as to make it malleable. And silver is too soft for the first of these purposes and too costly for the second.

It is, however, a fact that small quantities of silver are discoverable in very ancient specimens of pewter. But the silver is there, not because any one put it in, but because no one could then get it out. Silver and lead are almost always found together in nature. The crude methods of early smelting were unable completely to separate out the more precious metal. And it therefore followed that some silver was occasionally present as (one might say) an impurity in the lead used in the making of pewter. Thus do great oaks of popular tradition grow from small acorns of metallurgical error.

The discovery of pewter antedates all records. But it was probably contemporary with that of bronze — the other alloy of copper and tin that gave its name to the age of man's dawning mastery over metals.

Copper, tin, and lead were naturally among the first metals mined, smelted, and experimented with.

Copper, with about ten per cent of tin added, makes the "bronze" of the early weapons.

Tin, with about twenty per cent of copper added, makes the finest of pewter.

The two facts could scarcely have escaped being twin discoveries.

However, our ancestors of the Bronze Age being more concerned over weapons with which to kill their enemies than over dishes off of which to eat them, the softer alloy may not have interested its original discoverers.

The craft's actual beginnings, at any rate, are deep buried in the back of beyond.

Coming down to historic times, the Greeks knew pewter well. The Romans appear to have used it freely. The Chinese were early experts in its esthetic and utilitarian employments. When Europe began to emerge from the Dark Ages, the pewterers' craft came back with it, everywhere, into the light again — in Italy and in Spain, in Germany and in the Netherlands, in France and in England.

As the medieval machinery of trade control — the guilds — developed, organizations of pewterers, both on the Continent and in England, took over under Government authority the supervision and guidance of the handicraft.

On the Continent these organizations were generally local in scope, deriving authority from city and district. In England the London Guild became nationally supreme.

This body appears to have existed and functioned for many years before it was recognized and backed by the authorities. The so-called Ordinances of 1348 probably gave official sanction to trade rules already developed in this way. The organization was finally given a charter by Edward IV in 1473; and by this document "The Craft of Pewterers" was authorized to assay all pewter brought into London and even to search the premises of pewterers throughout

England, confiscating all pewter found to be below the established standards of the company.

For over two hundred years this famous "Company of Pewterers" (as it came to be officially styled after 1612) was the autocrat and arbiter of the. trade in the British Isles and, in spite of its stormy career and varying authority, ruled on the whole to the honor of the craft and the good of the public. Early in the eighteenth century changing economic conditions began to undermine its prestige, and from that time on the slowly losing fight of pewter against more modern wares continued to sap its strength. Like many of the old guilds, however, The Worshipful Company of Pewterers is still in existence and continues to maintain a Guildhall on the original site in Lime Street.

There has perhaps never been another example of so complete an abandonment of a material that had been so widely used for so long a period as that furnished by the disappearance of pewter from employment in the modern world.

A hundred years ago there were numberless unfashionable but well-to-do households, both here and abroad, where pewter was still the ordinary tableware. Fifty years back of that there were few homes whose owners were not either inordinately wealthy or very poor where this was not the case. And yet, to-day, there are not only hundreds of thousands of Americans who do not know what pewter is or what it was used for; but there are astonishing numbers of people whose pleasure derives largely from their interest in antiques who are actually in the same case. The fact that people ate off of pewter seems to be the most incredible part of the matter. "Doesn't it make things taste?" they ask. And people, all of whose drinking-water reaches their faucets in lead pipes and much of whose food comes to their kitchens in tin cans, are sure that pewter must poison things if they stand in it.

There is, however, a penumbra of half-knowledge surrounding this core of complete ignorance.

There are ladies who, when brought face to face with a garniture of the old metal, glance at it with raised eyebrows and say, with a decided lorgnette intonation, "Pewter? Oh, yes, that was kitchen ware."

Now fashions come in at the top and go out at the bottom. At least they used to do so when they moved slowly enough for their course to be observed, through a society that had a recognizable top and a bottom that knew itself as such. To-day, of course, fashions merely rage and subside, like other epidemics. If you will take the trouble to compare the course of Spanish influenza with that, say, of bobbed hair, you'll get what I mean.

Pewter, however, was a creature of slower centuries. It took it something like four hundred and fifty years to make the journey from the castle gate, through the state banquet hall and the lesser dining-rooms, down to the servants' quarters, and so to the kitchen and out by the back door.

People who happened — along in the eighteen-forties and eighteen-fifties — to see this final exit may be pardoned for not suspecting that the disreputable-looking creature had seen better days.

There has perhaps never been a generation for which it was as difficult to grasp the conditions of their near ancestors' lives as it is for ours.

We live in a world literally flooded with goods and gear; a world where economic well-being is somehow, apparently, conditioned upon waste; a world where it is only when all of us are buying, and using up, and throwing away as fast as possible, that the mines and the farms and the factories can all produce full tilt, and so supply the funds that will enable us to keep on buying and using up and throwing away.

If this phase of our world had been described to our ancestors, they would have thought us mad.

On the other hand, our ancestors by only a few removes lived in a world where a silver spoon or a pewter bowl were *possessions*, worthy of being specifically mentioned in a last will and testament. And when this phase of their world is brought to our notice, we think them poverty-stricken.

And yet, while we remain convinced that they were queer fish, these ancestors of ours, with few possessions and nothing to do evenings, let us remember — we of the world of interchangeable parts and quantity production, of quick discards and easy replacements, of aluminum utensils and ironstone china — that in that world that has passed, each article, whether of silver or of wood, of pewter or of porcelain, was made in the pride of craftsmanship by a man who took joy in the making, and was intended to be used with some sense of permanence by a man who not only expected to be proud of it during his lifetime, but to hand it down to his descendants — all joys that we have lost.

One needs only to push back to the Golden Age of Queen Bess to arrive at a period when, for most plebeian newly-weds, a wooden bowl to serve the stew in would have completely furnished the pantry. If a horn spoon accompanied it, so much the better. For the rest — fingers were forks, even at court, and the sheath knife at one's belt was the proper use for each of the twenty or more courses that composed the state banquets of the day.

In fashionable circles, however, plates — or "trenchers" as they were called — were coming in. Squares of coarse bread served the purpose well, and, being eaten at the end, saved trouble. But the really *chic* thing was wood. Square, flat slabs, at first. Then these same with shallow, plate-like depressions turned in their surfaces. This form frequently had a little supplemental depression turned in one corner for salt. And the squared shape of these early trenchers fitted in with the early custom of placing a number of them at each place at table, ready for use with successive courses. As many as six or eight — set square edge to square edge and sometimes two deep — were set at a great noble's place at table; and fewer for those of less rank. After use, they were scraped clean much as are our butcher blocks to-day.

Antonio De Navarro, in his delightful "Causeries on English Pewter," from which many of these facts about early wooden tableware are quoted, calls attention to Shakespeare's making Caliban sing,

> "No more dams I'll make for fish;
> Nor bring in firing at requiring
> Nor scrape trenchering, nor wash dish;"

and also to the fact that Pepys, under date of October 29, 1663, complains that they "had no change of trenchers" at the Lord Mayor's banquet that day.

It must not be thought, however, that because the use of wood thus continued, the vogue for pewter had not come in. Nor, indeed, that the possession of silverware in the great families had not been contemporary with the use of both wood and pewter. The facts are that the few who could afford to do so owned services of silver; although they normally used these for dining-room display, while eating from either pewter or wood, or both. And that the many of the next financial rank owned pewter in greater or lesser quantity — using much of this, normally, as a garnishment of the room while eating from wooden trenchers. This custom was practically universal. Pepys again (January 4, 1667) mentions serving to some guests "ale and apples, drunk from a wooden cup . . . and they full of admiration at my plate." The custom, indeed, is embalmed in the language of the day, like a fly in amber. A "garnish" became the pewterers' trade term for a complete set of a dozen platters, a dozen flat bowls, and a dozen small flat plates.

The wealth of England was now increasing fast. By the beginning of the eighteenth century the use of pewter was practically universal among people of any means whatever. Yet just about the same time imported porcelain from China, followed before long by that of European make, began in its turn to knock at that Castle Gate through which first wood and then pewter had made their initial bows to Society some centuries earlier. Thus for a little while the great trinity of tableware materials — wood, pewter, china — coexisted in English usage. But wood soon disappeared — leaving, of course, by the kitchen door. Before the nineteenth century was well started, pewter was following wood — using the same exit. Even porcelain, at last, was forced to take refuge in collectors' cabinets to escape the same fate.

It was the twilight of the gods of the hand-wrought. Before long, by those who were wakeful, the first hesitant cock-crows of our machine-made age could be heard in the night.

Le roi est mort. Vive le roi!

The finest old pewter contains no lead; but either copper alone, antimony alone, or combinations of the two, with, occasionally, a little bismuth added. The resulting grades of the alloy were chiefly used for the making of trenchers, chargers, and other flat-ware. A tin-antimony combination of low tin content was used for the making of spoons, salts, and other small articles by a branch of the trade known, in England, as "triflers," and was, in consequence, itself known as "trifle."

"Ley" metal was the name given in England to the tin-lead form of pewter where the lead content amounted to about twenty per cent; and most drinking-vessels were made of this alloy.

Candle-moulds, organ pipes, and such bulky articles were made out of pewter that was approximately forty per cent lead.

Practically every one who begins to be interested in pewter has (and has to get over) a desire to know just which, and just what proportions of, these ingredients are contained in his specimens. He wants to be able to say, "This is tin and copper — about four of tin to one of copper. That's what gives it that clear ring and that lovely surface. On the other hand, *this* is the antimony alloy. Do you notice how different it sounds when you strike it?"

But he has to get over this particular craving, because the only way to satisfy it would be for him to cut a piece out of each of his precious specimens; have all the pieces assayed; and then be careful to pin the right report on what was left of the right trencher, tankard, or porringer — "Which," as our old friend Euclid used to say, "is absurd."

You see there used, in the old days, to be as many formulæ for making pewter as there were recipes for mixing rum punch. And just as, in the latter case, the results, for the layman, merely divided themselves into extra good punch, good punch, and punch; so in the former the multiplicity of formulæ finally boils down into extra fine pewter, fine pewter, and pewter. And the modern amateur of the metal cannot hope to do more than become proficient in distinguishing between these classes.

It is said that some forty or so of the old formulæ have come down to us. And it is no doubt true that many times that number have failed to do so, except it be in the cipher message of some pot or porringer that it would take a chemist to decode. It is, then, more to satisfy a natural curiosity than to aid in differentiating the several classes of pewter that I print some characteristic formulæ, taken from a longer list given by Mr. H. J. L. J. Massée:

	Tin	Copper	Lead	Antimony	Bismuth
Fine pewter (early)..................	112	26			
Plate pewter (1).....................	100	4		8	
Plate pewter (2).....................	112			8	
Plate pewter (3)	90	2		6.7	
Trifle.............................	83			17	
Ley metal..........................	80		20		
Organ pipe metal....................	60		40		
Queen's metal.......................	100	4		8	
Good britannia metal................	150	3		10	
Limoges pewterers...................	100		4		
Montpelier pewterers................	90		10		
Spoons.............................	95.6	1.06	3.64		

In one respect, however, this list can do more for the beginning collector than just satisfy his idle curiosity. It affords him an opportunity of meeting under informal circumstances — quite *en famille*, in fact — that accredited villain of the American pewter drama, Britannia.

As a matter of fact, "britannia" was a trade name given to a superfine grade of pewter by some English makers along about the middle of the eighteenth century. That it then differed little if at all from other tin-copper-antimony alloys in occasional use can be seen by taking the fourth formula in the above list, calculating it for one hundred fifty parts of tin instead of for ninety parts as given, and comparing the result with the ninth formula. We then get the following:

	Tin	Copper	Antimony
Plate pewter (3)	150	3.33	11.
Good britannia metal....................................	150	3.	10.

It looks as though the name may have been more of an advertising dodge than indicative of a metallurgical innovation. And it may not be altogether a coincidence that this advertising name was adopted just at the time when pewter's monopoly of the tableware business was being first seriously threatened by the growing use of china.

In the records of the Pewterers' Society for the year 1710–11 there is an entry referring to the state of the trade as "now reduced to a verry deplorable condicion in this kingdom and in fforeign parts."

In 1715, in Burslem Parish in Staffordshire, there were forty-two potters, their total expense accounts for the year being calculated at £6400. By 1786 the number of these establishments in the district had increased to eighty, and by 1802 to one hundred and forty-nine. By 1851 the value of the district's output was well over one million pounds sterling and the making of pewter had practically ceased.

It is, then, no great wonder if the pewterers of 1750 in England thought that a good patriotic name given to a good grade of English pewter might start a backfire of fashion against the newfangled china stuff that was beginning to keep them awake nights.

And the idea proved a good one. The newly named ware became very fashionable; although, in the long run, it was as a competitor of Sheffield plate that it made its success and that it managed to survive after pewter had lost its fight and gone under.

For britannia, slowly at first, but later with increasing rapidity, changed its pewter-like character and ceased to be worthy of its parentage. At first it was merely that what had been superfine pewter came to be bred a bit *too* fine. Then it came about that in the effort to correct the more obvious faults of pewter — its softness and its liability to damage from heat — these faults were, as the lens-makers say, *overcorrected*. Gradually the moonlight glow of the old metal's surface faded, and the cold, repellent light of practicality took its place. That which was hard in fact became hard in feature. Then the toughness that underlay the looks was found to lend itself admirably to the machine-rolling and power-pressing of the new factory methods of manufacture; and soon the new demand for cheapness at the expense of taste and quality was being satisfied with the thin, skeletonized imitations of earlier forms and with the new decorative enormities of the middle nineteenth century.

Actually then — and the early realization of this fact will save the beginning American collector infinite trouble and confusion — the tin-copper-antimony alloys that are indubitably fine, and to be called "pewter," merge into those that are progressively less fine, until they come to coincide with our later-day notions of "britannia," so gradually that no hard-and-fast line of differentiation exists between them.

On the other hand, the beginning collector is certain to hear britannia spoken of as though it were a pariah, and to see it referred to in all the known terms of human misprisement. He is therefore liable, long before he knows when this metal is really despicable or whether a given article has any of the horrid substance in its make-up, to conclude that anything is ugly and inferior to which the name of "britannia" is attached. This attitude, undiscriminating as it is, matters little in an English collector, to whom all "britannia" is merely a late manifestation of a prolific and hence uncollectible pewter period. It is, however, a quite superfluous handicap for a student of American pewter, whose interest is specifically centered upon, and whose activities have precisely to do with, just that hundred years during which this transition took place.

Let us put it that at some point of this process of development and transformation will be found the finest pewter of the tin-copper-antimony type. The exact spot, like the exact character of the alloy, is a matter of taste, not a matter of fact. But whatever specific mixture may make, for a given judge, the chosen "best pewter" of this type, from this metal, as from a continental divide, *the country runs downhill both ways*. On the pewter slope it declines toward "leadiness." On the britannia side it falls off toward "tin-panishness." And when the beginner has once grasped this situation, he has received about all the real help that is likely to come to him on this point except what reaches him through his own handling and observation of the different alloys.

Books, let us pause to note, may be a valuable aid to the student. Like maps to the traveler, they are in many cases indispensable guides to the busy and un-instructed beginner. They offer him analyzed and ordered information through which he may orient himself in the country of connoisseurship. But they are no more a practicable substitute for experience than are those same maps the equivalent of personal familiarity with a countryside.

Connoisseurship consists, in large measure, in trained sensitiveness to particular values. It is only, as Pater says, "the roughness of the eye" that ever makes any two things look alike to us. Let us amplify his statement and add that it is but the "roughness" of the ear, of the palate, and of the finger-tips, that ever make any two things sound or taste or feel alike to us. Connois-seurship, then, comes with the more or less superficial smoothing down of these sensuous roughnesses — be these of eye or of ear, of touch or of taste. And the only abrasive that can do this polishing for us is contact and more contact with the actual experiences themselves.

The unquenchable desire and the unending quest, therefore, of the student and collector of pewter should be opportunity, and more opportunity, and still more opportunity to handle pewter — pewter of all types and grades, of all nationalities and periods. Opportunity to hold it and heft it; to run inquisitive fingers over its differing surfaces; to take in its varying sheens with appreciative and discriminating eyes; to test its many tensions and listen to its revealing rings. This, and the firm resolve to take no man's word for it, but to find out for one's self what pewter does to one's own senses. For only so can come to us the joy of feeling our own sensitivenesses develop and refine. And only so, when at last we have to make up our own mind and declare our own opinion, can we base a decision firmly on what we feel, and not gropingly on what we think some favorite author meant, or disingenuously on what we think it will be expected that we say.

CHAPTER III

PEWTER IN AMERICA BEFORE 1750

WHEN America was settled, pewter was still ware for the wealthy. Taken by and large, in the England of the day, woodenware was the vogue and habit of everyday life. Yet there were few households of the thrifty that did not include among their treasures a pewter salt, a pewter dish or so, perhaps even a silver spoon. And it was of course the dearest desire of every housewife, and no doubt of most householders, to see the dresser shelves garnished with enough gleaming pewter bowls and platters to brighten the living-room, to establish their social position beyond need of inquiry, and fittingly to set forth the main viands of the Christmas board, the marriage feast, and the funeral ditto.

And it was, on the whole, no different in New England.

All students of early Colonial conditions, and all of us who are interested in American pewter — and in pewter in America — are indebted to Mr. George Francis Dow for his "Notes on the Use of Pewter in Massachusetts during the Seventeenth Century," published in the July, 1923, number of "Old Time New England," the bulletin of the "Society for the Preservation of New England Antiquities." More enlightening information, culled from original sources, has seldom been compressed into four pages of print.

He tells us of a list of "such needeful things as every planter doth or ought to provide to go to New England," sent back to Old England in 1629 by a member of Governor Endicott's staff. It mentioned no pewter. On the other hand, it included "wooden platters, dishes, spoons and trenchers," among the things "needeful." By the way, not only these dishes, but something to eat off of them was advised. One of the items on the list was a year's provisions.

This list went to England on one of the vessels of a small fleet that had brought supplies to the colonists. Among these supplies were seed grain, potatoes, tame turkeys, copper kettles, brass spoons and ladles, and "pewter botles of pyntes and qrts." If any such have survived, I have not been lucky enough to see them. No doubt the fact that there has always been a modest money value attached to the metal contained in pewter articles has militated against their continued survival after they had ceased to be of use. Bottles — of any sort — were treasures in the early days. Not only were they as convenient as they are to-day (there were, indeed, more uses for them than now); but, for another hundred years after the date we are discussing, they were hard to come by and not to be replaced quickly when broken. Glass was scarce, costly, and fragile. No doubt "pewter botles" were in good demand. And they doubtless proved better sailors than their breakable relatives. They could not, however, have been as satisfactory for household use as glass, if for no other reason than that they hid what was in them. And this may account for their disappearance into the melting-pot, when glass bottles of approximately like date of origin have survived. One used frequently to find old glass bottles that had been kept in use and handed down from one generation to another. I recall a tottering old codger in Allowaystown, New Jersey, close to the site of the Wistarburg glass factory, who had his birdshot stored in a very early bottle which, he said, his father had used for a like purpose. It had been made, he said that his father told him, "out yonder" — that is to say, at the Wistarburg factory. As a matter of fact, the bottle was English, but very early.

It was not very long, however, before the New England settlers were receiving other pewter articles than "botles" from the home market. We shall examine in a few moments the invoice of a pewter shipment made from London to Boston in 1693 — an invoice which Mr. Dow tells us came to light recently in the Massachusetts archives. But, meanwhile, a glance at some of the bequests and inventories of the intervening years as given by him will afford us a notion of the well-to-do-ness of some of the colonists as gauged (and there were few better gauges at the time) by their possessions of pewter. There is, of course, no way of telling how many of these articles were brought over by the settlers when they came, and how many of them were subsequently bought as their venture in the New World prospered. But as we find "pewter botles of pyntes and qrts." arriving for sale in 1629, and lots of the value of £76 being landed in 1693, it is safe to conclude that quite a lot of the inventoried metal was of post-emigrational acquirement.

In 1635 Sarah Dillingham, a widow, died at Ipswich. She owned 40½ pounds of pewter, valued at £2.14.0.

In 1640 Bertha Cartwright, of Salem, disposed, by will, of three pewter platters, a double salt cellar, six spoons, and a porringer.

In 1643 Robert Massey, of Ipswich, left four pewter platters to each of his three children and divided five silver spoons among them.

In 1645 Lionell Chute, also of Ipswich, died possessed of pewter salts, saucers, and porringers to the number of fourteen; of two pewter candlesticks and a pewter bottle. He also owned one silver spoon.

Mary Hersome, of Wendham, in 1646, owned one pewter platter and two spoons; while Michael Carthrick, of Ipswich, had ten pewter dishes, two quart pots, one pint pot, one beaker, one small cup, one chamber pot, and a salt.

In 1647 William Clarke, a rich merchant of Salem, died. His estate included an interesting list of furniture, six silver spoons and two small pieces of plate, and a great array of pewter which (I can hear a triumphant "I told you so" from certain quarters) was kept in the kitchen. It seems almost superfluous to note that "kitchen," "dining-room," and, for the most part, "living-room," were one and the same in Massachusetts in the sixteen-forties.

He had twenty platters, two great plates and ten little ones, one great pewter pot, one flagon, one pottle (a "pottle" was half a gallon), one quart, three pints, four ale quarts, one pint, six beer cups, four wine cups, four candlesticks, five chamber pots, two lamps, one tunnel, six saucers, and miscellaneous old pewter; the whole valued (shades of the auction room!) at £7.

Mr. Dow gives us a look in upon many other interesting wills, inventories, and bequeathments. But we will go no further than to note the case of Matthew Whipple, of Ipswich, the inventory of whose estate totaled £287.2.1, and included eighty-five pieces of pewter weighing 147 pounds and valued at £16.9.16. A silver bowl and two silver spoons are listed. Also twenty-one "brass alchimic spoones," valued at four shillings and fourpence each, and nine pewter spoons. He also owned six dozen wooden trenchers, besides wooden trays, platters, bowls, and dishes.

In one will a "salt seller," a "tunell," and a "great dowruff" are mentioned. A tunnel is an old name for a funnel. I take a "dowruff" to be a mixing-bowl, since "dow" was "dough" in provincial England, and to "ruff" or "rough" means to shape up. In other documents such articles as pewter "basons," "sawcers," cullenders, and bedpans were listed. There is even one mention of a mustard pot.

In 1693 John Caxy, of London, shipped to Joseph Mallenson, his agent in Boston, a consignment of merchandise, the invoice of which by some rare good luck got into the Massachusetts archives; from which, by luck plus industry, no doubt, it has now emerged again. Cloth, clothing, hardware, implements, and pewter were included in the shipment. The portion of the invoice referring to pewter is reproduced in full by Mr. Dow and is most enlightening. I copy it with grateful acknowledgments.

When I first struck this list I was so puzzled by the question as to what a "Drume Fatt" might be that I could only half take in the list of that mysterious container's contents. I find that a "fat" or "vat" was an archaic term for a measure of about nine bushels. I assume, therefore, that this shipment of pewter came in drum-shaped hogsheads or whatever of about that size. For the other odd names, a "pottle" was, as already stated, a half-gallon. An imitation gold of the seventeenth century was known as "alchemy." We have just seen Matthew Whipple disposing of his twenty-one "brass alchimic spoones" that the appraisers "spoke of so highly." The "alcamy" spoons of this invoice were probably of the same nature. I take the "powder" ones that immediately follow to mean "pewter." It is quite evident that pewter came into use before spelling-bees.

Here is the list:

One Drume Fatt No. 2 Containing

12 Pottle Tankards at 3s. 10d. ps		£2. 6.0.
12 Quart ditto at 3s.		1.16.0.
24 Midle ditto at 2/6		3. 0.0.
24 Small ditto at 2s.		2. 8:0.

12 doz. Large Poringers at 9s. 6d. per doz.	£5.14.0.
12 doz. Small ditto at 8/	4.16.0.
3 pr New-fashon'd Candlesticks at 4s.	12.0.
3 pr. ditto at 3s.	9.0.
2 pr. Round ditto at 2s. 10d.	5.8.
a Fatt Cost	7.0.

One Drume Fatt No. 3 quantity

18 Large Chamber Potts at 2/10 ps	£2.11.0.
30 Middle ditto at 2s. 8d.	3.10.0.
40 Small ditto at 2s.	3.10.0.
12 doz. Alcamy spoons at 2/9	4. 0.0.
24 doz. Powder ditto at 2.3d. p doz.	2.14.0.
12 Large Salts at 2s. 2d. ps	1. 6.0.
24 Middle ditto at 20d. ps	2. 0.0.
48 Small ditto at 12d. ps	2. 8.0.
18 Basons. 32 qts at 12d.	1.12.6.
2 doz Sawcers at 9s. p doz.	18.0.
4 doz Small ditto at 7s. p doz.	1. 8.0.
2 Pottle Wine Measure Potts at 5/6	11.0.
6 Quart ditto Potts at 2/8	16.0.
6 Pint dotto Potts at 22d. ps	11.0.
6 halfe Pint ditto at 14d.	7.0.
6 Quartern ditto Potts at 9d. p ps	4.6.
a Fatt Cost	7.0.

One halfe Barell Fatt No. 4 cont.

78 dishes qt 265 at 9d½	£10. 9.9½
A Fatt Cost	3.6.
	£76. 2.5½

Where data are as hard to come by as they are in the American pewter field prior to the Revolution, it behooves us to extract as much information as possible from every find. It is therefore worth while to analyze this list into its significant elements. It boils down, then, to the following:

24 dozen spoons	1d. and 2d. each
24 dozen porringers	6d. and 9½d. each
7½ dozen chamber pots	2s. to 2s. 10d. each
7 dozen salts	12d. to 2s. 2d. each
6½ doz. dishes; total capacity 265 quarts	9½d. per quart
6 dozen covered tankards	2s. to 3s. 10d. each
6 dozen "sawcers"	7d. and 9d. each

1½ dozen "basons" total capacity 32 quarts at   1s. a quart
½ dozen sets tavern measures 1 quart to 1 gill   6s. 5d. the set
2 half gallon measures for big taverns   5s. 6d. each
8 pair candlesticks   2s. 10d. to 4s. the pair

This arrangement gives us, quite graphically set forth, both the shipper's estimate as to the probable requirements of the New England market at the moment, and his rating of the probable demand as between the various types of articles included in the list.

Probably the first thing that would strike a collector of American-made pewter — which is to say, of such pewter articles as the market called for one hundred years after this shipment was made — would be the almost total absence of flat ware. The list includes no trenchers, no platters, no chargers.

It should be noted in this connection that an almost complete absence of pewter trenchers is shown by the wills and inventories just quoted (as well as by those from which these were selected). The "two great plates and ten little ones" belonging to William Clarke, of Salem, are the only indication of such ownership contained in these documents. Even the wealthy Matthew Whipple, whose eighty-five pieces of pewter weighed 147 pounds (not much room there for light eight-inch plates) owned six dozen wooden trenchers besides trays, platters, bowls, and dishes of the same material.

Perhaps the six dozen "sawcers" in the two sizes included in this shipment may be regarded as the entering wedge, colonially speaking, of what was then the growing vogue among the well-to-do in England — namely, the substitution of pewter trenchers, or eating-plates, for the old-time wood. The prices asked for these "sawcers" (7d. and 9d. each), being very high compared to most of the shipment, would bear out this notion; indicating that they were a fashionable novelty for which fancy figures could be asked. It is also to be noted that Mr. Whipple, the sole recorded possessor of pewter plates, is also the only recorded owner of these "sawcers." He was evidently very much up to the minute.

We are told by Mr. Massée that the dishes then called "sawcers" were really (in shape) small flat plates. And dishes that exactly answer this description were still being made by the post-Revolutionary American pewterers. The sizes of these small plates seem to have ranged from four and a half inches to six and a quarter inches in diameter; and they were used well into the nineteenth century as sauce dishes and cup plates. In one case that I know of (Christ's Church, Middletown, New Jersey), one of them, made by Boardman & Hart — a firm that started business in 1828 — was used as a paten. So that it would seem as though this "saucer" model not only led the vanguard of pewter plates into use, but also brought up the rear guard as they retreated into oblivion.

Coming back, now, to a consideration of the list of this 1693 shipment as revelatory of the pewter "best sellers" of its day in America, it is no surprise to find that spoons at 1d. and 2d. were at the head of the polls. Then, as now, only the poor "got the horn." In the matter of the next item on the list — the twenty-four dozen "poringers" — we are somewhat at sea. The English are said to have applied the name "porringer" to a two-handled dish of similar design (sometimes called a "caudle-cup") much used both there and on the Continent, but little seen, in later days, in America; and to have called what we know as a porringer a "bleeding dish." The latter was also, on occasion, called a "blood porringer." It is therefore likely that the twenty-four dozen dishes of this importation were of the two-handled, English type.

The next item on the list — seven and a half dozen of them — is eloquent of the beginnings of luxury among the pioneers. It will be recalled that our friend William Clarke, rich merchant of Salem, already owned five in 1647. No installer of open plumbing in the eighteen-nineties was prouder than William, probably. How he would have sympathized with the modern slogan of "2000 rooms with 2000 baths."

The seven dozen salt cellars in three sizes that follow, and the high prices attached to them, are quite in line with what we would expect. The salt cellar was probably the most thought of, and, as the Japanese would say, "honorable," vessel of the entire household economy. Something of the ceremonial glory of its feudal status and use still clung to it. And the chances are that the first piece of pewter plate installed in a new home or aspired to by the newly successful was, in the seventeenth century, a salt cellar. On the other hand, unlike porringers and other dishes in active use, one salt cellar would generally last a lifetime.

The "dishes" of the next item doubtless included, beside the "great" and other "dowruffs," handled and handleless vessels for the serving of soup and stews, and even punch. The habit of pricing deep serving dishes of all kinds by the quart strikes us as curious; but only because we are accustomed to another way of expressing what is doubtless an equivalent method of grading prices according to cost. One is, however, left undecided as to whether the difference in price between nine and a half pence a quart for this lot of large dishes and one shilling a quart for the "basons" lower down the list is due to the wholesale character of their greater size or to an inferior pewter being used in them. One ventures to guess the latter.

The tankards, as we have seen from the inventories, were for private use as well, possibly, as for the supplying of taverns and hostels. The dozen and a half of "basons" were dishes of the shape still called basins by collectors, but they were used as vegetable dishes, as pudding-dishes, and, in the case of the small ones, as dishes from which to eat soup, bread and milk and such like food. Their name derived, probably, from their use in forkless times as "finger-bowls" — to use our equivalent phrase.

The six sets of graded measures — from a quart to a gill — were no doubt for tavern use. Occasionally they may have figured in the kitchen of some well-to-do housewife. But these sets, so very plentiful in England, have never been much more frequently met with in this country than this list would indicate to have been the case in its own day. No specimens of American make have ever come to my notice.* The limiting of the top-size measures of the set (the pottle or half-gallon) to two is quite of a piece with the scant numbers of the smaller sizes. These measures also came in gallon size, and a really complete set would include this monster. The eight pairs of "New Fashon'd" candlesticks were manifestly in the nature of a feeler. These, in the wilderness, bordered on magnificence.

---

* A half-gallon, "baluster," measure by Timothy Boardman & Co. has come into my possession since this was written. Also a pint measure by Philip Fields.

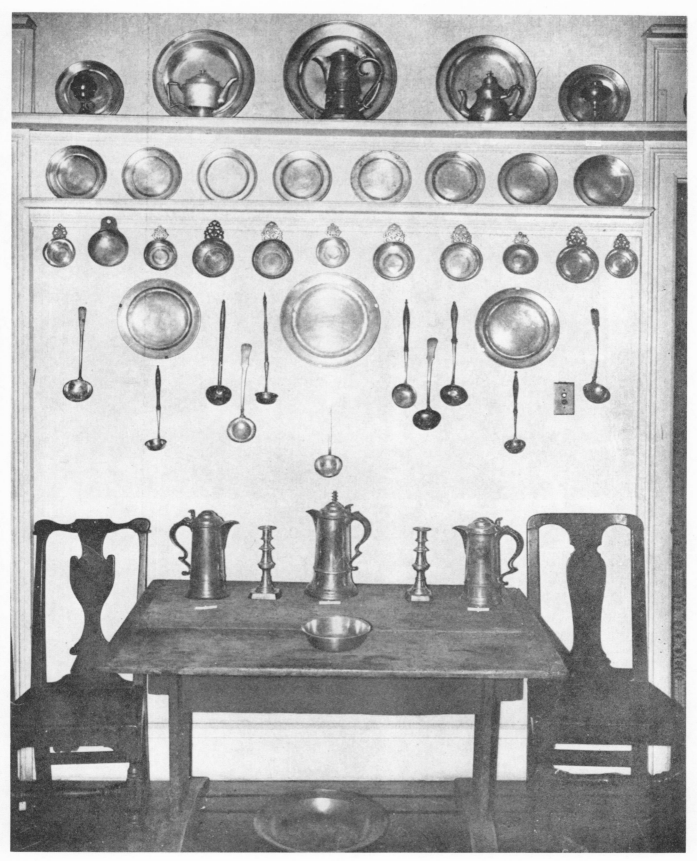

Fig. 1

PANEL ON NORTH WALL OF AUTHOR'S PEWTER ROOM

Fig. 2

A REMARKABLE BASIN WITH DOMED COVER

Diameter, 14 inches
Total height, 9 inches
Marked "Boardman Warranted"

Fig. 3

A SCREW–TOP TANKARD BY ROSWELL GLEASON

$4\frac{3}{4}$ inches high
4 inches wide at base

Fig. 4

CABINET OF MARKED LAMPS

From author's collection

Fig. 5

CABINET OF CANDLESTICKS

From author's collection

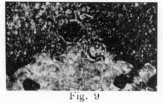

Fig. 9

Fig. 8

Fig. 10

Fig. 7

Fig. 6

Fig. 11

Fig. 12

A GROUP OF THE INITIALED PORRINGERS FOUND IN NEW ENGLAND TOGETHER WITH THEIR RESPECTIVE MARKS

No definite information is as yet available as to the origin of these pieces

Fig. 13

A GROUP OF AMERICAN MARKED BASINS AND MUGS IN THE AUTHOR'S PEWTER ROOM

Fig. 14

PEWTER FRAMES USED IN THE SECOND QUARTER OF THE NINETEENTH CENTURY

3¼ inches in diameter

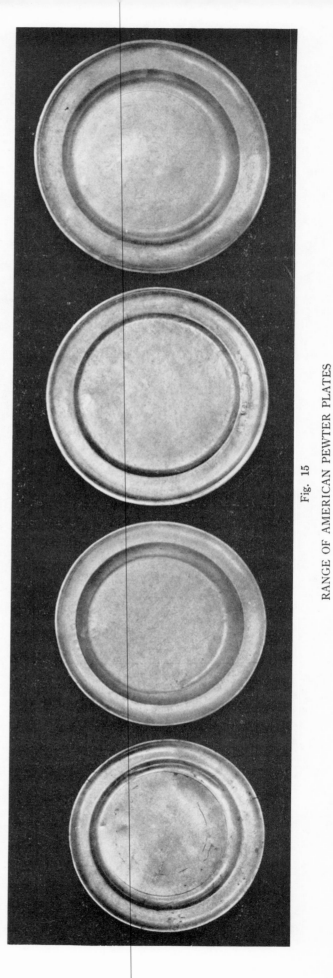

Fig. 15

RANGE OF AMERICAN PEWTER PLATES

5½ to 15 inches

There is no reason to believe that up to this time, or indeed for half a century afterward, much pewterware was made in the American Colonies. It is true that the names of a few men are known to us who lived in Boston, Philadelphia, and New York in the seventeenth century and who were known as pewterers. But without exception, so far as I am aware, these names are trophies of hunts through old records — no one of them, to my knowledge, being anywhere known to exist impressed upon a surviving specimen of its bearer's handiwork.

In a sense, of course, this is to be expected; and cannot, by itself, be regarded as indicating that no marked pieces by these men existed or exist. But it is really only one of a number of facts, the joint consideration of which inclines me, for the present at least, to this opinion.

There is, indeed, only one fact that might lead us to believe it possible that much pewter was made and marked here before 1750. This is the fact that the desperate need of the American armies for raw material came near, during the Revolution, to sweeping the country clean of metals. To us who, in wasteful twentieth-century America, have seen discarded tinfoil wrappers gathered by charitable ladies to be sold for war purposes for the benefit of the poor; who know how copper roofs and all other secular metal hoards were confiscated in Germany; — to us this melting-down of the pewter plate in the revolting Colonies is easily seen to have been inevitable. But while a ruinously large percentage of the existing pewterware of America disappeared during the Revolution, *it did not all disappear*. And for the purposes of our inquiry the portion that survived is legitimately to be regarded as an assayer's sample.

Now during the past twelve years a great quantity of pewter — many thousands of plates, for example — all from sources where it had lain *perdu* in this country since the metal's use was discontinued here, has passed through my hands for examination. This may seem rather an amazing statement, considering the present comparative scarcity of such pewter. But a dozen years ago the "runners" — local dealers who make a business of house-to-house searching for salable articles — derived a small but fairly steady return from the purchase and resale of old pewter. One seldom visited one of their shops without finding a pile of from ten to fifty plates, brought in within a few weeks from the countryside roundabout, and waiting only for the shop's clientèle to have a chance to pick them over before being sold to the junkman for old metal.

My personal observation of this stream of pewter led me to believe that it contained on the average about one American marked plate to from one hundred to one hundred and twenty-five English ones. A good five per cent of the English pewter in this stream antedated the Revolution, most of this being older than 1750. But while quite a little — three or four per cent — of the American plates bore the marks of the makers who worked just before, as well as just after, the Revolution, I have never seen or heard of a marked piece of American pewter antedating 1750.

I do not, of course, mean to deny the possible existence of a few such pieces. But I do contend that this absence of American pewter of the seventeenth and early eighteenth centuries is exactly what the then prevailing conditions would lead us to expect. For not only was the America of those days far from wealthy and by no means given to luxurious indulgence, but the few people of means who did gratify their taste for fine things quite naturally preferred the London article to its local imitation.

Even in so fine a product as the lovely output of the Stiegel glasshouse at Manheim, Pennsylvania, we know from the advertisements printed in the journals of the day that the owner was driven to appealing (and appealing in vain) to the patriotism of his fellow Americans to try to overcome the preference of the provincial public for the imported article. Moreover, breakable as the Stiegel offerings were, and difficult as he found it to induce the home market to absorb them, there are probably hundreds of times as many Stiegel articles surviving to-day as there are pieces of marked American pewter of even the same late — that is to say immediately pre-Revolutionary — period (1765–74).

How much more unlikely is it, then, that the individual artisan pewterers of Boston, Philadelphia, and New York, of the generation before Stiegel and of the generation before that again, should have been able successfully to compete with the exporting members of the all-powerful organization of the Society of Pewterers of London? Or how likely is it that many of those listed in the old records as pewterers by trade owned the valuable outfit of expensive gun-metal moulds needed for the full practice of that craft?

At any rate, there were pitifully few of them, whatever their real activities may have consisted of. Here follows the entire list of those who are even reputed to have been pewterers in America during the seventeenth, or during the first half of the eighteenth, centuries.

> Richard Graves, Salem, 1635–69
> Thomas Bumpsteed, Boston, 1654
> Henry Shrimpton, Boston, 1665 (dealer?)
> John Comer, Boston, 1678
> Thomas Clarke, Boston, 1683
> Samuel Grame, Boston, seventeenth century
> William Horsewell, New York, 1708 (dealer?)
> Simon Edgell, Philadelphia, 1718
> James Everett, Philadelphia, 1718
> John Holden (or Halden), New York, 1743.

And for most of these, even, our authority is hazy. Thomas Bumpsteed, John Comer, and Thomas Clarke are mentioned as pewterers in the Suffolk Deeds. Henry Shrimpton is there set down as a "brazier." His will, however, dated in 1665, makes mention of several thousand pounds of pewterware and of "tools for pewter and brasse." And these possessions (in the village of Boston, forty-five years after the landing of the Pilgrims) carry with them a strong suggestion that their owner was an importer of English pewterware and prepared, when need arose, to make repairs for his customers. Some thousands of pounds of finished pewterware would, at that time, have been worth some hundreds of pounds sterling — a very respectable but by no means unthinkable investment for a merchant so situated. But some hundreds of pounds sterling worth of pewterware of his own make, in a tiny provincial settlement where London pewter must have had an overwhelming "selling edge" over that of local origin, is simply not thinkable either as a speculation or as a business venture.

The other names — Samuel Grame, William Horsewell (also reputed to have been, perhaps, only a dealer), Simon Edgell, James Everett, and John

Holden, or Halden, are here set down simply because their names have been included in one or more of the tentative lists of American pewterers that have from time to time found their way into print. In no case has the compiler's authority for the inclusion of the name been given.

Remains only Richard Graves, of Salem; and here, at least, is one seventeenth-century American pewterer of whose activities we have a record and whose character is not hidden from us. I quote once more from Mr. Dow's invaluable four pages:

Graves came to Massachusetts in the Abigail, arriving in July, 1635. He settled at Salem and was a proprietor there in 1637. Sometimes he is styled "husbandman." He got into trouble with the authorities very soon, and in December, 1638, was sentenced to sit in the stocks for beating Peter Busgutt in his own house. . . . In 1641 Graves was brought into court again, and William Allen testified that "he had herd Rich Graves kissed Goody Gent twice." Richard confessed that it was true, and for this unseemly conduct was sentenced to be fined and whipped. . . . He was presented at a quarterly court on February 28th 1652–3 for "oppression in his trade of pewtering" and acquitted of the charge. Then he was accused of neglecting to attend the ferry carefully, so that it would seem that pewtering occupied only part of his time. This he acknowledged, but said that he had not been put to it by the Court and also that it was necessary to leave the ferry when he went to the milk, a quite apparent fact. He seems to have been a somewhat reckless fellow in his dealings with his neighbors, for he was accused of taking fence rails from Christopher Young's lot and admonished by the Court. At the same time he was fined for stealing wood from Thomas Edwards and for evil speeches to him, calling him "a base fellow, & yt one might Runn a half pike in his bellie & never touch his hart." . . . In 1645 he was in Boston in connection with some brazen molds that were in dispute. A Mr. Hill and a Mr. Knott were concerned in the affair, and very likely the molds were for pewterers' use. On another occasion, a few years later, when Graves went to Boston, he got drunk at Charlestown, and in consequence was mulct by the Quarterly Court. Only a month later he was complained of for playing at shuffle-board, a wicked game of chance, at the tavern kept by Mr. Gedney in Salem, but this time he escaped the vengeance of the law, for the case against him was not proved. He was still pursuing his trade of pewterer in 1665 when he so styled himself in a deed to John Putnam, and some time between that date and 1669 he passed out of reach of the courts to that bourne from which no pewterers ever return.

For myself, I take it that these early pewterers, where they were not primarily dealers in imported pewterware, were on the whole more menders than makers; repairers and refinishers of worn and broken dishes, rather than manufacturers of new ones. And quite possibly, since the use of an identifying mark in a competitive industry is evidence of a conscious ability to compete, they deliberately omitted to mark even such articles as they did make.

Henry Shrimpton, thrifty trader at a frontier settlement; and Richard Graves, tinker, rolling-stone, and ne'er-do-well; perhaps, after all, these two out of a list of ten — these two of whom alone we catch some glimpse through the mists — may be allowed to sum up for us the range and the character of most pewter activities in America during the seventeenth and early eighteenth centuries.

CHAPTER IV

PEWTER-MAKING IN AMERICA

1750–1850

I T is not, I trust, too much to hope that the publication of this pioneer report upon the topography of the American pewter country will eventually lead to its complete exploration. There is invaluable information still to be dug out of forgotten manuscripts and run to ground in neglected publications. There must be many names of as yet unlisted makers hiding on the backs of undiscovered plates. Even the touch-marks of Henry Shrimpton and Richard Graves may yet turn up and give to their discoverers "the thrill that comes once in a lifetime" — not to mention the pleasure of knocking holes in my arguments of the last chapter.

But at this time of writing, the fact remains that, to the best of my knowledge, no marked specimens of pre-Revolutionary American pewter exist whose makers did not work at their pewter-making craft after the Revolution as well as before it. And it seems to me that this fact admits of but one interpretation. And this is that it was, roughly speaking, the generation whose life-span bridged the Revolution that first found it possible to make a "go" of the pewterer's craft in America. Before the men of that generation came upon the scene, we find few names and no pewter. After their advent, we find a sudden galaxy of names and — in spite of the small demand there seems to have been for their wares — a most satisfactory percentage of representation by surviving examples.

It may be noted in this connection that Stiegel, the beloved hero of the American glass world, belonged to this generation. So did Richard Wistar, Caspar Wistar's son, who inherited the Wistarburg Works in 1752, and managed them during two thirds of their existence. So did Benjamin, Simon, and Aaron Willard, the most famous of American clock-makers. So did Paul Revere, ranked Number One in the All-American team of silversmiths. It was also in the seventeen-sixties and seventies that William Savery carved his highboys in Philadelphia and John Goddard made his block-fronts in Newport. In fine, the same 1750-to-1770 increase in the wealth of the Colonies, that both drew the fire of English taxation and gave us the self-confidence to resist it, also created a colonial demand for luxuries large enough to enable local craftsmen, for the first time, to live on the crumbs that fell from the importers' tables.

To this same generation belonged the following pewterers, those with the asterisk before their names being represented by surviving specimens of their work:

*Francis Bassett	New York
*Frederick Bassett	New York
Robert Boyle	New York
William Bradford	New York
*Thomas Danforth (1)	Norwich, Conn., and Taunton, Mass.
*Joseph Danforth	
*Gershom Jones	Providence
James Liddell	New York
*Richard Lee	Taunton, Mass.
*Henry Will	New York
*William Will	Philadelphia

It is quite possible that fuller data as to their histories may show Nathaniel Austin, of Boston (b. 1741 – d. 1816), and Daniel Melvil, who was working in Newport in 1788, to be entitled to inclusion in this list. For the present, however, these names are relegated to the next later, but closely related, group. At any rate, here are eleven names, eight of them belonging to actual pewter-making and pewter-marking pewterers, and all related in their beginnings to the third quarter of the eighteenth century. It is but natural to compare this group to the earlier one of about the same size that we examined in the last chapter. And, having compared them, it is difficult to escape the conclusion that the middle years of the eighteenth century were somehow determinative in the history of American pewter-making. So much so, indeed, that I think we are justified in regarding 1750 as a convenient boundary between prehistoric and historic times in American pewter — a dividing-line between the era of Romantic Legend and the age of Realism. And since pewter-making in this country dwindled off to a practical vanishing point about the middle of the ninteenth century, the heading of this chapter, "Pewter-Making in America, 1750–1850," really bounds and includes the effective life-span of the craft in this country. The object of the chapter is to get an airplane view of this life-span; of the influences that determined its development; and of the periods into which it is, in consequence, logically divisible. Afterward, we shall go on to a more detailed and analytical examination of the work and the workers that characterized these several divisions. Of course it scarcely needs to be pointed out that this tiny and distant craft-drama in America was really a far-flung reflection of the final European struggle between pewter and china.

The battle on this front had been joined, in England, during the early years of the eighteenth century; and by the seventeen-eighties there was no longer much question as to the ultimate victor — china having, by then, made a clean sweep of the fashionable world, so far as dress occasions went; and pewter being manifestly destined to no more than informal use among the well-to-do, if not to exclusively lower-class employment.

At the beginning of the eighteenth century, however, the American Colonies were far removed from the Old World. Wooden trenchers were no uncommon sight here in ordinary households up to the very threshold of the Revolution. It thus came about that the final victory of pewter over wood on the American side of the Atlantic almost coincided with the preliminary triumphs of china over pewter on the European side. Even before the Revolution, however, the clipper ships of New England were beginning, not only to reduce our distance in time from the Old World, but to close the gap between us in wealth. And so, in the end, the final defeat and unconditional surrender of pewter on the main issue at stake came only about ten years earlier in England than with us. A struggle that lasted for a full century and over on the other side was thus dramatically compressed into half that time in America. The making of pewter plates for table use was finally abandoned in England between 1810 and 1815. In America this took place between 1820 and 1825. After this, in both countries, pewter maintained a more or less successful guerrilla warfare until about 1850. After this it disappeared.

It is important for us, since the main division in the classification of American pewterers depends upon it, to understand just why the dropping of the table plate from the list of the pewterers' output should have signified a final defeat and have constituted a change of era. And the simplest path to a working realization of this fact and of the cause of it is a "close-up" of our attitude toward our own familiar tableware — china.

We shall find that plates are the basis and background of our whole "china" notion.

Serving plates, soup plates, dinner plates, breakfast plates, dessert plates, bread-and-butter plates — take these away and nothing remains of a "set of china" except the frills. And what is more, these "frills" — the soup tureen, the meat platters, the gravy boat, the vegetable dishes, the salad bowls, the pickle dish, and so on — might just as well not be china at all. Silver, or plated ware, or, in some cases, glass, would do just as well, or even better, and very often do. If we are curious as to the seventeenth-century attitude in these matters, all we have to do is to translate these feelings into the materials then in vogue. The ordinary table of that day was as normally served in wood as are ours in china. Platters and serving dishes, drinking vessels, and eating plates, all were habitually made of it. Of course the platters and bowls and salt cellars — the frills, in short — not only might be, but often were, made of silver or pewter — the frill materials of the time. But the plates — the thing was regarded as a matter of course — the plates were made of wood.

Wood, pewter, china — these three have been the successive rulers of the tableware world. Each has won its spurs as a frill material. Each has fought its way to complete command. And each, when its triumph was won and its time came to rule, has had the scepter handed to it on a *dinner plate*.

Pewter, then, was done for as a tableware material when the dinner plate was finally struck from its lists. This did not, of course, mean that it was otherwise done for. The excellent business the craft created for itself from the exploiting of secondary issues during the next quarter-century proves this; and proves that it was not this defeat, but the trend of the times, that finally banished the metal from modern life.

We shall see, indeed, that the twenty-five years from 1825 to 1850, furnish us, in America, with more names of local makers, and that they very likely produced as much local pewter and near-pewter, as did the seventy-five years from 1750 to 1825. Nevertheless, and allowing for the fact that, as in most periods of transition, the line of demarcation is at first somewhat blurred, the exploiters of these second-string specialties — the makers of coffee-pots and cuspidors, the manufacturers of candlesticks and whale-oil lamps — belonged to a new era. The last American plate-maker of 1825 was more nearly related to the first American plate-maker of 1750 (or, for that matter, to the English sadware men of the sixteenth and seventeenth centuries) than to his coffee-pot-making neighbor in the next block. One of them belonged to the passing order and looked backward to the guild-controlled world of the Pewterers' Society. The other belonged to the coming order and looked forward to Big Business. Our century of pewter-making in America, therefore, divides itself logically into two main divisions — that of the plate-makers and that of the non-plate-makers.

It may be well at this point to call the attention of such readers as are unfamiliar with the history of pewter-making in England, to the fact that from very early times, there, the makers of flatware constituted a separate division of the craft. They were known, in the trade, as sadware men, and flatware in general was known, in the trade, as sadware. They were required to use a finer grade of metal than the "triflers" or the "ley men," and they looked down on both of these classes in consequence. The "triflers" made all sorts of pewter odds and ends from an alloy known as "trifle" and containing much antimony. The "ley men" made hollow-ware from a grade of pewter containing about twenty per cent of lead, and known as "ley" metal.

No such organization as the Pewterers' Society, and no such division of labor in the trade as that thus countenanced and enforced, ever existed in America. There was neither need for, nor possibility of maintaining, such a central authority in the struggling Colonies; and it was not always possible there for a pewterer, even though he practiced all the known branches of his craft, to make a living without having other irons in the fire — let alone his being able to devote himself to a single type of pewter-making. We have already seen Henry Shrimpton quoted as both pewterer and brazier, besides being, probably, more dealer than either. We have seen Richard Graves figuring as a pewterer, a husbandman, and a ferry-tender — not to mention his less official activities. Paul Revere is known to have made pewter. Nathaniel Austin was primarily a goldsmith. And while, in the eighteen-twenties and thirties, the beginnings of modern manufacturing methods are traceable in the sizable enterprises of the Boardmans and of the Taunton britannia firms, still, by many of the pewterers of even the last period, tinsmithing, brass-, copper-, and German-silver-working, japanning, and even plumbing, were followed concurrently with that of pewter-making.

In fact the craft in America appears to have reverted, quite naturally and no doubt of necessity, to very much the methods prevailing in England during the thirteenth and early fourteenth centuries, when the ability to do work in pewter was rather one of an expert metal-worker's many accomplishments than a separate craft. In 1320, for instance, we read of one "Peter the Wire Drawer" doing pewter work at York. And Cotterell, in his treatise on Irish pewter, speaks of "Walter the Goldsmith" making pewterware for Holy Trinity Priory in Dublin in 1344. Even so, Sam Rust, printing-press-maker of New York, made pewter lamps in the eighteen-thirties, and Eben Smith, of Beverly, Massachusetts, manufacturer of hose nozzles, made pewter Communion sets for New England churches in the eighteen-forties.

Our division of American pewterers, then, into plate-makers and non-plate-makers does not imply that these American plate men made plates only. On the contrary, it may probably be taken for granted (and this in spite of the fact that some of them are as yet only represented by flatware) that most of the men entitled to rank in this division made many or most of the other pewter articles then in common demand. But, as we have already seen, it is precisely the fact that they made plates — or rather that they made eating plates — that definitely associates them with the old order. To say "plates," simply, might prove misleading, because, for a time after eating plates had ceased to be made, larger plates and large deep plates of the charger type, often of britannia, and often for Church use as patens and collection plates, continued to be made by the transition workers.

We will, then, since we must needs have a name by which to distinguish it, call the first of these main divisions the "Eight-Inch-Plate Period," and the men who worked in it the "Eight-Inch-Plate Men." For the eight-inch plate was the typical dinner plate of the time.

At present there are thirty-seven men, known to us by their marked handiwork, who made pewter in America during what we are calling the "Eight-Inch-Plate Period." Thirty-five of them made eight-inch plates.

One of the two exceptions is George Coldwell, of New York, "pewter spoon and candle mold maker" from 1792 to 1796. The other is Samuel Hamlin, who worked in Providence, Rhode Island, in the early eighteen-twenties. He, unlike Coldwell, seems to have been a normal, all-around pewterer of the older order; making whatever the demand of the day offered him a market for. He made eleven-, thirteen-, and even fifteen-inch plates and chargers; but nothing in flatware by him smaller than eleven inches has turned up, to my knowledge. It may be that he saw the writing on the wall and was a believer in "safety first." It may well be, too, that, like some of his fellow workers of the later years of his period, he made a few eight-inch plates and that a specimen or so will be found later. At any rate, in all other regards he was a worthy representative of the best traditions of the old order.

Thirty-five out of the thirty-seven men, then, whose work thus represents for us the old-order tradition, made eight-inch plates. Moreover, eight-inch plates are the only article, so far as we know, that they all did make. And I submit that these facts amply evidence the justness, as well as the convenience, of this classification.

"But what, exactly, did they make?" I seem to hear more than one reader asking. Let us put the query in a slightly different form. If a housewife, desirous of furnishing her pantry shelves, or of replacing articles thereon that had passed their usefulness, went into an American pewterer's shop, say in the seventeen-nineties, what sort of dishes, and in what variety, would she have found displayed there for her to choose or order from? Because, as far as we can judge from the marked specimens that have come down to us, the craft of the pewterer in the young United States was firmly founded upon the housewife's patronage. If there were "triflers" in their ranks, they do not seem to have marked their output. Snuffboxes, buckles, ornamental or fashionable jimcracks — the chances are that most such were imported. The local makers seem to have confined themselves pretty closely to the essentials and fundamentals of their craft. And this, of course, meant tableware.

And since plates were the basis and background of the whole tableware world, the first and most important question that needs answering is, "What variety of American-made plates was at the service of the shopping housewife?" The answer is given in Fig. 15.

I believe all of these plates to be of American origin, although the three smallest are unmarked. Beginning with the fourth plate from the small end, each plate here pictured bears the touch of an American maker, and so offers an incontrovertible and graphic reply to our question.

Plates from six and a quarter inches in diameter up to fifteen inches, of marked American origin, are here shown. The smallest unmarked plate measures five inches. It, and its three next larger brothers, all probably come under the old definition of "saucers" that we met with in the 1693 invoice. The other sizes above the four "saucer" sizes are eight, nine, eleven, twelve, thirteen, fourteen, and fifteen inches. I have never, myself, seen or heard of a smaller marked plate than the six-and-a-quarter-inch size. The unmarked smaller sizes here shown may or may not be of American make; it is impossible to say with certainty. They are here shown merely to complete the picture of the types of flatware that were, apparently, in use here during the seventy-five years of the eight-inch-plate period. No ten-inch plate is introduced into the series because I know of no example of this size that was made here for household use. Later we shall see one or two specimens of this size, made during the later period as patens in communion sets. Very handsome pieces, too, in some cases. But they do not belong here.

To those familiar with the larger sizes of English chargers and plates, fifteen inches will seem rather small for the top item in this series. But thirteen inches appears to have been, normally, the largest size made by American pewterers. The fifteen-inch size, whether in the plate form or in the dish (deep plate) type, is one of the rarities of American pewter. So far as we know now, only six makers in this country put out specimens of this size, and so few of them are known that it will be a good collection that can boast one. In England sixteen- and eighteen-inch plates were not unusual, and twenty-inch ones turn up on occasion. I believe they even exist larger still.

Next to the plate, the basin seems to have been the most important thing for the housekeeper. These were evidently used both as mixing bowls and as serving dishes. The range of sizes of local make that were obtainable is graphically shown in Fig. 16. The bottom basin in this pyramid is the only one of its size (twelve inches in diameter) made in America that I have ever seen. On the other hand, thirteen-inch ones of English make turn up here on occasion. The twelve-inch one here shown is by Thomas Danforth (3), who worked from 1807 to 1813 in Philadelphia. The next above it is ten inches wide and is by the same maker. Then comes a nine-inch specimen by Thomas Danforth (2), both of these men being members of one of the leading pewter-making families in America. Above this follow in order an eight-inch basin by Nathaniel Austin, of Boston; a seven-and-a-quarter-inch one by Thomas D. Boardman, of Hartford; and a six-and-a-half-inch one by Samuel Hamlin. These basins made their exit in company with the eating plates. No single specimen to my knowledge has turned up bearing the mark of a coffee-pot era maker. Indeed, I have seen but one, I think, by a transition worker.

It must be borne in mind, in discussing these American marked types, that an overwhelming majority of the pewter used in this country was imported from England. There was a whole series of dishes, made with double bottoms and with a small hinged lid leading to the enclosed space between, through which hot water could be introduced. These were used both for the serving of food and for the individual to eat food off of. I have never seen a specimen of this class of hot-water dishes, whether platter or plate, marked by an American maker. Neither have I ever seen an oval platter, large or small; or a scalloped-edged plate, such as were common on the Continent, and made by one or two makers in England, notably by the Flackmans. Neither in strict truth do I imagine that it would have been possible for any housewife in any city of the New World to find, in any one American pewterer's shop, anything approaching the complete line of types and sizes here illustrated as constituting the composite output of the craft in America. Indeed, the chances are that most purchases of any size or variety made from the local pewterers were orders, not selections; and the chances are very strongly against many complete or even extensive orders being placed at one time for pewter services. In pewter, as in silver, the evidence from surviving metal is all the other way. It is seldom, indeed, that one finds an entire communion service, even, made by one maker. And the same thing holds good in the matter of tea sets. Of course, it has come to be regarded as almost a matter of course that silver tea services of the late eighteenth and early nineteenth centuries should contain pieces of differing types and often by different makers; showing that these services, far from being bought at once, were slowly saved for and assembled as the family means permitted. The same process of successive savings-up and modest spendings would seem to have been responsible for most of the pewter communion services of the country churches during the early years of the nineteenth century. And seldom are all the pieces of one type or of identical markings. Many of these services had tankards — covered or uncovered — in lieu of chalices; and not a few of them had the type of vessel that we call a "covered water pitcher" (a type belonging to the second era of pewter-making in America) instead of the more normal flagon. All in all, there are two considerations that we must constantly bear in mind in trying to understand the conditions faced by our early pewterers; one of which is the essential poverty of the communities where they lived, and the other the overwhelming competition that they had to face in order to get even a small share of the trade of the well-to-do.

All this being understood, we can go on to consider the other standard products of the eight-inch-plate man on this side of the ocean. Next to the plate and the basin, the porringer was doubtless the popular article of table-ware. Unfortunately, the porringer, because of the vulnerability of its fascinating but structurally weak handle, is a form that stood little chance of surviving the rough usage of daily employment. Those specimens of this form that were made by the men who worked during the last years of the continuance of pewter in active table service, have survived because, presumably, their time of actual service was short and their beauty and oddity have won careful preservation for them. But even these are scarce. And specimens of earlier American porringers are rare, indeed. Yet this fact does not for a moment persuade one that few of them were made here.

Fig. 18 shows the range in sizes of these beautiful little dishes that appear to have been made in this country during the first period.

Five and a quarter inches seems to have been the greatest diameter in vogue here. And four and seven eighths, four and a quarter, four, three and a quarter, two and three quarters, and two and a quarter, form the notes in the descending scale of sizes. The smallest of these are said to have been used as measures by physicians in bleeding their patients. I do not vouch for the report. Such doctors as still follow this practice do not use measures. They make a generous incision in the bank account and take what flows.

The family group shown in Fig. 18 (those were the days when family groups normally took this stepladder form) is made up as follows:

At the large end is a five-and-a-quarter-inch porringer by Thomas D. Boardman, of Hartford. Next to this is a four-and-seven-eighths-inch specimen by William Calder, of Providence. Both of these men worked near the dividing-line between the two chief divisions of the craft in this country, and they and the firm made up of this T. D. Boardman and his brother Sherman, the makers of the fourth porringer in this row, are, between them, responsible for the great majority of the surviving porringers of early American origin.

Next below the Calder specimen is a four-inch example by Joseph Belcher, a maker who worked perhaps thirty years earlier than these others. This is a very rare piece. Then comes a three-and-a-quarter-inch porringer by T. D. and S. Boardman, dating from somewhere about 1828; and then a two-and-

Fig. 16

SIZES OF "BASONS" MADE BY AMERICAN PEWTERERS

Beginning at the top, these are by Samuel Ham¹in, Thomas D. Boardman, Nathaniel
Austin, Thomas Danforth (2), T. Danforth, Philadelphia, and T. Danforth, Philadelphia.
Their sizes, given in diameters and again reading from the top, are: 6½ inches, 7¼ inches,
8 inches, 9, 10, and 12 inches.

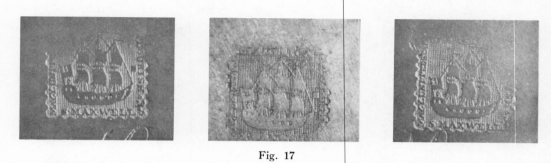

Fig. 17

RARE MARKS USED BY S. MAXWELL, OF LONDON, ON PEWTER EXPORTED TO THE
UNITED STATES

The inscription around the ship reads: "May the United States of America flourish. S. Maxwell."

Fig. 18

RANGE OF AMERICAN PEWTER PORRINGERS

From 2¼ to 5¼ inches. Left to right, by Richard Lee, Richard Lee, T. D. & S. B., Joseph Belcher, William Calder, and Samuel Hamlin

Fig. 19

AN EARLY PORRINGER BY DANIEL MELVIL

Fig. 20

MAGNIFICENT FLAT-TOPPED TANKARD BY FREDERICK BASSETT

7½ inches to top of thumb piece
5 inches in diameter at base

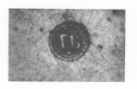

Fig. 21

MARK ON INSIDE BOTTOM OF THIS TANKARD

Fig. 22

A SPLENDID QUART MUG BY FREDERICK BASSETT

Height, 6 inches
Width at base, 4⅞ inches
Width at lip, 4 inches

Fig. 23

MARK ON INSIDE BOTTOM OF THIS MUG

Fig. 24

A COMMODE FORM BY FREDERICK BASSETT

Height, 8 inches
Extreme width, 12 inches
Marked "F.B." on outside bottom

Fig. 26

MARK ON BOTTOM OF SAME

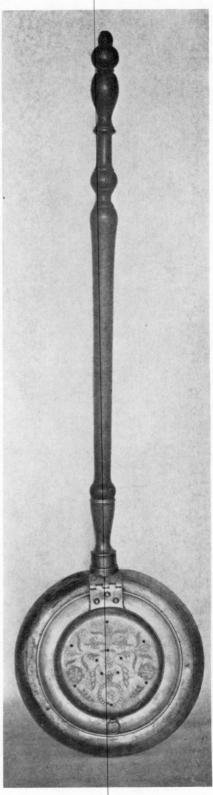

Fig. 25

PEWTER WARMING PAN BY WILLIAM WILL

three-quarter-inch beauty by Richard Lee, of Taunton, one of the men who belong to the small, Revolution-spanning group of American pewterers. The last little porringer in the line is also, I believe, by Richard Lee. It bears on the handle the initials "R. L." at any rate; and very probably came from his workshop. Fig. 19 pictures another fine early porringer with a type of handle typical of early times. The piece is by Daniel Melvil, of Newport, Rhode Island.

We must not, of course, forget the ubiquitous spoon, which enjoys the distinction of having, so far as we know, bred the only specialist in the craft here — our friend Mr. Coldwell, recently held up as one of the two non-plate-makers in the whole trade catalogue of his period. An example of his handiwork is shown in Fig. 104. One of a set of six tablespoons by Colonel William Will, one of the pre-Revolutionary workers, a member of Assembly in Pennsylvania, and an innkeeper in Philadelphia, as well as a pewterer, is shown in Fig. 73. Spoons, like porringers, were subjected to a strain under which they were ill-calculated to stand up. Add the fact that they were little thought of, and it is small wonder that few early ones have come down to us. It is quite likely, however, that more of them were made here, marked or unmarked, than of any other one pewter form in use at the time. This belief is largely based on the quantity of moulds for pewter spoons that one used to see banging round in forgotten corners of old junk shops. In fact, it is more than probable that "rolling your own" was the spoon order of the day in most outlying communities. It must be recalled that, although pewter spoons broke at the waist and pewter dishes got holes melted in their bottoms, the material they were made of could be used over and over, provided only that one had the necessary implements at hand and a modicum of skill in using them. This, of course, did not guarantee much neatness or patina to the finished job.

We come now to the drinking vessels that kept the plates and basins, porringers and spoons, company on the table. In England, the pewter mug, or tankard, survived in pretty habitual use in the bar parlors of inns and in the "publics" of city corners and village greens, well up to the middle of the nineteenth century and beyond. Even to-day, the elements of the old pewter "measure" sets, ranging from a quarter gill to a half-gallon or gallon, are a common sight in English shops; and the common mugs of nineteenth-century pattern are discoverable in droves there. But no such popularity seems ever, over here, to have developed for this form of drinking vessel. The covered tankard of marked American pewter, like its aristocratic silver relative, belongs among the greater rarities; and the flat-topped variety of the breed marked by one of the early men is only to be mentioned with reverence. Even the uncovered tankard, or tall mug, is rare in its American manifestation; and when it bears a rare name it becomes comparatively priceless. One of the former, by Frederick Bassett, is shown in Fig. 20. I consider it by all odds the rarest piece of American pewter illustrated in this volume. In Fig. 22 is shown a quart-sized mug, or uncovered tankard, by Frederick Bassett. The type is much less rare than the covered tankard type just referred to, but both of these pieces are in the first ranks of rarity, besides being good examples of important products of their day.

We have already seen the influx of "Chamber Potts" that was taking place in the Boston of the late seventeenth century. In Fig. 24 is shown an eighteenth-century equivalent of local make — a commode form, by Frederick Bassett. In the eighteenth century humble usage was no bar to beauty.

Mention has been made of the likelihood that much work — perhaps even most work — by local pewterers in the early period was done on order. Fig. 25 shows a most interesting example of pewter work by Colonel Will, which must, one imagines, have been thus undertaken. The fact of its being the only pewter warming pan I have ever heard of, would make me think this. But the fact that the lid is made of an eight-inch plate used bottom-side up makes me certain of it. Perhaps it would be more correct to say that the lid of this vessel has been cast in the mould used ordinarily for eight-inch plates. Another, more detailed picture of the pewter pan itself will be found in Fig. 80. The touch shown in Fig. 26 is from the bottom of this warming pan, which is the property of Mr. J. Stogdell Stokes, of Philadelphia, and is here pictured by his very kind permission.

The very great majority of the communion vessels in pewter, of American make and mark, that turn up are by makers of the later period. I take this, however, to be indicative of the mortality among early pewter specimens rather than of our earlier pewterers' failure to make these pieces. I have heard of a communion set by Thomas Badger, of Boston, although I have never seen it. In Fig. 27 is shown a fine specimen of a communion flagon by Thomas D. Boardman, of Hartford. It will have to represent, here, the earlier Church pewter with American markings.

And this about covers the field of the activities of the eight-inch-plate men in this country as represented by the surviving examples of their output.

There is one department of the craft that we must not forget, however, and that is the maker of pewter buttons. We no longer — we of the masculine persuasion, at least — live in an age of metal buttons for decorative use. But the eighteenth and early nineteenth centuries were eminently given to this sort of display. Blue coats and brass buttons persisted well into what we used, when I was a kid, to call modern times. I well recall the picturesque figure of old Doctor Davis, the living embodiment to my youthful eyes of Holmes's "Last Leaf," who still walked the streets of Chicago, when I was a boy, in all the curious Old-World dignity of a stock and a blue swallow-tailed coat with brass buttons front and back.

Caspar Wistar, it must be remembered, made the money with which he started the Wistarburg glass factory by being "Caspar Wistar, Brass Button Maker of Philadelphia." And pewter buttons, one gathers, were worn by the thousands. Fig. 28 pictures the under side of two that happen to carry the maker's mark. I have many that are not marked. But the smooth side of a pewter button does not sit well for its likeness. One of those here pictured is marked "N H & B ** Patent.**" The other is marked "A C * Hard White.*" Neither of these makers has as yet been identified.

Before coming to the second of our main divisions — that of the non-plate-makers — we find, as we might, indeed, expect to find, that there are a few transition workers who refuse to fit uncomplainingly into either of our other-

wise valid definitions. They are, in fact, the few men who, in their own persons, bridged the gulf between the old order and the new. There are, all told, outside the Boardman group, which was itself the chief landmark and protagonist of the transition, but four of these *liaison* workers. By definition, however, they made nothing of their own invention. Their peculiarity consists merely in the fact that, to some extent, they made types characteristic of both periods.

And after that, in a sense, came the deluge. It was not only in the pewterers' craft, but in the whole contemporary world of human industry, that an old order was dying and a new one coming into being. Individualism; personal pride in personal performance — this was the keynote of the old, guild-taught order. Organization; quantity, speed of production, and cheapness of resulting output — these were the lodestars that more and more were to draw and guide the new. The Boardmans, with their central workshops in Hartford and their apparently independent branches or agencies in New York and Philadelphia, appear not only to have catered both to the old-fashioned users of the passing forms and to the progressive adopters of the new ones, but to have at the same time retained the appearance of individual craftsmanship for their several shops while taking early advantage of the economies of centralization. And to a large extent they set the fashions for the final period.

For the rest, with here and there an outstanding exception, as in the cases of such men as Roswell Gleason and Israel Trask — instances where natural ability and personal efficiency enabled an adherer to the old methods to succeed under the new conditions — the makers of the final period appear to have been for the most part economic opportunists and industrial graspers-at-straws. This was the time when it first began to dawn upon a scientifically naïve world that oxygen had something to do with candle-power. Hence a rush of new inventions looking to an improvement on the tallow dip and the Betty lamp. Result, twenty-eight makers of pewter lamps, patented and unpatented, among the sixty-six pewter-represented names of our last division. Twelve of these actually seem to have made nothing else. Two of them seem to have made nothing but lamps and candlesticks. While fourteen of them merely added lamps to their other output. An exceptional pair of these pewter lamps is shown in Fig. 29.

This, too, was the time when the old open hearth began definitely to give place in the homes of America to the kitchen stove; and when the luxury of tea and coffee drinking began to spread downward through the social fabric. Which is perhaps why the opportunists who could pewter, took to making pewter coffee-pots and tea-pots. At any rate thirty-six of the makers whose names figure in the last division made one or both of these articles; some of them appear to have made little else and seem not to have done a very big business at that. The truth is that many of the makers of this final period will be completely ignored by those collectors of American pewter who can afford to indulge their preference for the better men and for the earlier era. But the work of no one of them is plentiful. The appearance of most of their handiwork has at least quaintness and some textural quality to commend it. And it is certain that no one of them will long go begging for appreciators among the more modest-minded (and pursed) of the collectors of Americana. This being, to my mind, quite beyond question, it becomes the manifest business of a manual on American pewter to be as informative as it can be about the least of the pewterers who can claim the title. Nor is this last statement to be taken as in any sense an apology for the inclusion of these humble brethren. My greatest quarrel with the authors of most collectors' manuals is that only "museum specimens" — if you get what I mean — appear to have been thought worthy of their notice; so that the things that the ordinary poor devil picks up and wants to know about are never mentioned. In consequence, he is left wondering whether he has acquired something beneath contempt, or something so rare that the authorities themselves never heard of it. An assortment of tea- and coffee-pots is shown in Fig. 31.

But the "Coffee-Pot Period" is not without its own glories. Its pitchers, alone, would give it distinction. Of these, the magnificent specimen by Roswell Gleason, shown in Fig. 32, will serve as an example. Reference has already been made to the fact that covered pitchers of this general type, although of course much smaller than this monster, were frequently used in the middle years of the nineteenth century as flagons in churches. Mugs, covered tankards, beakers (the right-hand specimen in Fig. 33 was so used), and goblet-shaped pieces, both high- and low-stemmed, were used at the same period as chalices. The true early chalice shape is seldom seen.

There was quite a vogue, toward the middle of the nineteenth century, for a pair of silver or Sheffield goblets of the chalice shape to flank the family water pitcher withal. To-day these pieces are almost certain to be taken for sacramental pieces. It is more likely that some of the similar drinking cups or goblets of the eighteen-thirties and forties — mostly by the successive Taunton makers — were intended for similar use. Fig. 33 shows the range of this period's typical table drinking vessel, the beaker. Beakers appear to have been in very general use; and as those of English make that I have seen marked have differed very materially from the typical American form shown in the second largest of the four illustrated, I incline to the belief that these dainty little flare-mouthed cups are, at least largely, of local origin. They are, however, hardly ever seen with a maker's touch on them. And as for the little whiskey-glass sizes at the left, I have never seen one of these so-called "baby-beakers" bearing a maker's touch. They look, however, too exactly like their elders not to be classed with them. The large beaker on the right of this picture is by Israel Trask, of Beverly, Massachusetts.

Perhaps it would have been more according to Hoyle to have named the coffee-pot first in cataloguing and picturing the typical output of the coffee-pot period. However, as these twenty-five years have to stand a lot of knocks and need all the encouragement they can get, I preferred to put their best foot forward by leading off with the water pitchers. Fig. 34 shows the coffee-pot in its most attractive form. This particular example is one made in Hartford by the Boardmans, and marked for sale by Boardman & Hall, of Philadelphia, sometime during or after 1845. Later chapters will show the many types of this vessel that were developed during the period.

In Fig. 35 is shown a coffee-urn by Roswell Gleason, which is a type, surely, that the era need not be ashamed of. Gleason made them in at least two sizes;

and I have also seen one marked Boardman & Hall. It is an odd fact that all the marked specimens of American candlesticks that have come under my notice date from this final period of craft activity here. We have already seen pewter candlesticks coming into Boston for sale in the necessarily economical communities of those early days. It is hardly thinkable that the demand did not keep up and grow during the following century and more. Yet the facts are as stated. The pewter whale-oil lamp, in spite of its frequent ascription to earlier times, belongs, I am firmly convinced, in this list of typical coffee-pot period products. My reasons for so believing are set forth fully in the chapter on lamps. The candlestick is not, of course, assignable to any period comprised in the life-history of American pewter-making. Yet all the marked specimens shown in this volume belong to the period now under discussion.

As an example, finally, of the casual uses to which this alloy was put in these years, I show, in Fig. 14, two silhouettes and an engraved portrait of Andrew Jackson, each one framed in an ingenious pewter frame, so made that the easily bent metal would allow of several insertions and removals of its intended contents.

CHAPTER V

LARGELY STATISTICAL

IT was in 1910 that I first heard of the existence of American pewter; Mr. W. R. Lawshe, of Trenton, New Jersey, happening to mention having seen an occasional piece with an eagle mark. At the time I was deep in preliminary investigations about Stiegel and Wistarburg glass, and going about quite a little in New Jersey, Pennsylvania, and Maryland; and I began to keep a lookout for some of these eagle-marked plates. Later on a friend sent me a copy of N. Hudson Moore's "Old Pewter, Brass, Copper, and Sheffield Plate" and I, metaphorically speaking, pasted the list of American pewterers there given in my hat when I went hunting. And for a time I was very greatly puzzled by the fact that none of the pewterers whose names I found on pewter — B. Barns, T. Danforth, and R. Palethorp, Jr., of Philadelphia, and S. Kilbourn, of Baltimore, for instance — were down on this printed list. But finally it dawned on me that I had to do with a list of names gathered, not from pewter, but from records. And at first I felt very superior, indeed, telling myself that the old bookworms who had dug out the list probably did not know a piece of pewter when they saw one. But one day I found a plate, evidently very early, indeed, and certainly American because it was stamped "New York," but with the mark so blurred that I could not be certain of the maker's name. In desperation I turned to the despised and long-neglected list and, with its help, made out to decipher the name of Francis Bassett. And so I got my first inkling of the fact that, after all, both approaches — the direct one by the way of the pewter itself, and the oblique one through the printed records — must be used and made to supplement each other, if we are to wring all the information possible from the secretive past. And our task in this and the succeeding chapter is going to be just that: to subject all the data that we have at command, whether pewter-derived or record-derived, to as searching a cross-examination as we can devise, in order to wring from it all the information and understanding possible.

Of course, to the collector, a name on a dish is, and always will be, worth two in a directory. And to all of us, collectors and students alike, it is a great satisfaction to find that, as our information piles up, and as the combined list of pewter-derived and record-derived names of American pewterers grows, the percentage of those represented by discovered specimens increases steadily. Because, after all, it is only for the sake of the discoverable pewter that the list has value; and so our success as investigators and students of American pewter is roughly measurable by the shrinking discrepancy between the two catalogues.

Let us, therefore, before proceeding, see how we stand to-day, in this regard, as compared with the days of the old list. There were thirty-three names on the list as published in Mrs. Moore's book, and even now only eleven of these have been verified — so to put it — by discovered, marked specimens. On the other hand, the list as it stands, at the moment of going to press and as printed in this chapter, contains a total of two hundred and fourteen names, one hundred and thirteen of which are, to my knowledge, represented by existing specimens of marked pewter. Indeed three hundred and fifty-three specimens by one hundred of these makers are actually illustrated in this volume, and two hundred and eleven marks, used by one hundred and three of these makers, are here reproduced.

It has seemed to me that the most practical way to go about "cross-examining our known data" will be, first, to place these data on view in the most concise form available; after which we can proceed to examine them from as many angles and under as many classifications as we shall find need for.

First, then, I propose to publish the complete list of American pewterers as it stands to-day to the best of my knowledge; marking with an asterisk (*) those names whose pewter is known to have turned up; and giving, in each case, such data as to dates and place of residence as I can. As some method of differentiating is needed between verified information and mere tradition or report, I shall place in parenthesis, after each date, either a capital (D) to indicate that the date is the first or the last appearance of the name in a city directory; a small (b) or (d) to mean "born" or "died"; or a question mark (?) to indicate that I owe the date to a report not verified by me. Where a place of residence is given without qualification, it indicates that the fact is definitely known. Where the information is taken from some earlier list or from report, and has not, to my knowledge, been verified, this will be indicated by a question mark after the place name, as, for example, "Philadelphia (?)." "W.A." after a name or date means "Wadsworth Athenæum Bulletin."

Before coming to the list itself, attention should be called to the fact that quite a few names have appeared from time to time in earlier lists of American pewterers which do not, I believe, belong there. To include these in our new list, together with the reasons why they should not be there, would be a somewhat clumsy procedure. Yet to leave them unmentioned would do nothing toward correcting the error of their former inclusion. All these names, therefore, appear in the general index at the end of the book, and all the information I have concerning them is gathered in a list supplemental to the main list in this chapter and immediately following it.

Here is the general list:

GENERAL LIST OF AMERICAN PEWTERERS

NAMES	ADDRESSES	DATES
Anthony Allaire	New York City Hester Street	(D) 1815 1821 (D)
* Austin	Boston, Massachusetts	
*Nathaniel Austin	Boston, Massachusetts Back Street	(b) 1741 (d) 1816 (D) 1789 1816 (D)
*Richard Austin	Boston, Massachusetts 16 Marlboro Street Franklin Street after 1803	(D) 1796 1810 (D)
*Babbitt, Crossman & Co.	Taunton, Massachusetts	1824 (?)
*Thomas Badger	Boston, Massachusetts Prince Street	(D) 1789 1813 (D)
O. & A. Bailey (dealers?) "Lamps"	New York City 116 Grand Street	(D) 1845 (D)
*Bailey & Putnam		
C. Bancks	Chelmsford, Massachusetts (?)	
*B. Barns	Philadelphia, Pennsylvania Filbert and Thirteenth Streets	(D) 1812 1817 (D)
*Stephen Barns		Before 1825
*Francis Bassett	New York City 218 Queen Street	(D) 1786 1799 (D)
*Frederick Bassett	New York City 4 Burling Slip Later, 218 Pearl Street	(D) 1787 1798 (D)

GENERAL LIST OF AMERICAN PEWTERERS — *continued*

NAMES	ADDRESSES	DATES
S. Bast	New York (?)	19th Cent. (?)
*Joseph Belcher	New London, Connecticut	Late 18th Century
*William Billings	Providence, Rhode Island	1791 (?)
James Bird	New York City	(D) 1816 1820 (D)
	75 Harman Street	
*Boardman	Hartford, Connecticut (?)	Circ. 1825
Lion mark		
*Henry S. Boardman	Hartford, Connecticut	1841 (W.A.)
	67 Trumbull Street	
	Philadelphia, Pennsylvania	(D) 1845 (D)
	106 North Third Street	
J. D. Boardman	Hartford, Connecticut	1828 (W.A.)
	58 Main Street	
*L. Boardman		After 1825
Sherman Boardman	Hartford, Connecticut	1828 (W.A.)
	52 Main Street	
*Thomas D. Boardman	Hartford, Connecticut	Before 1820 (?)
	59 Main Street	
*T. D. & S. Boardman	Hartford, Connecticut	Circ. 1828–1854
("T.D.&S.B.")	Main Street	
*Timothy Boardman & Co.	New York City	(D) 1822 1824 (D)
	178 Water Street	
*Boardman & Co.	New York City	(D) 1825 1827 (D)
	178 Water Street	
*Boardman & Hall	Philadelphia, Pennsylvania	(D) 1844 (D)
"Britannia Ware Mnfrs."	436 High Street	
*Boardman & Hart	New York City	(D) 1828 1850 (D)
	178 Water Street	
	After 1831, 6 Burling Slip	
*Parks Boyd	Philadelphia, Pennsylvania	(D) 1798 1819 (D)
	Various locations on North Second Street	
Robert Boyle	New York City	1745 (?) 1780 (?)
	Dock Street	
	"Sign of the Gilt Dish"	
Cornelius Bradford	Philadelphia, Pennsylvania	Pre-Rev. (?)
William Bradford	New York City	1750 (?) 1780 (?)
*——n Brigh——		Before 1825
*Brook Farm	West Roxbury, Massachusetts	1841 1847
David S. Brooks	Hartford, Connecticut	1828 (W.A.)
	27 Trumbull Street	
Thomas Bumsteed	Boston, Massachusetts	1654
*William Calder	Providence, Rhode Island	1824
	166 North Main Street	
*Capen & Molineux	New York City	(D) 1848 1853 (D)
Ephraim Capen	132 William Street	
George Molineux		
Thomas Clarke	Boston, Massachusetts	1683 (?) 1687 (?)
*Cleveland & Bros.	Providence, Rhode Island	After 1825
*George Coldwell	New York City	(D) 1792 1796 (D)
"Pewter, Spoon, & Candle	23 Gold Street	
Mold Mnfr."		
John Comer	Boston, Massachusetts	1678 (W.A.)
Thomas Connell	Philadelphia, Pennsylvania	(D) 1839 1840 (D)
(See Palethorp & Connell)	144 High Street	

GENERAL LIST OF AMERICAN PEWTERERS — *continued*

NAMES	ADDRESSES	DATES
*Crossman, West & Leonard	Taunton, Massachusetts	After 1824 (W.A.)
*D. Curtiss		Circum 1825
*I. Curtis		
Curtis & Co.	New York City	(D) 1868 (D)
Stephen Curtis, Jr., formerly of Yale & Curtis.	90 Fulton Street	
*Edward Danforth	Hartford, Connecticut (?)	18th Cent.
*J. Danforth	Middletown, Connecticut	Circ. 1825
*Joseph Danforth		18th Century
*Samuel Danforth	Hartford, Connecticut	Circ. 1810
*Thomas Danforth (1)	Norwich, Connecticut, and Taunton, Massachusetts	(b) 1703 (d)c. 1786
*T. Danforth (Thomas) (3)	Philadelphia, Pennsylvania	(D) 1807 1813 (D)
	Corner Thirteenth and High Streets	
Thomas Danforth (2)	Rocky Hill, Connecticut	(b) 1792 (d) 1836
	Philadelphia, Pennsylvania	(W.A.)
	Augusta, Georgia	
*Will Danforth		Before 1825
*T. S. Derby		After 1825
John Dolbeare	Boston, Massachusetts	
	New Haven, Connecticut (?)	
*R. Dunham	Portland, Maine	After 1830
*R. Dunham & Sons	Portland, Maine	After 1830
Eastman & Co.	Albany, New York	
Simon Edgell	Philadelphia, Pennsylvania	1717 (?) 1718 (?)
William L. Elsworth	New York City	(D) 1789 1797 (D)
Also listed in early directories as William J. and William I. In 1795 appears as "Pewterer and Coroner."	1, later 4, Cortland Street	
Edm. Endicott	New York City	(D) 1852 1853 (D)
Once of Endicott & Sumner	195 William Street	
*Endicott & Sumner	New York City	(D) 1846 1851 (D)
Edm. Endicott	106 Elm Street	
Wm. F. Sumner	195 William Street	
James Everett	Philadelphia, Pennsylvania	1717–18 (?)
*Gaius and Jason Fenn	New York City	After 1830
	35 Pack Slip	
*Philip Fields	New York City	(D) 1799 (D)
	16 Bowery Lane	
*Fuller & Smith	Connecticut (?)	After 1830
Lewis Ganty	Baltimore, Maryland	(D) 1802 (D)
Also given "Geanty"	72 French Street	
Gerhardt & Co.		19th Cent. (W.A.)
*Roswell Gleason	Dorchester, Massachusetts	Circ. 1830
Glenmore Company		
(See G. Richardson)		
Samuel Grame	Boston, Massachusetts	17th Century (?)
*Henry Graves	Middletown, Connecticut	1849 (W.A.)
*J. B. and H. Graves	Middletown, Connecticut (?)	After 1830
Richard Graves	Salem, Massachusetts	1635 c. 1669
Andrew Green	Boston, Massachusetts	(D) 1789 1798 (D)
	Temple Street	
*Samuel Green	Boston, Massachusetts	(D) 1798 1810 (D)
	Milk Street, Sweetser's Alley	

GENERAL LIST OF AMERICAN PEWTERERS — *continued*

NAMES	ADDRESSES	DATES
Thomas Green	Boston, Massachusetts Dock Square	(D) 1789 (D)
Henry Grilley	Waterbury, Connecticut	1790 (W.A.)
*Ashbil Griswold		Before 1825
Franklin Hall	Hartford, Connecticut	1840 (W.A.)
Hall, Boardman & Co.	Philadelphia, Pennsylvania	(D) 1846 1857 (D)

Hall & Boardman after 1848
  F. D. Hall
  Hy. S. Boardman
	104 North Third Street
	95 Arch Street after 1855	

*Hall & Cotton		After 1825
*Samuel Hamlin	Providence, Rhode Island 109 North Main Street	Circ. 1825
William (?) Hamlin	Providence, Rhode Island	(b) 1772 (d) 1869 (W.A.)

*Harbeson
  Benjamin Harbeson
  Joseph Harbeson
  "Tin & Copper Smiths"
	Philadelphia, Pennsylvania
	44 South Second Street
		(D) 1793 1803 (circ)

*Lucius Hart
  Of Boardman & Hart
  "Lucius Hart & Co."
  after 1864
	New York City
	178 Water Street
	6 Burling Slip after 1830
		(D) 1828 1863 (D)

Christian Hera	Philadelphia, Pennsylvania 230 North Second Street	(D) 1813 1818 (D)
*C. & J. Hera	Philadelphia, Pennsylvania 230 North Second Street	(D) 1805 1811 (D)
Christian & John Hera	Philadelphia, Pennsylvania 230 North Second Street	(D) 1801 (D)
John Hera	Philadelphia, Pennsylvania 230 North Second Street 61 Walnut Street after 1819	(D) 1802 1804 (D) (D) 1819 1822 (D)
Charlotte Hero	Philadelphia, Pennsylvania 170 North Second Street 230 North Second Street after 1795	(D) 1791 1798 (D)
Christian Hero	Philadelphia, Pennsylvania 170 North Second Street	(D) 1791 (D)
Christopher Hero	Philadelphia, Pennsylvania 230 North Second Street	(D) 1797 1798 (D)
Christiana Herroe	Philadelphia, Pennsylvania Callowhill, between Second and Front Streets	(D) 1785 (D)
John Holden (or Halden)	New York City Market Slip	1743 (?)
*Holmes & Sons	Baltimore, Maryland	After 1825
*Homans & Co.	Cincinnati, Ohio	After 1825
*Henry Hopper	New York City 234 Second Street	(D) 1842 1847 (D)
William Horsewell (dealer?)	New York City	1708 (?)
*Houghton & Wallace		After 1830
Edwin House	Hartford, Connecticut	1841 (W.A.)
*M. Hyde		After 1830
Mary Jackson	Boston, Massachusetts Cornhill	Early 19th Century (?)
Daniel H. Jagger	Hartford, Connecticut	1844 (W.A.)

GENERAL LIST OF AMERICAN PEWTERERS — *continued*

NAMES	ADDRESSES	DATES
James H. Jagger	Hartford, Connecticut	1843 (W.A.)
Walter W. Jagger	Hartford, Connecticut	1839 (W.A.)
*Gershom Jones	Providence, Rhode Island	Pre-Rev. Post-Rev.
Keene	Rhode Island	
*Samuel Kilbourn	Baltimore, Maryland	(D) 1814 1824 (D)
	89, later 93, North Howard Street	
Kilbourn & Porter	Baltimore, Maryland	(D) 1816 (D)
	Saratoga Street	
William Kirby	New York City	(D) 1786 1793 (D)
"Kirkby" in 1786 D.	23 Great Dock Street	
Ran china, glass, and		
earthenware store		
after 1793		
W. W. Knight	Philadelphia, Pennsylvania	
Knowles & Ladd (W.A.)	(?)	
*L. Kruiger	Philadelphia, Pennsylvania	(D) 1833 (D)
(Lewis Kruger in D.)	119 Callowhill	
Moses Lafetra	New York City	(D) 1812 1816 (D)
	Beekman Street	
Lafetra & Allair	New York City	(D) 1815 1816 (D)
	277 Water Street	
James Leddel	New York City	1744 (?) 1780 (?)
	Dock Street	
	Wall Street	
*Richard Lee	Taunton, Massachusetts	Circ. 1770 Post-Rev.
Richard Lee	Providence, Rhode Island	1832 (?)
*Leonard, Reed & Barton	Taunton, Massachusetts	1835 1845 (?)
*George Lightner	Baltimore, Maryland	(D) 1810 1812 (D)
	High Street near Mr. Miller's	
	blacksmith shop	
John Lightner	Baltimore, Maryland	(D) 1814 (D)
	144 High Street	
*J. D. Locke	New York City	(D) 1835 into 1870's
	Various addresses on Water and Cliff Streets	
Locke & Carter	New York City	(D) 1837 1845 (D)
	241, later 193, Water Street	
Bartholomew Longstreet	Buck's County, Pennsylvania	C. 1810 (?)
Malcolm McEwen	New York City	(D) 1787 1792 (D)
	160 Water Street	
Malcolm & Duncan McEwen	New York City	(D) 1793 (D)
	160 Water Street	
Malcolm McEwen & Son	New York City	(D) 1794 1797 (D)
After 1797 listed as	Water and Beekman Streets	
"Plummers"		
*William McQuilkin	Philadelphia, Pennsylvania	(D) 1845 1853 (D)
"Mfr. Britannia Ware"	91 North Second Street	
Thaddeus Manning	Middletown, Connecticut	1849 (W.A.)
Marcus Maton	Hartford, Connecticut	1828 (W.A.)
*Daniel Melvil	Newport, Rhode Island	(?) — 1788 — (?)
Joshua Metzger	Germantown, Pennsylvania	1806 (?) 1820 (?)
Andre Michel	New York City	(D) 1795 1797 (D)
Also Andrew Michal	255 Broadway	
"Tinman & Pewterer"		
S. Moore (W.A.)	Kensington, Connecticut	C. 1820–30 (?)

GENERAL LIST OF AMERICAN PEWTERERS — *continued*

NAMES	ADDRESSES	DATES
*Morey & Ober David B. Morey R. H. Ober	Boston, Massachusetts 5 and 7 Haverhill Street	(D) 1852 1854 (D)
Morey, Ober & Co.	Boston, Massachusetts 5 and 7 Haverhill Street	(D) 1855 (D)
*Morey & Smith	Boston, Massachusetts	1857
*J. Munson	55 North Sixth Street 144 High Street	
*J. H. Palethorp "Ink Powder & Pewter Mfr."	Philadelphia, Pennsylvania 50 North Second Street	(D) 1828 1845 (D)
J. H. & Robert Palethorp, Jr.	Philadelphia, Pennsylvania 50 North Second Street	(D) 1820 1825 (D)
*Robert Palethrop, Jr.	Philadelphia, Pennsylvania 444 North Second Street	(D) 1817 1822 (D)
*J. H. Palethorp & Co. (Mark "Palethorp & Connell") John H. Palethorp Thomas Connell	Philadelphia, Pennsylvania 144 High Street	(D) 1839 1841 (D)
*C. Parker & Co. Caleb Parker, "Whitesmith"	New York City Twenty-Ninth Street near Seventh Avenue	(D) 1849 (D)
Robert Pearse	New York City 13 Chatham Street	(D) 1792 (D)
*Samuel Pierce		Before 1825
*A. Porter	Southington, Connecticut	After 1830
Edmund Porter	Taunton, Massachusetts	Circ. 1800 (W.A.)
Edmund Porter (another?)	Taunton, Massachusetts	Circ. 1847 (W.A.)
*F. Porter	Westbrook, Connecticut	After 1825
James Porter	Baltimore, Maryland North Street	(D) 1803 (D)
Lincoln Porter	Taunton, Massachusetts	Circ. 1800 (W.A.)
Samuel Porter	Taunton, Massachusetts	Circ. 1800 (W.A.)
*Putnam		After 1825
*Reed & Barton	Taunton, Massachusetts	Est. 1845
Paul Revere	Boston, Massachusetts	(b) 1735 (d) 1818
*G. Richardson	Cranston, Rhode Island	1824 (?)
George Richardson	Boston, Massachusetts Oliver Place	1825
Thomas Rigden	Philadelphia, Pennsylvania (?)	Early 19th Century (?)
Leonard M. Rust "Lampmaker"	New York City 8 Dominick Street	(D) 1849 (D)
John N. and Samuel Rust "Lamps"	77 William Street later, 38 Gold Street	(D) 1842 1845 (D)
*Samuel Rust "Formerly Printing Press Maker"	New York City 125 Fulton Street	(D) 1837 1842 (D)
*Sage & Beebe		After 1825
*Savage	Middletown, Connecticut	After 1825
*Savage & Graham	Middletown, Connecticut	After 1825
*Sellew & Co.	Cincinnati, Ohio	After 1830
*"Semper Eadem"	Boston, Massachusetts	
*Sheldon & Feltman	Albany, New York	After 1825
Henry Shrimpton	Boston, Massachusetts	1660–1665

GENERAL LIST OF AMERICAN PEWTERERS — *continued*

Names	Addresses	Dates
*Samuel Simpson	New York City 272½ Pearl Street	(D) 1843 1845 (D)
Simpson & Benham (Same Simpson as above)	New York City 272½ Pearl Street	After 1845
John Skinner	Boston, Massachusetts Newberry Street	(D) 1789 (D)

*E. Smith
  Eben Smith, an employee of
  Israel Trask, who later made
  pewter, britannia, and hose
  nozzles
	Beverly, Massachusetts	After 1825

*Smith & Co.	Connecticut (?)	After 1825
*Smith & Feltman	Albany, New York	After 1825
*H. Snyder	Philadelphia, Pennsylvania	
*S. Stafford	Albany, New York	Before 1825
William H. Starr (dealer?) "Lamps"	New York City 67 Beekman Street	(D) 1843 (D)
S. Stedman (W.A.)		
Jireh Strange	Taunton, Massachusetts	Circ. 1800 (W.A.)
Joseph Strange	Taunton, Massachusetts	Circ. 1800 (W.A.)
*Taunton Britannia Mnfg. Co. "T.B.M.Co."	Taunton, Massachusetts	Est. 1830
*Israel Trask	Beverly, Massachusetts Cabot Street	(b) 1786 (d) 1867 Worked 1825–1842
John Trask	Boston, Massachusetts	(D) 1822 (D) 1826
*Oliver Trask	Beverly, Massachusetts	After 1825 (b) 1792 (d) 1874
*Vose & Co.	Albany, New York	After 1825
Lester Wadsworth	Hartford, Connecticut	1838 (W.A.)
R. Wallace (W.A.)		
*H. B. Ward & Co.	Guilford, Connecticut	After 1825
James Ward	Hartford, Connecticut	1795 (W.A.)
*J. Weekes	New York City (?)	After 1825
*Weekes & Co.	New York City (?)	After 1825
E. Whitehouse		Late 18th Century (W.A.)
Whitlock (dealer?)	Troy, New York	After 1825
George and William Wild	Bucks County, Pennsylvania	19th Century (?)
*Thomas Wildes	New York City Hester and Second Streets	(D) 1832 1840 (D)

George Will
  Also listed "Wills"
  in 1805 and 1806
	Philadelphia, Pennsylvania
	97 North Second Street
	22 Elfreths Alley after 1800
		(D) 1797 1806 (D)

*Henry Will	New York City 3 Water Street 41 Chatham Street in 1793	1765(?) 1793 (D)
*William Will	Philadelphia, Pennsylvania 177 and later 66 North Second Street	(D) 1785 1797 (D)
*Lorenzo L. Williams "Block tin Mfr."	Philadelphia, Pennsylvania Third Street and the Railroad	(D) 1838 1842 (D)

Richard Williams
  Son-in-law and partner of
  Thomas Danforth (3)
	Rocky Hill, Connecticut	

*J. B. Woodbury
  "Japanner & Britannia
  Maker. German Silver Ware."
	Philadelphia, Pennsylvania
	361 Cedar Street
		(D) 1837 1838 (D)

Fig. 27

COMMUNION FLAGON BY THOMAS D. BOARDMAN

13½ inches high

Fig. 28

UNDER SIDE OF TWO PEWTER BUTTONS

Actual size

Fig. 29

EXCEPTIONAL PAIR OF PEWTER WHALE–OIL LAMPS MARKED WITH THE COAT OF ARMS OF
MASSACHUSETTS

Fig. 30

MARK ON ABOVE LAMPS

Fig. 31

A COFFEE-POT PERIOD CONVENTION IN THE AUTHOR'S PEWTER ROOM

Fig. 32

MAGNIFICENT COVERED WATER PITCHER BY ROSWELL GLEASON

The finest type evolved by the Coffee-Pot Era
Height of this specimen, 12½ inches

Fig. 33

RANGE OF THE AMERICAN PEWTER BEAKER

From 2 to 4 inches high

Fig. 34

TYPICAL PEWTER COFFEE-POT OF THE EARLY COFFEE-POT ERA

Specimen by Boardman & Hart
Height, 11 inches

Fig. 35

COFFEE-URN BY ROSWELL GLEASON

Height, 16 inches

GENERAL LIST OF AMERICAN PEWTERERS — *continued*

NAMES	ADDRESSES	DATES

*Woodbury & Colton
  J. B. Woodbury
  O. Colton
	Philadelphia, Pennsylvania
	  22 Library
		(D) 1835 1836 (D)

*Woodman, Cook & Co.	Portland, Maine	After 1830

*Charles Yale
  "Britannia Ware"
	New York City
	  80 Pine Street
		(D) 1832 (D)

*H. Yale & Co.	Wallingford, Connecticut	After 1825
*W. & S. Yale	Wallingford, Connecticut	After 1825

William Yale
  "Lampmaker"
	New York City
	  115 Beekman Street
	  Later, 271 Pearl Street
		(D) 1830 1832 (D)

*Yale & Curtis
  Henry Yale
  Stephen Curtis
	New York City
	  67 Beekman, 90 Fulton,
	  and 45 Gold Streets
		(D) 1858 1867 (D)

George Youle	New York City 294 Water Street	(D) 1798 1828 (D)
George Youle & Co.	Same address	(D) 1829 (D)
Thomas Youle & Co.	New York City 594 Water Street	(D) 1810 1812 (D)
Thomas Youle	New York City 334 Water Street	(D) 1813 1820 (D)
Widow Youle (of Thomas)	New York City 594 Water Street	(D) 1821 1822 (D)

NAMES THAT HAVE APPEARED IN SOME LISTS OF AMERICAN PEWTERERS BUT THAT HAVE BEEN OMITTED, FOR CAUSE, FROM THE ABOVE LIST

Broadhead, Gurney & Co.	English.
Hale.	English.
Christian Heave, Philadelphia, Pennsylvania.	Not in the Philadelphia directories, and probably a misreading of the name "Christian Heavo," as given by mistake in the 1799 and 1800 issues for Christian Hero.
Lewellyn & Co.	Probably English.
E. B. Manning Circ. 1862 (W.A.)	Too late to concern us.
Marshes & Shepherd.	English.
Padelford & Palenthorp, Philadelphia.	Not found in the Philadelphia directories, and apparently an oral confusion of the Palethorp family name.
W. R.	The English touch used during the reign of William IV —?
Joseph Roby Boston 1789.	In directory for one year only, and then as "Tin plate worker." Henry Roby, presumably his brother, has even a better right to be listed, since he figures in the directory from 1789 to 1803. But only as "Tin Man" and as "Tin Plate Worker and Ship Chandler." Joseph and Henry appear as partners again in 1805 for one year.

Joseph Tucker,
  302 Mulberry Street,
  New York City, 1845.
	Appears for this year only with the notation "Britannia." Presumably a dealer.

Watts & Harton.	English.
John Welch, Union Street, Boston.	In 1789 directory as "Ironmonger." In 1796 directory as "Pewterware." In 1800–1803 as "Hardware." No business given in 1788 or from 1805 to 1810. Manifestly a dealer and not a maker.
Yates.	All pieces I have seen marked with this name have been English.

A count shows that this list contains a total of two hundred and fourteen names, but fourteen of these prove, on examination, to be identified and vouched for neither by specimens of surviving pewter nor by dates and places of residence. In short, they are present only as a hint to students that their right to stay is under investigation. And since we cannot codify information that we do not possess, we shall, in the following tables, take cognizance only of the two hundred useful, because informative, names that remain.

The fourteen omissions are as follows:

NAMES OF MAKERS PRINTED IN GENERAL LIST BUT OMITTED FROM FOLLOWING TABLES BECAUSE NO STATISTICAL INFORMATION COULD BE HAD FROM THEM

O. & A. Bailey, New York.	Probably dealer. In 1845 directory only. "Lamps."
C. Bancks.	Probably Chelmsford, Massachusetts, but date unknown.
S. Bast.	Said to be New York, but date unknown.
John Dolbeare.	Said to be Boston and perhaps New Haven. Date unknown.
Gerhardt & Co.	No data.
Keene.	Said to be Rhode Island, but date unknown.
W. W. Knight.	Said to be Philadelphia, but date unknown.
Knowles & Ladd.	No data.
William H. Starr, New York.	In 1843 directory only. "Lamps." Probably dealer.
S. Stedman.	No data.
R. Wallace.	No data.
E. Whitehouse.	Said to be late eighteenth century. No further data.
Whitlock, Troy, New York.	Probably dealer. Known from his name stamped over "Boardman" on a water pitcher. (See Fig. 211.)
Richard Williams.	No data.

We shall not, as a matter of fact, detain even these two hundred for long, because it is, of course, quite evident that the bulk of our information must come from actual specimens of American pewter and what these can teach us about the habits of the craftsmen that made them, rather than from mere data about as yet pewterless pewterers. In other words, the ultimately important part of the general list for our purposes are the one hundred and thirteen men whose pewter we possess and can examine.

The two hundred can, however, tell us something about the numbers engaged in the craft in America at successive periods; and also something of the comparative prominence of the various localities in these same successive periods. And, in the following table, I have therefore divided them up according to habitat, indicating, moreover, by an asterisk (*) in the proper column whether each maker is represented by surviving specimens of his handiwork, and whether he belonged to the period before 1750, to the period between 1750 and 1825, or to the final period between 1825 and 1850. The transition workers are entered in the 1750–1825 column, but are indicated by a "T" instead of an asterisk (*).

LIST OF AMERICAN PEWTERERS
SHOWING THEIR DISTRIBUTION AT SUCCESSIVE PERIODS

TOWN NAME	NAME OF MAKER	PEWTER?	BEFORE 1750	BETWEEN 1750–1825	AFTER 1825
Albany, N.Y.	Eastman & Co.				*
	Sheldon & Feltman	*			*
	Smith & Feltman	*			*
	S. Stafford	*		*	
	Vose & Co.	*			*
Baltimore, Md.	Lewis Ganty			*	
	Holmes & Sons	*			*
	Samuel Kilbourn	*		*	
	Kilbourn & Porter			*	
	George Lightner	*		*	
	John Lightner			*	
	James Porter			*	
Beverly, Mass.	Israel Trask	*			*
	Oliver Trask	*			*
	Eben Smith	*			*
Boston, Mass.	—— Austin	*		*	
	Nathaniel Austin	*		*	
	Richard Austin	*		*	
	Thomas Badger	*		*	
	Thomas Bumsteed		*		
	Thomas Clarke		*		
	John Comer		*		
	Samuel Grame		*		
	Andrew Green			*	
	Samuel Green	*		*	
	Thomas Green			*	
	Mary Jackson				*
	Morey & Ober	*			*
	Morey, Ober & Co.				*
	Morey & Smith	*			*
	Paul Revere			*	
	George Richardson				*
	"Semper Eadem" mark	*		*	
	Henry Shrimpton		*		
	John Skinner	*		*	
	John Trask				*

LIST OF AMERICAN PEWTERERS — *continued*

TOWN NAME	NAME OF MAKER	PEWTER?	BEFORE 1750	BETWEEN 1750–1825	AFTER 1825
Bucks County, Pa......	Bartholomew Longstreet			*	
	George & William Wild				*
Cincinnati, O.........	Homans & Co.	*			*
	Sellew & Co.	*			*
Cranston, R.I.........	G. Richardson	*			*
Dorchester, Mass.......	Roswell Gleason	*			*
Germantown, Pa......	Joshua Metzger			*	
Guilford, Conn........	H. B. Ward & Co.	*			*
Habitation Unknown...	Bailey & Putnam	*			*
	Stephen Barns	*		*	
	——n Brigh——	*		*	
	L. Boardman	*			*
	D. Curtiss	*		T	
	I. Curtis	*		T	
	Joseph Danforth	*		*	
	Will Danforth	*		*	
	T. S. Derby	*			*
	Fuller & Smith	*			*
	Ashbil Griswold	*		T	
	Hall & Cotton	*			*
	Houghton & Wallace	*			*
	M. Hyde	*			*
	J. Munson	*			*
	Samuel Pierce	*		*	
	Putnam	*			*
	Sage & Beebe	*			*
	Smith & Co.	*			*
	J. Weekes	*			*
	Weekes & Co.	*			.*
	Unidentified marks				
	Eagle 1	*		*	
	Eagle 2	*		*	
	Eagle 3	*		*	
	Eagle 4	*		*	
	Arms of Mass. mark	*			*
Hartford, Conn.	Boardman (Lion Mark)	*		T	
	J. D. Boardman				*
	Sherman Boardman				*
	Thomas D. Boardman	*		*	
	T. D. & S. Boardman	*		T	
	David S. Brooks				*
	Edward Danforth	*		*	
	Samuel Danforth	*		*	

LIST OF AMERICAN PEWTERERS — *continued*

Town Name	Name of Maker	Pewter?	Before 1750	Between 1750–1825	After 1825
Hartford, Conn.	Franklin Hall				*
	Edwin House				*
	Daniel H. Jagger				*
	James H. Jagger				*
	Walter W. Jagger				*
	Marcus Maton				*
	Lester Wadsworth				*
	James Ward			*	
Kensington, Conn.	S. Moore				*
Middletown, Conn.	J. Danforth	*		T	
	Henry Graves	*			*
	Thaddeus Manning				*
	Savage	*			*
	Savage & Graham	*			*
New London, Conn. . . .	Joseph Belcher	*		*	
Newport, R.I.	Daniel Melvil	*		*	
New York City	Anthony Allaire			*	
	Francis Bassett	*		*	
	Frederick Bassett	*		*	
	James Bird			*	
	Timothy Boardman & Co.	*		*	
	Boardman & Co.	*		T	
	Boardman & Hart	*		T	
	Robert Boyle			*	
	William Bradford			*	
	Capen & Molineux	*		*	*
	George Coldwell	*		*	
	Curtis & Co.				*
	William L. Elsworth			*	
	Edm. Endicott				*
	Endicott & Sumner	*			*
	Gaius and Jason Fenn	*			*
	Philip Fields	*		*	
	Lucius Hart				*
	Lucius Hart & Co.				*
	John Holden			*	
	Henry Hopper	*			*
	William Horsewell		*		
	William Kirkby			*	
	Moses Lafetra			*	
	Lafetra & Allaire			*	
	James Leddel			*	
	J. D. Locke	*			*
	Locke & Carter				*
	Malcolm McEwen			*	
	Malcolm & Duncan McEwen			*	

LIST OF AMERICAN PEWTERERS — *continued*

Town Name	Name of Maker	Pewter?	Before 1750	Between 1750–1825	After 1825
New York City.......	Malcolm McEwen & Son			*	
	Andre Michel			*	
	C. Parker & Co.	*			*
	Robert Pearse			*	
	Leonard M. Rust				*
	John N. & Samuel Rust				*
	Samuel Rust	*			*
	Samuel Simpson	*			*
	Simpson & Benham	*			*
	Thomas Wildes	*			*
	Henry Will	*		*	
	Charles Yale	*			*
	William Yale				*
	Yale & Curtis	*			*
	George Youle			*	
	George Youle & Co.				*
	Thomas Youle			*	
	Thomas Youle & Co.			*	
	Widow Youle			*	
Norwich, Conn.........	Thomas Danforth	*		*	
Portland, Me..........	R. Dunham	*			*
	R. Dunham & Sons	*			*
	Woodman Cook Co.	*			*
Philadelphia, Pa........	B. Barns	*		*	*
	Henry S. Boardman	*			
	Boardman & Hall	*		T	
	Parks Boyd	*		*	
	Cornelius Bradford			*	
	Thomas Connell				*
	T. Danforth	*		*	
	Simon Edgell		*		
	James Everett		*		
	Hall, Boardman & Co.				*
	Harbeson	*		*	
	Christian Hera			*	
	C. & J. Hera	*		*	
	Christian & John Hera			*	
	John Hera			*	
	Charlotte Hero			*	
	Christian Hero			*	
	Christopher Hero			*	
	Christiana Herroe			*	
	Lewis Kruiger	*			*
	William McQuilkin	*			*
	J. H. Palethorp	*			*
	J. H. and Robt. Palethorp, Jr.	*			*
	Robert Palethorp, Jr.	*		*	*
	Palethorp & Connell	*			*

LIST OF AMERICAN PEWTERERS — *continued*

Town Name	Name of Maker	Pewter?	Before 1750	Between 1750–1825	After 1825
Philadelphia, Pa.	Thomas Rigden				*
	H. Snyder	*			*
	George Wills			*	
	William Will	*		*	
	Lorenzo L. Williams	*			*
	J. B. Woodbury	*			*
	Woodbury & Colton	*			*
Providence, R.I.	William Billings	*		*	
	William Calder	*		T	
	Cleveland & Bros.	*			*
	Samuel Hamlin	*		*	
	William (?) Hamlin			*	
	Gershom Jones	*		*	
	Richard Lee				
Rocky Hill, Conn.	Thomas Danforth	*		*	
Salem, Mass.	Richard Graves		*		
Southington, Conn.	A. Porter	*			*
Taunton, Mass.	Babbitt, Crossman & Co.	*			*
	Crossman, West & Leonard	*			*
	Richard Lee	*		*	
	Leonard, Reed & Barton	*			*
	Edmund Porter			*	
	Lincoln Porter			*	
	Samuel Porter			*	
	Reed & Barton	*			*
	Jireh Strange			*	
	Joseph Strange			*	
	Taunton Britannia Mfg. Co.	*			*
Wallingford, Conn.	H. Yale & Co.	*			*
	W. & S. Yale	*			*
Waterbury, Conn.	Henry Grilley			*	
Westbrook, Conn.	F. Porter	*			*
West Roxbury, Mass.	"Brook Farm"	*			*

In this form the list offers a convenient reference list for those who want, for any purpose, to examine the New York City or the Boston or Philadelphia pewterers' lists; or, indeed, for any one who recalls that a man whose name he has forgotten worked in Providence, and wants to identify him. But as yet it is not sufficiently condensed to give us at a glance the specific information we are in search of. In order, therefore, to extract from it the essence of this information, the following summary by cities has been compiled:

Town Name	Number of Makers	Pewter	Before 1750	Eight-Inch-Plate Period	Transition Workers	Coffee-Pot Era
New York City........	49	19	1	24	2	22
Philadelphia, Pa........	32	17	2	16	1	13
Habitation unknown...	21	21		5	3	13
Boston, Mass.........	21	9	5	10		6
Hartford, Conn........	16	5		4	2	10
Taunton, Mass.........	11	6		6		5
Baltimore, Md.........	7	3		6		1
Providence, R.I........	7	5		4	1	2
Albany, N.Y...........	5	4		1		4
Middletown, Conn......	5	4			1	4
Beverly, Mass.........	3	3				3
Portland, Maine.......	3	3				3
Bucks County, Pa......	2			1		1
Cincinnati, Ohio.......	2	2				2
Wallingford, Conn......	2	2				2
Cranston, R.I.........	1	1				1
Germantown, Pa.......	1			1		
Dorchester, Mass.......	1	1				1
Guilford, Conn.........	1	1				1
Kensington, Conn......	1					1
New London, Conn.....	1	1		1		
Newport, R.I.........	1	1		1		
Norwich, Conn........	1	1		1		
Rocky Hill, Conn	1	1		1		
Salem, Mass..........	1		1			
Southington, Conn.....	1	1				1
Waterbury, Conn.......	1			1		
Westbrook, Conn......	1	1				1
West Roxbury, Mass....	1	1				1
Totals.........	200	113	9	83	10	98

We note, then, after studying this revealing summary, that from first to last — as far as we now know — pewter was made in twenty-eight American cities, all but two of which are situated in the East; and that specimens of pewter known to have been made in twenty-three of these twenty-eight cities survive. We see that but nine makers out of the total number of two hundred considered, worked during the period before 1750, and that they were located in but four cities; one in New York City, two in Philadelphia, five in Boston and the remaining one in Salem (although according to some accounts he also worked in Boston). We find that the pewterer's craft so increased in this country between 1750 and 1825 that a total of eighty-three makers, distributed among seventeen cities, are recorded as working during the latter period. We see that the leadership, which belonged to Boston in the earlier period, had now shifted overwhelmingly to New York; that Philadelphia, while still retaining the second place that it had previously held, had also, meanwhile, outstripped Boston; and that of the thirteen new cities where the craft had sprung up, six were in Connecticut, two in Rhode Island, two in Pennsylvania, and one each in New York, Massachusetts, and Maryland.

We see that a total of only ten men — five of whom, moreover, seem to have been partners or agents of one Hartford firm — made articles characteristic of both the eight-inch-plate and the coffee-pot periods, and are consequently classed by us as transition workers. And, finally, we see that in the coffee-pot era itself, the total number of makers rose to ninety-eight; and the total number of cities where pewter was made, to twenty-two; and that of this number eleven had never before sheltered the craft, while six cities had given over making pewter altogether. Indeed, when we note that Boston, with five makers in the first period and ten in the second, had fallen back to six in the third; that Philadelphia, with two makers in the first period and thirteen in the second, had fallen to twelve in the third; that New York, with but one in the first period and twenty-four in the second, had fallen to twenty-two in the third; while six lesser cities represented in the second had ceased to be so in the third; and that Hartford, with none in the first period and five in the second, had grown to ten in the third, while eleven cities were making in the third that had never made before — we get a vivid glimpse of how wholly the locale of the trade as well as its character and its personnel had altered after the passing of the eating-plate era.

For the purpose of presenting the information contained in this grouping of makers by sections and periods in still more concentrated form, the following table by States and the succeeding statement of summaries are here given:

State Name	Number of Makers	Pewter	Before 1750	Eight-Inch-Plate Period	Transition Workers	Coffee-Pot Era
New York.............	54	23	1	25	2	26
Massachusetts.........	38	20	6	16		16
Connecticut...........	31	17		8	3	20
Pennsylvania..........	35	17	2	18	1	14
Habitation unknown....	21	21		5	3	13
Rhode Island..........	9	7		5	1	3
Maryland.............	7	3		6		1
Maine................	3	3				3
Ohio.................	2	2				2
Totals............	200	113	9	83	10	98

Period	Total Number of Known Makers	Total Number Represented by Pewter	Known from Pewter only	Known from both Pewter and Records	Known from Records only
Before 1750..........	9	0	0	0	9
Eight-inch plate......	83	37	5	32	46
Transition workers....	10	10	3	7	0
Coffee-pot era........	98	66	13	53	32
Totals..........	200	113	21	92	87

Commenting upon this last tabulation of our data, we note — a fact not shown by the former arrangements — how rapidly the number of names not represented by surviving pewter increases in proportion to the whole number as we go backward in time.

Out of the entire list of two hundred, we have pewter by one hundred and thirteen makers. The ten transition workers are naturally all represented by pewter, since our definition of them is based on the character of their output. But only thirty-seven of the total of eighty-three names belonging to the eight-inch-plate period are so represented, while sixty-six of the total of ninety-eight names belonging to the coffee-pot era have pewter surviving.

This is quite natural, of course; and is no doubt due to two causes. In the first place, the earlier pewter has largely disappeared. And in the second place, the earlier records have been much more thoroughly examined. For the city directories back of 1825 are, to our eyes, accustomed to the huge compilations of modern telephone and business directories, absurd little pocket-sized affairs, easily searched through from cover to cover. And they have repeatedly been so searched by students of American handicrafts. On the other hand, I dare say that I have, individually, done more searching of the later directories, in attempting to locate late makers whose names I had found on pewter, than has ever before been done by people who would have noted a pewterer's name had they come across one.

Here's good hunting to those who, one hopes, are going to keep a sharp watch for specimens by the forty-six missing makers of the eight-inch-plate period, as well as for such of their fellow workers who may be still unknown as well as missing. I need hardly say that I would greatly appreciate reports from the lucky ones as to their discoveries, including rubbings of any marks not illustrated in this book.

CHAPTER VI

THE EIGHT–INCH–PLATE MEN

IT has already been set down that it is only by contact with pewter itself that the understanding that rewards the student or the responsiveness that marks the amateur of this metal can be developed. Yet it is, of course, impossible for the author of a treatise like the present one to pass real pewter round while he writes. And it is also, unhappily, seldom feasible for the reader of such a volume to have simultaneous access to a sufficiently comprehensive collection. But while the aids of touch and hearing are thus denied you, dear Mr. and Mrs. Reader, the eye at least can be half-persuaded that it is looking upon the actual specimens under discussion.

Yet even a "roving eye" does not like to rove too far from the text in order to look at an illustration. And the most industrious and painstaking student is apt to rebel at a too constant necessity for turning pages in search of cuts. Indeed, I am sure that I will evoke a "You said it, Bo!" when I confess to never having been able to make up my mind as to which of the usual arrangements I disliked most — the one by which the illustrations are nicely scattered at even intervals through the book; or that by which all the illustrations, Quaker-meeting fashion, are segregated, bunched and rendered *incomunicado*, in a special *corral* at the end of the volume. Add to either of these methods of distribution the usual scheme of printing the "List of Illustrations," not in the alphabetical order of their subjects, but in the same sequence as the page numbers where they are to be found (so that it is only relatively less wasteful of time to hunt through this list than it is to look through the pages), and the likelihood of the reader's keeping on looking up the references to illustrations dwindles to a vanishing point.

I hope, in the present and succeeding chapters, to bid a temporary adieu, at least, to both of these time-honored arrangements; and shall there try to induce descriptive text and illustrative cuts to run in double harness. There will, of course, be times when one or another will hang back on its running mate or momentarily take the bit in its teeth and forge ahead. But be patient with them. They've only worked together a few times.

Here follows the list of the makers of the eight-inch-plate period, given in the approximately chronological order in which they will then be successively taken up, illustrated, and discussed.

AMERICAN PEWTERERS OF THE EIGHT-INCH-PLATE PERIOD SPECIMENS OF WHOSE WORK ARE KNOWN, ARRANGED CHRONOLOGICALLY

Thomas Danforth (1)	Taunton, Massachusetts; Norwich, Connecticut	(b) 1703	(d) c. 1786
Joseph Danforth			
Francis Bassett	New York City	Pre-Rev.	1799 (D)
Frederick Bassett	New York City	Pre-Rev.	1798 (D)
Henry Will	New York City	1765 (?)	1793 (D)
Gershom Jones	Providence, Rhode Island	Pre-Rev.	Post-Rev.
Richard Lee	Taunton, Massachusetts	1770 (?)	Post-Rev.
—— Austin	Boston, Massachusetts		
Nathaniel Austin	Boston, Massachusetts	(b) 1741	(d),1816 (D)
William Will	Philadelphia, Pennsylvania	Pre-Rev.	1797 (D)
D. Melvil	Newport, Rhode Island	1780	
Joseph Belcher	New London, Connecticut		
"Semper Eadem"	Boston, Massachusetts		
Thomas Badger	Boston, Massachusetts	(D) 1789	1810 (D)
John Skinner	Boston, Massachusetts	(D) 1789 (D)	
Edward Danforth	Hartford, Connecticut (?)		
Samuel Pierce			
William Billings	Providence, Rhode Island	1791 (?)	
George Coldwell	New York City	(D) 1792	1796 (D)
Benj. and Joseph Harbeson	Philadelphia, Pennsylvania	(D) 1793	1803 (?)
Richard Austin	Boston, Massachusetts	(D) 1796	1813 (D)
Samuel Green	Boston, Massachusetts	(D) 1798	1810 (D)
Parks Boyd	Philadelphia, Pennsylvania	(D) 1798	1819 (D)
William Danforth			
C. & J. Hera	Philadelphia, Pennsylvania	(D) 1805	1811 (D)
Thomas Danforth (2)	Rocky Hill, Connecticut		
Thomas Danforth (3)	Philadelphia, Pennsylvania	(D) 1807	1813 (D)
Samuel Danforth	Hartford, Connecticut	Circ. 1810	
George Lightner	Baltimore, Maryland	(D) 1810	1812 (D)
B. Barns	Philadelphia, Pennsylvania	(D) 1812	1817 (D)
Samuel Kilbourn	Baltimore, Maryland	(D) 1814	1824 (D)
Robert Palethorp, Jr.	Philadelphia, Pennsylvania	(D) 1817	1822 (D)
Samuel Hamlin	Providence, Rhode Island	(D) 1824	
S. Stafford	Albany, New York		
Stephen Barns			
—— n Brigh ——			
Unidentified Eagle 1			
Unidentified Eagle 2			
Unidentified Eagle 3			
Unidentified Eagle 4			
Thomas D. Boardman	Hartford, Connecticut	Before 1825	

THOMAS DANFORTH (1)

Thomas Danforth, of Taunton, Massachusetts, and Norwich, Connecticut, is not only one of the earliest American pewterers whose work has survived, but he founded one of the great pewter-making dynasties of American pewter history. Thomas (1) — for there were, later on, two more of the name — was born in Taunton in 1703 and died about 1786. He is said to have worked in Norwich, Connecticut, as well as in his native town. His pewter, naturally, is rare, and I have seen nothing attributable to him except flatware. The eight-and-three-eighths-inch plate shown at the left, in Fig. 36, I believe to be a specimen of his Norwich work. It bears an indistinct touch showing the name "Danforth" and the separate touch with the name "Norwich," shown in Fig. 37. Besides this I have seen only a few seven-and-three-quarters-inch plates — one of which is shown at the right in Fig. 36 — a few eight-inch plates, and the twelve-and-a-quarter-inch plate in the same illustration.

Thomas Danforth's normal mark appears to have been that shown in Fig. 38, accompanied by the hall marks shown in Fig. 39. These are the marks on the twelve-and-a-quarter-inch plate here shown, as well as upon half of the smaller plates that I have seen. The touch shown in Fig. 40 appears upon the remainder of the smaller plates that I believe to have been made by Thomas Danforth (1). My reason for this belief is that this touch, wherever I have seen it, has been accompanied by the identical hall marks illustrated in Fig. 39. It is possible that the lion mark with his name in full (Fig. 38), which is quite in the English style of the middle eighteenth century, is the mark used by Thomas Danforth (1) before the Revolution, and that the lion mark with the initials (Fig. 40) was used by him later. But of course this is only surmise. An occasional impression of this mark (Fig. 40) is found in which the "D" looks like an "I." That this is a broken or defaced die, however, is proved by the fact that the hall marks accompanying these impressions have the "T.D." lettering as usual. Another Thomas Danforth, called "Thomas Danforth (2)" in this volume, used somewhat similar marks. For purposes of comparison see Fig. 127. Thomas Danforth (1) will be found included in the third grade of comparative rarity in the list printed in Chapter XI.

JOSEPH DANFORTH

The placing of Joseph Danforth in a list chronologically arranged is to some extent a matter of guesswork. A "James Danforth," with the birth date of 1745 attached to him, and said to have been a pewterer, has been reported to me by a connection of the family. I have wondered whether this rumored "James" was not really a "Jos." instead of a "Jas." and whether it is not, therefore, his pewter that we are about to discuss. At any rate one thing is beyond much possibility of error; and that is that work of Thomas (1) and the work of Joseph belong to approximately the same period. Both are distinctly eighteenth-century English in their markings. And, indeed, the marks of the two men are so very similar that it requires close attention and an expert familiarity with the two designs to tell them apart when, as often happens, an impression fails to show the Christian name. Even the two sets of hall marks bear identical symbols in the same order; differing only in the sizes of the four shields and in the presence of the letters "T.D." in the first shield of Thomas's set and of "I.D." in that of Joseph's. And even there, the "T" and the "I" are so much alike as to puzzle one at times. By far the quickest way to identify an imperfect impression of one of these touches is to remember that the small grid (it looks like the head of a steel garden rake) on which, in both marks, the lion's hind foot rests, comes, in Thomas's touch, above the "OR" of the name "DANFORTH"; while in Joseph's this grid is immediately over the "FO" of that name. A comparison of Fig. 38 with Fig. 42 will show this clearly. As between the two men, the work of Joseph is the rarer. I have seen about twice the number of pieces by Thomas (1) as by Joseph. Both are hard to find, however, and there are not enough pieces by either to make it possible for very many collections to display specimens by them. I know of no pieces by Joseph that are not plates. Indeed, he has credit on my check list for only five eight-inch plates and one thirteen-inch one. This fine example and two of the eight-inch size are shown in Fig. 41. His marks are reproduced in Fig. 42. His name will be found in the second grade as to rarity in the list in Chapter XI.

FRANCIS BASSETT

Francis Bassett shares with Henry Will the distinction of being the earliest
represented members of the pewterer's craft in New York. We do not, as yet,
know the exact date at which either of these men began work. The date of
1765 has been assigned to Henry Will, but I do not know with what authority.
Both men appear as pewterers in the earliest edition (1786) of the New York
City Directory; and both are shown by their work and marks to have worked
before the Revolution. We give Francis Bassett precedence because "he spells
his name with a B."

All things considered, I am inclined to regard Francis Bassett as being, from
the collector's point of view, the most desirable of all the American makers,
and his work as the most valuable. There are several factors in this estimate.
To start with, his name has figured in all the lists of American pewterers ever
published, and has consequently been before the eyes of students of this
subject from the beginning. Then, he belongs to the Revolution-spanning
group of our earliest pewter-represented makers, and is the only pewterer
listed in the first issue of the New York City Directory. And, finally, he is as
far as I know represented by but a single specimen of his marked work — the
eight-inch plate illustrated in Fig. 43, the marks on which are shown in Fig.
44. I have already mentioned finding this plate and identifying its maker by
the aid of the little list of makers published in N. H. Moore's book. This was
somewhere back in 1911 or 1912. Naturally, I have been on the lookout for
other pieces by him ever since; and I have never seen another.

I have, it is true, thought that I had found at least two other specimens of
Francis's work. For one of the mysterious traditions that get themselves
born, apparently without parents, and are found actively engaged in guiding
the blind in all collecting fields, has had it for years that, of the two small
Bassett marks with the letters "F.B." in a roped circle, the one with fleur-de-
lys decorations belonged to Francis, while the one with the dots was used by
Frederick.

Now the proving or disproving of such persuasive-looking traditions as

Fig. 36

THOMAS DANFORTH (1), 1708–1786

8¼ inch plate · · · · · · · · · · · · · · 12¼ inch plate · · · · · · · · · · · · · · 7¾ inch plate

Fig. 38

Fig. 37

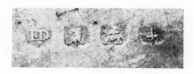

Fig. 39

Fig. 40

MARKS USED BY THOMAS DANFORTH (1)

Fig. 41

JOSEPH DANFORTH

8 inch plate   13 inch plate   8 inch plate

Fig. 42

MARKS USED BY JOSEPH DANFORTH

Fig. 43

FRANCIS BASSETT, PRE–REVOLUTION TO 1799

8 inch plate

Fig. 44

MARKS USED BY FRANCIS BASSETT

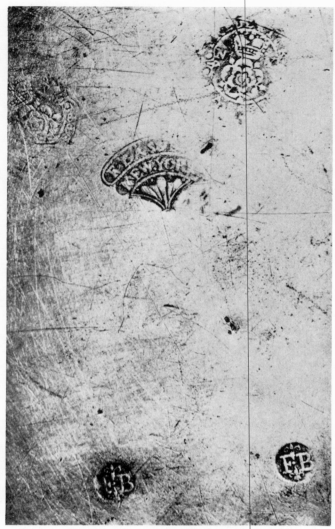

Fig. 45

Fig. 46

Fig. 45A

Fig. 46A

MARKS USED BY FREDERICK BASSETT

Fig. 47

FREDERICK BASSETT, PRE–REVOLUTION TO 1798

8 inch plate   14¾ inch plate   8½ inch plate
13½ inch plate
Flat-topped tankard

Fig. 48

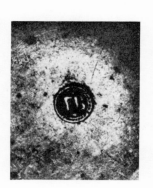

Fig. 49

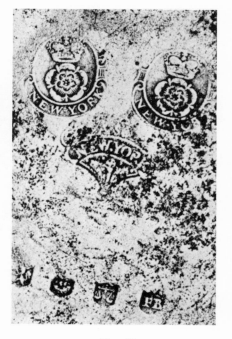

Fig. 50

MARKS USED BY FREDERICK BASSETT

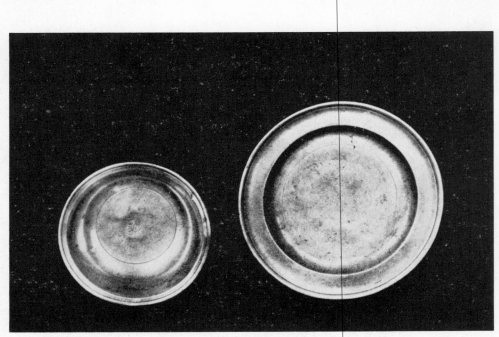

Fig. 51

HENRY WILL 1765 (?)–1793

6½ inch basin   9 inch plate

Fig. 52

Fig. 53

Fig. 54

MARKS USED BY HENRY WILL

Fig. 55

GERSHOM JONES
Worked before and after the Revolution

8¾ inch plate   15 inch charger   8¾ inch plate

Fig. 56

Fig. 58

Fig. 59

Fig. 57

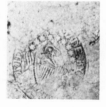

Fig. 60

Fig. 61

Fig. 62

MARKS USED BY GERSHOM JONES

Fig. 63

RICHARD LEE, 1770 TO POST-REVOLUTION

7¾ inch basin   Ladle   8¼ inch plate
                                                          2¾ inch porringer

Fig. 64 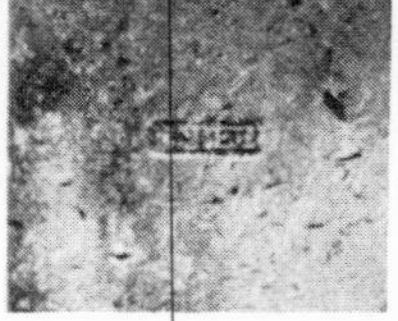   Fig. 65

MARKS USED BY RICHARD LEE

Fig. 66

AUSTIN (OF THE MASSACHUSETTS COAT OF ARMS MARK)

15 inch plate
12¼ inch plate
8 inch plate

Fig. 67

Fig. 68

MARKS USED BY THIS AUSTIN

Fig. 69

NATHANIEL AUSTIN, 1741–1816

15 inch plate
8 inch basin

8 inch plate

Fig. 71

Fig. 70

MARKS USED BY NATHANIEL AUSTIN

Fig. 72

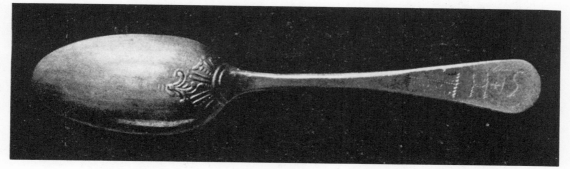

Fig. 73

WILLIAM WILL, PRE–REVOLUTION TO 1797

8 inch plate   Tablespoon   Dome-topped tankard

Fig. 74

Fig. 75

Fig. 76

Fig. 77

Fig. 78   Fig. 79

MARKS USED BY WILLIAM WILL

Fig. 80

WARMING PAN BY WILLIAM WILL

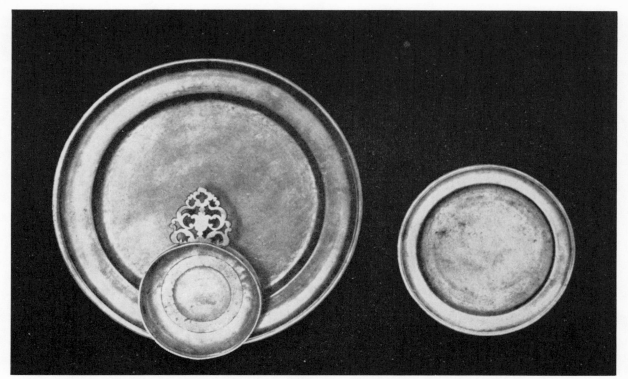

Fig. 81

DANIEL MELVIL, 1780

14 inch plate   8¼ inch plate
5¼ inch porringer

Fig. 82

Fig. 83

Fig. 84

Fig. 85

MARKS USED BY DANIEL MELVIL

Fig. 86

JOSEPH BELCHER, LATE EIGHTEENTH CENTURY

8 inch plate
4 inch porringer   5¼ inch porringer

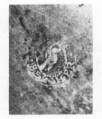

Fig. 87   Fig. 88   Fig. 90

Fig. 89

MARKS USED BY JOSEPH BELCHER

Fig. 91

"SEMPER EADEM" (THOMAS BADGER?)

8 inch plate

Fig. 92

Fig. 93

MARKS USED BY "SEMPER EADEM" MAKER

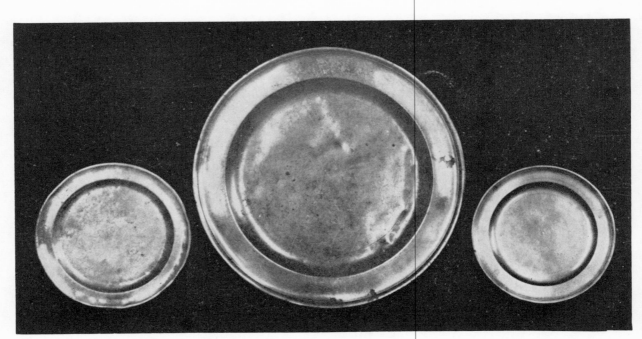

Fig. 94

THOMAS BADGER, 1789–1810

8 inch plate   14¾ inch plate   8 inch plate

Fig. 95   Fig. 96

MARKS USED BY THOMAS BADGER

this — at the very least the refusal to take them at their face value — is part of the duty of the investigator. And the successful confirmation of a long-familiar ascription may be as exciting as the taking of a wily old square-tail that has long looked askance at one's most appetizing flies. Several such adventures will be referred to later on. But in the case of the Bassetts it has been my fate first to think that I had successfully verified the accuracy of tradition's ascriptions, and then to find that both tradition and my supposed verification of it were wrong.

It must be remembered that these small initialed touches were intended for use on articles where it was inconvenient or impossible to use the larger marks that the maker habitually applied to his flatware and other large pieces. It is, therefore, only at very rare intervals, if at all, that one can — by finding one of these small marks applied to a piece of flatware in company with the usual name-plate touches of the maker — secure an absolute identification of it. I was, therefore, very much elated when I got hold of an eight-inch plate by Frederick Bassett, upon the back of which, in addition to both his usual name-plate touch and his oval mark showing the crowned rose, two impressions of the small initialed mark showing the letters "F.B.," and the famous dots above and below, had been impressed. The marks on this plate have been reproduced in Fig. 45a.

Quite naturally, I think, I concluded that, since the traditional ascription of this one of the two initialed marks to Frederick Bassett was thus proved beyond question, it followed that the other form of this circular, initialed "F.B." mark (Figs. 45, 46 and 46a) had been properly ascribed to Francis. The more so, since a reference to Fig. 44 will show that Francis actually did use the fleur-de-lys as a decorative motif in his small initialed mark that has a lion on it. Please note that above the lion on this mark appear not only the fleur-de-lys, but two stars. And then note that in the hall marks used by Frederick Bassett (Figs. 48 and 50) the lion is used in the first shield, and that the famous "dots" in Frederick's initialed mark (Figs. 45a and 49) prove, on examination, to be stars. These facts make one think it likely that these two Bassetts were near relatives, and that the lion, the fleur-de-lys, and the stars were perhaps heraldic fragments from their common family arms. At any rate, it is evident that these items were *Bassett* stigmata and not *Frederick* or *Francis* ones. For one of the last adventures I had before going to press with this volume, was the finding of a fourteen-and-a-half-inch plate with the marks shown in Fig. 45. Here, as will be seen at once, are the familiar and unmistakable Frederick Bassett touches, accompanied by two impressions of the initialed touch that has always been assigned to Francis Bassett. The evidence, I take it, is beyond quarreling with. It deprives my collection of two very fine specimens of what I had supposed to be Francis Bassett mugs; one a quart-sized one, shown in Fig. 22, and the other a pint one, not illustrated. But as I have received in exchange for these, two Frederick Bassett mugs and the truth about these marks, I feel that I have made a good bargain!

FREDERICK BASSETT

It is quite possible that, in placing Frederick Bassett next to his earlier name-bearer, Francis, we are doing a slight violence to the chronological order we are attempting to maintain. But it is evident from Frederick's work that he also began making pewter before the Revolution, and while he is very probably later than Henry Will, it is too important to place his marks within comparing distance to those of Francis to stand too meticulously on a possible few years of priority. Frederick's name does not appear in the 1786 New York City Directory. It is first found in the 1787 issue, and then continues to appear until the issue of 1798, when it is printed for the last time. This makes it look as though Frederick did not begin work until 1787. But not only do his work and his marks seem definitely to contradict this evidence, but no one who has familiarized himself with the rather catch-as-catch-can methods of the compilers and issuers of the earlier city directories would take the non-appearance of a name as positive proof that the bearer of it was not at the time a resident of the town in question. Indeed, I have repeatedly found, in the course of tracing pewterers' careers through the pages of these valuable, if erratic, books of reference, that it was distinctly unsafe to take the disappearance of a name from one or two issues as evidence of the bearer's final retirement.

Personally, I believe that Frederick Bassett was out when the directory man called on him in 1786, and that this gentleman never came back to find out whom he had missed.

Specimens of Frederick's work are somewhat more frequently — or, more correctly speaking, are somewhat less infrequently — met with than specimens of the work of Francis. Nevertheless, they are among the great rarities and are in every way in the first flight of desirables from the collector's point of view. The covered tankard with the flat lid and the Charles II type of lip, illustrated in Fig. 47, is as beautiful an example of the work of an American pewterer as I have ever seen. A "close-up" of this piece appears in Fig. 20. In Fig. 24 is also shown another interesting specimen of Frederick's work. It is a commode form, eight inches high and twelve inches in diameter at the top, and bears his small "F.B." touch on the under side of the bottom. Of the plates illustrated, the left-hand one in Fig. 47 bears the marks shown in Fig. 48 (including the hall marks); while the marks shown in Fig. 50 are from the right-hand plate in the illustration. The two large plates shown at the back of the illustration are respectively thirteen and fourteen and three-quarter inches in diameter. Both are hammer-finished and both bear the marks shown in Fig. 48 without the hall marks. I rank them among the rarest pieces of American flatware extant. Frederick Bassett is marked in the second grade of comparative rarity.

HENRY WILL

Henry Will, as we have already said, is probably earlier than Frederick Bassett. He ceased work, too, earlier than either of the Bassetts, disappearing finally from the New York directories in 1793. And his work is of the first order of rarity. Indeed, I have seen but two specimens of his pewter — both of which are illustrated in Fig. 51. The plate is a nine-inch one and is one of the very few American plates that I have ever seen finished with the hammer after the method prescribed by the London Society of Pewterers. It also bears the touch of the crowned rose without initials or other personal insignia — which was the method of use prescribed by that Society's rules. In other words, this plate is the most typically English in style of any American plate I know of. It bears on the back the two touches reproduced in Figs. 52 and 53. The touch shown in Fig. 54 appears on the inside of the beautiful little six-and-a-half-inch basin shown in Fig. 51. This touch is very probably later than those upon the plate. At any rate, in it the crowned rose is combined with the maker's name and place of residence in a manner not permitted by the English rules.

GERSHOM JONES

It is distinctly a freak of whatever fate has control of the destinies of pewterware that Boston should score so heavily in the lists of earliest pewterers' names, and come off so poorly in the matter of earliest pewter. She has her innings, however, in the years immediately following the close of the War of Independence.

Gershom Jones, the next maker on our list, worked in Providence, and worked both before and after the Revolution. So much we can safely state from an examination of his marks and of his pewter. But I have no data as to when he began or, indeed, as to when he left off. The date 1784 has been assigned to him in some of the early lists. As usual no indication is offered as to the source of the information — if such it be. Specimens of his work are decidedly rare. I have come across but four pieces by him — all flatware.

One of these pieces is an eight-inch plate. Two are eight-and-three-eighths-inch plates. And the fourth is a magnificent fifteen-inch charger. The latter and two of the small plates are shown in Fig. 55.

Either the successful impressing of a maker's touch upon a piece of pewter-ware was an operation that required more skill than was usually possessed by the workmen entrusted with the job, or else these workmen were uniformly careless in performing this special duty. Perfect impressions of makers' touches are rare indeed. With a collection of seven hundred specimens of marked pewter to select from, it will readily be noticed how frequently I have been driven to reproducing two or more impressions of one touch in order to show the whole design — and haven't always done so then. In the case of Gershom Jones it has been necessary — or, at any rate, I have thought it desirable — to make reproductions from three different specimens, including five impressions all told, in order to place before the student a clear impression of all parts of Gershom's pre-Revolutionary touch and hall marks. (See Figs. 58, 61, and 62.) To me, this touch and its accompanying hall marks are among the most striking of all the touches on American pewter. They have about them something of what, in living people, we call personality; and, interesting in many ways as this maker's marks are in their post-Revolutionary form, these certainly do not equal his earlier designs. Something of primitive force-fulness seems to have flown out of the window when patriotism came in by the door.

However, the post-Revolutionary marks of this maker are distinctly interesting. The four examples shown in Figs. 56, 57, 59, and 60 are all from the back of the fifteen-inch charger which occupies the central position in Fig. 55. It is worth while comparing the later form of Jones's hall marks (Fig. 57) with the earlier form (Fig. 58). Note the use of the more modern "J." instead of the earlier, and less definite, "I." Note, also, the introduction of the anchor and stars from the Rhode Island coat of arms. And note the introduction of the suspended sheep — a symbol that was used from time immemorial by dealers in tin, and that was thus no doubt considered to be free from any distinctively British connection. The touch giving the name of the town of origin, Providence, with the Rhode Island coat of arms and the thirteen stars, is interesting as one of the comparatively few uses of this type of mark — Melvil, also of Providence, and Austin, of Boston, about completing the list. Finally the partly erased touch with the American eagle with a (comparatively) huge shield on its breast hiding all of the bird but its head and with an inscription that appears to have read "Made in Providence by G. Jones," actually introduces a touch of humor into the "touches" of the pewterers. For not only is this probably the earliest extant use of the eagle as a pewterer's touch, but the eagle itself seems to bear out this fact by appearing to be in the very act of emerging, half-fledged, from the shell.*

The fifteen-inch deep plate or charger in Fig. 55 is one of the grandest pieces of surviving American pewter on account of its great size, fine quality, and beautiful condition, as well as because of the rarity and early date of its maker. A fifteen-inch charger by Samuel Hamlin, also of Providence, is shown later on. These are the only two American pewterers by whom, as yet, pieces of this size and type have been discovered. The fifteen-inch pieces by the other four makers who are known to have put out dishes of this size in America are all of the shallow-plate type. A specimen by Frederick Bassett, of New York, has just been shown. The other men all hail from Boston.

We of to-day are familiar with the fact that Boston likes brunette eggs, while New Yorkers will pay fancy prices only for eggs with white shells. A somewhat similar difference of opinion in the matter of pewter flatware seems to have existed during the eight-inch-plate period. Practically all flatware made in Boston was of the "plate" type. A single eleven-inch deep plate by an unidentified Boston maker is the only exception that has come to my notice. Yet from Providence south, more "dishes" and "chargers" — plates of the "soup-plate" form — seem to have been made than any other, after the nine-inch size was passed. The exact figures are given in Chapter XI.

* The mark shown in Fig. 99 is a Gershom Jones touch, and not, as I had thought likely, one of Edward Danforth's. When completely seen, it shows the letters "G" and "I", one on either side of the lion. The "G" looks like part of the lion's tail. The "I" is in front of the animal's extended paws.

RICHARD LEE

Richard Lee is reputed to have been an English pewterer who, about 1770, settled in Taunton, Massachusetts, where he started the practice of his craft. Pewter buttons are said to have been one of his specialties, and he is said to have supplied the Continental troops with many of these during the Revolution. So far as I know, no examples of these buttons have turned up. But occasional pieces of Lee's other products are found — very occasional, by the way, since he is one of the very rare makers. He seems, however, if it is safe to judge from so scanty a showing of evidence, to have been one of the more versatile of the early makers in the variety of his output. Fig. 63 shows, at the left, a seven-and-three-quarters-inch basin; next, a very quaint and attractive ladle with a turned wooden handle, marked in the bowl with the touch shown in Fig. 65; and finally an eight-and-one-fourth-inch plate and a small porringer, two and three fourths inches in diameter. The basin, the plate, and the porringer all bear the touch shown in Fig. 64. All four pieces are of fine metal; are of excellent design and proportions; and bespeak for their maker the possession of taste and a touch of independence. In my personal experience, I have known no other instance where, out of four specimens found by one maker, four distinct types of article were represented.

Another Richard Lee, said to have lived in Providence, with the date 1832 assigned to him, has been reported to me by a Providence collector. I include the name in the general list for investigation; but know nothing of any pewter by this possible son or grandson of the original Richard, who, himself, is given first rating for comparative rarity.

AUSTIN, BOSTON

In Fig. 66 we reach the earliest of the represented pewterers of Boston Town. As is shown by the marks reproduced in Figs. 67 and 68, the maker of these plates was an Austin and worked in Boston. An initial belongs before the surname in the touch, but unfortunately it does not show legibly on any of the four pieces by this maker that I have seen. The touch itself, shown complete except for the maker's initial in the combined impressions here reproduced, bears the coat of arms of Massachusetts in an ornamental frame, with the maker's name below. It belongs, therefore, in all probability to the period immediately following the Revolution. And I shall be surprised, when a more perfect impression of the touch turns up and gives us definite knowledge of what Austin made these pieces, if Nathaniel Austin does not turn out to be the man responsible.

Be this as it may, however, pieces bearing this Massachusetts arms mark of the Austins are of extreme rarity. Fig. 66 shows a fifteen-inch plate (one of the rarities in American pewter by whomsoever made), a twelve-and-one-fourth-inch plate and a seven-and-three-fourths-inch plate. My collection contains one other plate of the latter size, but in very poor condition. The twelve-and-one-fourth-inch plate bears on the under side of the rim the engraved name of "King's Inn." Pewter bearing this Austin mark is of the second grade of comparative rarity.

It is to be noted that the "Boston" touch that accompanies this Austin mark bears a striking resemblance to the "Boston" touch used by Thomas Badger (Fig. 96) and to the one found on the "Semper Eadem" plates illustrated in Fig. 93. This fact will be discussed later.

NATHANIEL AUSTIN

We now come to the unquestioned work of Nathaniel Austin, specimens of which are shown in Fig. 69. Here again we have a fifteen-inch plate (the marks upon which are reproduced in Fig. 70). It is not altogether without possible bearing on the identity of the Austin of the Massachusetts arms pewter, to find that Nathaniel Austin made fifteen-inch plates. For, *so far as I know*, these were made by but four makers outside of the unidentified Austin — Frederick Bassett, Nathaniel Austin, D. Melvil and Thomas Badger. Nathaniel Austin is one of the most distinguished American craftsmen whose name is found on pewter plate.

He came of pioneer stock, his great-grandfather, Richard, having come to the province as a boy in 1632. His forbears had largely followed the sea — his own father being lost in 1745 at the age of forty-one. His own son, Nathaniel — "General Austin," high sheriff of Charlestown, a socially and politically prominent and picturesque figure — and his other son, William, the well-known author, carried on the family traditions. The Nathaniel with whom we have to do was born in 1741. His name appears as a goldsmith in the first edition of the Boston City Directory, in 1789, and continues so to appear there until the issue of 1816 — the year in which he died. As he was thirty-five years old at the outbreak of the Revolution, it is quite possible that he may have made pewter before that event. On the other hand, it is equally possible that he may have been led by post-Revolutionary conditions to add pewter-making to his goldsmith's work. Only the discovery of earlier documents bearing on the case, or of manifestly pre-Revolutionary pieces marked by him, can be looked to to settle this or similar matters of doubt.

Many of the early American goldsmiths and silversmiths are said to have supplemented their incomes from work in precious metals by the making of pewterware. But apparently few if any of them had the courage of their necessities and marked their less noble handiwork. One honors Nathaniel for his lack of this sort of false pride, and likes to trace, in the distinguished and tasteful character of his touches, evidences of his character.

It is quite natural that his later pieces should be more frequently met with than his earlier ones; and all of his later pieces are marked merely with his hall marks and his eagle touch, unless, indeed, as is the case with his basins, they bear the eagle touch alone. There was nothing, therefore, to make me sure that pieces thus marked were really by Nathaniel Austin. (See Figs. 70 and 71.) "N.A." suggested his name; and the fact that "R.A. Boston." had long been said to be the mark of Richard Austin made me the more ready to lean to this interpretation. Nevertheless, I was greatly elated when I first came upon a piece marked with the earlier touch shown in Fig. 70 and also with the hall marks. This placed the ascription practically beyond cavil. Of course it is still possible that the "N" here does not stand for Nathaniel, since it nowhere appears upon the pewter written out in full. But to hold such a view seriously would not be to have "come from Missouri," but to have taken root there. An examination of Nathaniel Austin's hall marks is well worth while. There is real distinction in the designs, as may be seen at once by comparing his figures of Britannia and of the leopard with others in the plate of American hall marks in Fig. 347. The third symbol in "N.A.'s" set of hall marks is peculiar to him. I incline to the belief that it is a Yankee-Doodle rooster. Whatever it is, it is a "swell bird." And it is due him to take a good look at his eagle. Of all the makers who — a few before him and many after — used this emblem as part of their touches, no single one ever approached Nathaniel Austin in the boldness, the beauty, and the distinction of this design.

Nathaniel Austin belongs, according to the table published in Chapter XI, to the third relative grade of rarity among the makers of the eight-inch-plate period. The exact figures upon which I have based this rating are three-fifteen-inch plates, two eight-inch basins, and eleven small plates by him. The men in the first grade are without exception those by whom I have never found but a single plate. Those in the second grade are men to whom only three or four pieces are credited on my records. It is an eloquent testimony to the essential rarity of all the makers of this period that there are but three names in the fourth grade, and that the commonest of these are down for only forty-five examples of all types.

WILLIAM WILL

The next name upon our roughly chronological list is that of Colonel William Will, of Philadelphia, member of the Pennsylvania Assembly, innkeeper and pewterer — another man of some distinction whose name graces our lists. His name, like that of Nathaniel Austin, appears in the earliest edition of the city directory of his home town — in this case 1785. He is there set down merely as "Member of Assembly." In the next edition of the directory (1791), he is listed as "Pewterer and Inn-Keeper." His name appears as a pewterer simply, in the three next issues — 1795, 1796, and 1797 — and then disappears. The impenetrable screen that cuts us off, for the most part, from any knowledge of the earlier activities of such American pewterers as are listed in the earliest directories of their respective places of residence has, in the case of William Will, been pierced at a single point by one of those strange freaks of good luck that occasionally come our way. Three pages from an old account book, on which appear a part of the business accounts of William Will, and Shinkle & Graff, who were his selling agents, apparently at Philadelphia, during the year 1780, have by chance come into my hands. These accounts show us just what articles these agents had for sale for "Col. Will"; what they got for them; and what sums, less their five per cent commissions, they turned over to him. And in three different places on the three sheets, William Will acknowledges, over his own signature, settlement and payment in full of the account to date.

The range of articles which these agents had on sale does not seem to have been great. Here is the entire list:

Plates
"Basons"
Pint Mugs
Quart Mugs
Table Spoons
Tea Spoons
Tea Pots.

When these papers first came into my hands, I was particularly pleased at what I took to be an opportunity of comparing the pewterers' prices in 1780 with those of 1693, as shown by the invoice from London printed in Chapter III. But no cipher code, cross-word puzzle, or rebus of sorts could have proved less amenable to first-sight use in this way than the itemized statement of receipts set down by Messrs. Shinkle & Graff. Even now, while I believe that I have a key to the puzzle, it unlocks only an outer door and leaves us still shut off from all real information.

In order to give my readers the pleasure of working a bit on this puzzle themselves, I copy a short section of the accounts for April and May, 1780.

SALES FOR COLO. WILLIAM WILL

		£.	s.	d.
'80 April 17th To Six Table Spoons 30 Ds.		11	5	0
To 1 Tea pott 140 Ds.		52	10	0
To 6 Tea spoons 15 Ds.		5	12	6
18th To 1 pewter Tea pott 140 Ds.		52	10	0
19th To six plates @ 250 Ds.		93	15	
To 1 Tea pott 140 Ds.		52	10	0
To 9 Tea spoons 22½ Ds.		8	8	9
20 To 1 Tea pott 150 Ds.		56	5	0
22 To 2 Basons @ 25 Ds. each		18	15	
To six plates 250 Ds.		93	15	0
24 To 1 Tea pott 150 Ds.		56	5	
25 To 5 Basons @ 25 Ds. each		46	17	6
To 5 Do. @ 25 Ds. each		46	17	6
To 6 Do. @ 25 Ds. each		56	5	
May 2 To 1 Tea pott 150 Ds.		56	5	
To six table spoons 30 Ds.		11	5	
To 3 Do. 15 Ds.		5	12	6
3 To 3 plates 125 Ds.		46	17	6
		771	11	3
Brought over		410	18	9
		1182	10	0
Deduct Commns. @ 5 P. Ct.		59	2	
		1123	8	0

Recd. May 5th 1780 of Shinkle & Graff eleven hundred and twenty three pounds for ware sold on commission to this day

(Signed) WM. WILL.

I take the abbreviation "Ds." to mean "dollars." This seems, indeed, to conduct one into a land where finance has gone mad, for $140 for a teapot and $5 for a spoon would appear to be quotations from such a country. Nevertheless, all the prices given in "Ds.," if you figure them as equal to seven and a half shillings to the dollar, figure out to exactly the sums in £. s. d. that appear opposite them in the last column. And when one recalls the hopeless state of the currency in this country toward the close of the Revolution (as well, indeed, as afterwards), one can well imagine that these "ds." units were sufficiently depreciated in value to figure out at the rates quoted.

At that they were more valuable than European currencies to-day.

I have never seen but the one plate by William Will. That is shown in Fig. 72. The covered mug (quart size) that accompanies the plate and the tablespoon shown in Fig. 73, together with a six-and-one-half-inch basin by him that I own, but that is not here shown, pretty well cover the list of articles made by him as revealed by these papers. Pint mugs and teaspoons remain; and the $140 "Tea Potts" of his 1780 style. It would greatly interest me to see one of the latter.

We are lucky, however, in being able, thanks to the kindness of Mr. J. Stogdell Stokes, of Philadelphia, to illustrate a piece by William Will that does not appear on the Shinkle & Graff lists, but that is surely one of the most beautiful pieces of American pewter extant. This is the pewter warming pan shown in Figs. 25 and 80.

By the way, my statement a few lines back that I had never seen but one plate by William Will needs to be qualified. The lid of this warming pan is made of an eight-inch plate! Or, rather, it has been cast in a plate mould and then used as the lid of this piece. It is unmarked. The maker's touch is on the bottom of the pan and will be found reproduced in Fig. 26. Note the similar use of a frame of concentric circles about the "W.W." touch shown in Fig. 78. This last-named touch, by the way, is from the inside of the covered tankard shown in Fig. 72. The touch shown in Fig. 75 is the one used on the tablespoon illustrated. This was one of a set of six (costing 30 Ds. in 1780!).* The eagle touch illustrated in Fig. 79 is from the back of the plate shown, and is there accompanied by an impression of the touch shown in Fig. 76.

How long before 1780, Colonel Will was making pewter we have, of course, no way of knowing. As, however, he disappears from the records as early as 1797, and as he was evidently already a prominent man and a successful pewterer in the spring of 1780, it is quite certain that he belongs with the small band whose pewter-making careers bridged the Revolution. His name will be found among those of the highest order of rarity.

---

* I paid thirty dollars for these spoons myself some time ago and sold them for one hundred in 1924, so the colonel was not so bizarre in his prices after all.

DANIEL MELVIL

The next name on our list is that of Daniel Melvil, of Newport, Rhode Island. I have but one way of placing him in time, beyond the manifestly early character of his work, and that is by a dated porringer from his hand, illustrated entire in Fig. 81, and shown in detail as to its marks and dating in Fig. 83. This proves that he was working in 1788. Even Boston did not boast of a city directory until 1789; and the hunting-up of early records in the smaller towns is almost a specialist's job. I have, I regret to say, been able to do but little of this scattered research. But I hope to see many of the missing facts about many of the earlier provincial pewterers ferreted out by the growing body of collectors of American pewter. The mark shown in Fig. 84 at once suggests a comparison with the arms of Massachusetts touch (Fig. 68) employed by the unidentified Austin we have already discussed. It shows the arms of Rhode Island, with the word "Newport" above and the motto "In God We Hope" below. Another comparison is invited between the hall marks here illustrated in Fig. 85 and the later hall marks of Gershom Jones, shown in Fig. 57. In both we find the same use of the elements of the Rhode Island arms; the same use of the suspended sheep of the tin men; the same type of general design and a similar spacing of the initials. Again the introduction of a conventional design (suggestive of the larger touch of the user) in the last shield is similar. Of course, this parallel between the marks of these two Rhode Island pewterers may merely indicate that Melvil (whom we know worked in 1788) began practicing his craft about the time that Gershom Jones adjusted his marks to the post-Revolutionary etiquette in such matters. But it also puts us on the lookout for possible pre-Revolutionary marks by Melvil.

Another porringer by this maker is illustrated in Fig. 19. The general character of this piece, in spite of its late mark, makes the suggestion of the last paragraph even better worth considering. Besides the fourteen-inch plate, the porringer, and the eight-and-a-quarter-inch plate shown in Fig. 81, I have an eight-inch basin by Melvil that is not illustrated.

Daniel Melvil will be found rated as belonging to the third order of rarity among the eight-inch-plate men. I have, all told, found twenty-one pieces of his make.

JOSEPH BELCHER

The placing of Joseph Belcher as twelfth in this list is an example of how very tentative the assigning of chronological precedence to these men must, as yet, be. Absolutely nothing is known as to his dates, beyond the fact that he evidently worked in the last quarter of the eighteenth century. Nothing was even known about his place of residence, or the State where he worked, until two plates, of which one is shown in Fig. 86, came into my hands; both of them bearing, in addition to the usual touch of Joseph Belcher, the "N. London" touch reproduced in Fig. 88. The form of his plates (he is credited with three examples in my rating list) shows that he worked early, or, at any rate, that he adhered to early lines. And if both the porringers shown as his in Fig. 86 are really by him, it is likely that he worked well back toward the time of the Revolution. The reason for speaking thus uncertainly about one of these porringers is that the larger and plainer of the two bears only the touch shown in Fig. 89; and while the initials "J.B." instantly suggest Joseph Belcher; and while the use of the dot as a decorative element is in perfect keeping with the way the same use is made of dots in his known marks — it is by no means beyond question that this piece is his. Even the smaller porringer, however, while later than the "J.B." one, is much earlier than the run of American pieces of the type. It, and all the other pieces here mentioned, bear the touch shown in Figs. 87 and 90. For the present, then, Joseph Belcher would seem to belong somewhere near where we have placed him in the procession of American pewterers.

In the matter of comparative rarity, he ranks well above Melvil and about even with Gershom Jones — the other Rhode Island makers of the same general period. His name will be found in the second list. I find him credited with a total of five pieces in my books.

"SEMPER EADEM" AND THOMAS BADGER

Thomas Badger seems to have been so prosperous a person in life, and he has, through some mysterious working of luck in his behalf, achieved so wide a fame as a pewterer in our day, that he could well bear the brunt of being numbered 13 on the present list. Moreover, he seems to be the logical claimer of the berth. For while we know nothing whatever about him until his name appears in the first Boston Directory of 1789, there is a strong likelihood of his having been the maker of the probably pre-Revolutionary and exceedingly rare plates that bear the mark of "Semper Eadem" with a crowned rose and a separate touch of "Boston" that is in all respects identical with the Boston touch of Thomas Badger.

However, as the matter is a bit too uncertain to include the "Semper Eadem" plates with the Badger work, and yet, as one does not feel warranted in altogether separating the two, I am giving "Mr. Eadem" the benefit of the thirteenth place and putting Mr. Badger next door.

The "Semper Eadem" marks are shown in Figs. 92 and 93, and one of the three plates known to exist with these markings is illustrated in Fig. 91. It may or may not be significant that all of Badger's small plates I have ever seen (and he is the one eighteenth-century worker whose name is found in the fourth order of rarity) are either of seven-and-seven-eighths-inch size, or else of eight-and-a-half-inch size; and that *of the three "Semper Eadem" plates known, two measure seven and seven eighths inches and one measures eight and a half inches in diameter.* It is an amusing incident worth quoting, perhaps, that the friend who turned up these "Semper Eadem" plates for me, wrote me in the first place that he had seen some plates "marked Eadem, Boston." It being a name that I had never heard, I naturally urged him to try to capture the plates. Later on, and quite a while before the plates came into my possession, I received from him the laconic message, "Have seen Eadem plates again. His first name is Semper."

* Since this was written, I have seen a twelve-and-a-quarter-inch plate bearing the "Semper Eadem" mark. This is an unusual size in American flatware. It was, however, also made by Thomas Badger.

Fig. 97

EDWARD DANFORTH, LATE EIGHTEENTH CENTURY

9 inch plate   8 inch plate   5 inch porringer

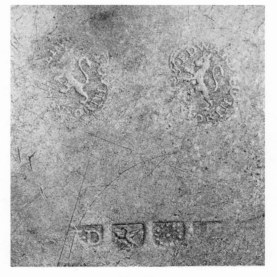

Fig. 99

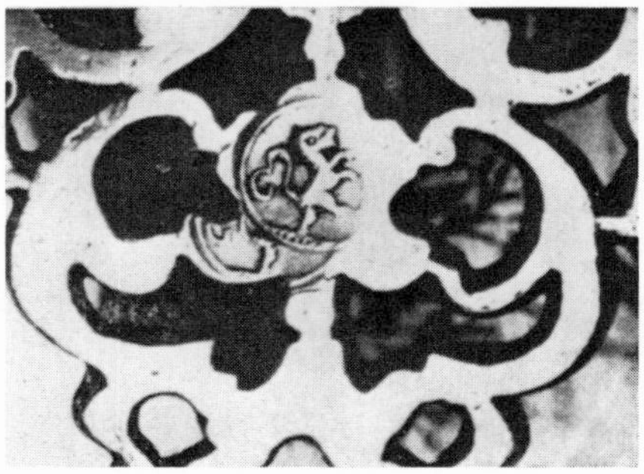

Fig. 98

MARKS USED BY EDWARD DANFORTH

Fig. 100

SAMUEL PIERCE

8 inch plate   8 inch basin   8 inch plate

Fig. 101

MARKS USED BY SAMUEL PIERCE

Fig. 102

WILLIAM BILLINGS, 1791

8 inch plate

Fig. 103

MARK USED BY WILLIAM BILLINGS

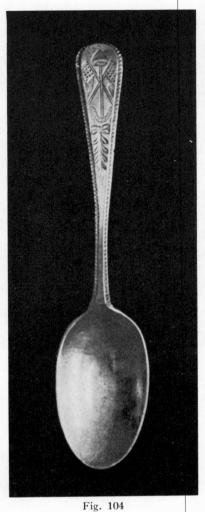

Fig. 104

GEORGE COLDWELL, 1792–1796

Pewter dessert spoon

Fig. 105

MARK USED BY GEORGE COLDWELL

Fig. 106

BENJAMIN AND JOSEPH HARBESON, 1793–1803

8¾ inch plate   8 inch plate   8¾ inch plate

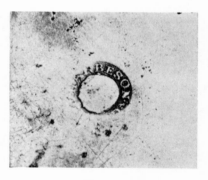
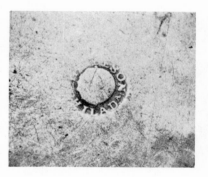

Fig. 107   Fig. 108

MARK USED BY THE HARBESONS

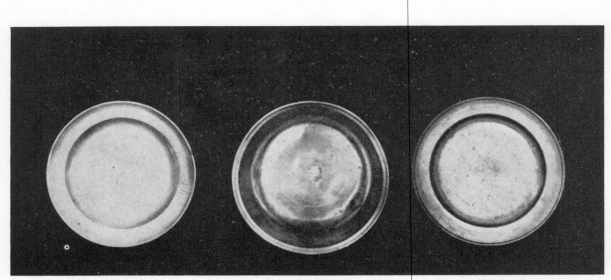

Fig. 109

RICHARD AUSTIN, 1796–1813

7¾ inch plate   8 inch basin   8½ inch plate

Fig. 110

Fig. 112

Fig. 111

MARKS USED BY RICHARD AUSTIN

Fig. 113

S. G. (SAMUEL GREEN), 1798–1810

13½ inch plate

Fig. 114

MARK USED BY S. G.

Fig. 115

PARKS BOYD, 1798–1819

11 inch deep plate
Pint mug

8 inch plate
6¼ inch plate

Fig. 116

Fig. 117

Fig. 118

MARKS USED BY PARKS BOYD

"Mr. Eadem," being represented by three extant pieces to my knowledge, is listed in the second order of rarity.

Whoever he was, it is not stretching the evidence to say that he probably worked before the Revolution. And Thomas Badger, in all the more than thirty examples of his work that I know, never used any mark except his eagle touch (Fig. 95); which he could scarcely have adopted much before the date at which we first find him in the Boston Directory. If, therefore, he were really the maker of the "Semper Eadem" plates, he would appear either to have ceased work for a time after the Revolution, or else it would seem that no pieces of his, made in these intervening years and marked with his transitional mark, have yet turned up.

Both of these surmises seem a bit unlikely. The only other explanation that suggests itself, of the use by both Badger and "Eadem" of the same "Boston" touch (Figs. 93 and 96), is that these touches were made for both men by one die-maker who did not take the trouble to make separate designs for them. This idea is strengthened by the fact, already noticed, that a very similar and possibly identical Boston touch is used by the unidentified Austin of the Massachusetts arms touch.

For the present, then, we list "Semper Eadem" separately, and yet (in spite of the difference in date) have placed "him" and Thomas Badger next to each other.

Thomas Badger himself made mostly flatware, apparently. An eight-inch basin by him is in the Bishop collection at the New Haven Historical Society. Outside of that I have seen nothing, myself, beyond plates of the following sizes; seven-and-seven-eighths-inch, eight-and-one-half-inch, twelve-and-one-fourth-inch, thirteen-and-one-fourth-inch, fourteen-and-three-fourths-inch, and fifteen-inch. I once heard much talk of a communion set by him, but I was never able to run it down, and do not know, except by hearsay, that it exists.

He is rated by me, as already stated, in the fourth order of rarity. One of his seven-and-seven-eighths-inch plates, one of his eight-and-one-half-inch ones, and a fifteen-inch one are shown in Fig. 95.

EDWARD DANFORTH

We now come to Edward Danforth, assigned, without much confidence apparently, to Hartford. His exact relationship to the earlier Danforths is not known either; but it is quite evident from his use of the lion in his marks that he belonged to the famous family; and his position, chronologically, in the family succession is pretty clear, notwithstanding our ignorance of other details. For not only does he use the form of touch-design that appears to have characterized their habit immediately after the Revolution, but he is the first of the family to introduce the eagle into his marks in any form. Indeed, he appears to have been one of the earliest users of this symbol among pewterers in general. His hall marks are, for this reason, very interesting; and examples of them ought to be much sought for by collectors who are trying to show the full development of the American touches during this early period. Examples will take a lot of seeking for, too, as specimens of Edward's work are very rare, indeed. So much so that his name will be found in the first division of the table of comparative rarities.

The only examples of pewter that I can positively assign to him are the eight-and-seven-eighths-inch plate and the eight-inch plate shown in Fig. 97, and an eleven-inch charger in the Wadsworth Athenæum collection at Hartford. All three of these bear the touch and hall marks shown in Fig. 98. The porringer included in the same group is there because of the touch impressed upon its handle, and reproduced in Fig. 99.* This interesting touch shows a lion rampant, which, while it faces the opposite way from the normal lion of the Danforths, might yet very easily be that same lion engaged, not in its usual act of going to school, but in the equally necessary one of coming home. The determining fact about the beast, however, in so far as its being assigned to Edward goes, is the fact that its tail is so waved as to make the letter "E." What a lion of this particular breed would be doing making "E's" out of its tail on the

---

* Another porringer with the same mark completely impressed has come into my possession since this was put in type. The mark is a Gershom Jones touch, and not an Edward Danforth one. It shows a "G" and an "I", one on either side of the lion—which is "a Jones lion coming home from school" (see Fig. 58), and not a Danforth one.

handle of a pewter porringer, unless it belonged to Edward Danforth, I am unable to imagine. And I have therefore placed the specimen in Edward's locker until some one shows me why it ought not to stay there.

JOHN SKINNER

All that is to be said of John Skinner — the one remaining Boston pewterer whose name figures in the 1789 directory — can be put into a sentence or two. He had his place of business in Newbury Street. His name appears in no subsequent issue of the Boston Directory. And he made eight-inch plates. This statement is made because a specimen, marked with his name, once came near landing in my collection. It was one of those things that one misses "by an hour." A strange woman, unknown to the dealer who had the plate, had just walked in and bought it.

He is, therefore, one of the comparatively few makers whose pewter is known to exist, whose mark is not reproduced in this volume.

Naturally, his name is found in the first division in my list indicating comparative rarity.

SAMUEL PIERCE

Samuel Pierce, another whose dates have not yet been definitely established, and whose residence is not known, ought, to judge by the character of the eagle design on his touch, to have worked early in the period when the national bird took to roosting on pewter.

His touch (Fig. 101) instantly, by its shape and general character, suggests an English touch of the last half of the eighteenth century. And only the unmistakable nationality of the eagle, and the joint facts that such pieces of Samuel Pierce's work as I have seen do not comply with the requirements of the Society of Pewterers and do bear the evidences of American work, have convinced me that he belongs in our catalogue of local makers. No Samuel Pierce, moreover, is listed in the most complete list yet issued of English makers — Mr. Massée's list of some two thousand names, published in his "The Pewter Collector" (1921) — a book, by the way, that all students of American pewter should own, if only for the sake of this same list. Several of the earlier and smaller lists of American pewterers include Samuel Pierce's name — their compilers evidently satisfied, as I have been, that he belongs there.

In Fig. 100 are shown all the examples of Samuel Pierce's work that I have seen, except one other eight-inch plate and a thirteen-inch deep plate. The middle piece in this group is an eight-inch basin of fine metal and workmanship. The flanking pieces are both eight-inch plates. Samuel Pierce's work is assigned to the second grade of comparative rarity.

WILLIAM BILLINGS

To William Billings the date 1791 has been assigned, but with what authority I do not know. His work and his touch make the ascription seem just, however; for it is at least probable, judging from these indications, that he worked in the interval between the Revolution and the wave of nationalistic feeling that expressed itself, among pewterers, in the eagle touch. His home was in Providence, Rhode Island, the home of a quite remarkable group of early workers in pewter. All that I have ever seen of his work has been three plates, two of them measuring seven and seven eighths inches, and the other eight inches and a quarter. One of these is here shown in Fig. 102, and a good impression of his touch is reproduced in Fig. 103. His name is assigned to the second rank as to rarity.

GEORGE COLDWELL

George Coldwell, "Pewter spoon and candle mold manufacturer" of 23 Gold Street, New York City, where he appears to have carried on his business for four years — 1792–1796 — is next in order.

He alone, of the pewter-workers of his day whose marked work has survived, does not seem to have made eating plates. The spoon by him shown in Fig. 104 is the only example of his work I have ever seen. It belongs to Miss M. I. Meacham, of New York, and it is through her kindness that it, and the mark from the back of it (Fig. 105), are here pictured.

The patriotic decoration of the spoon handle is worth examining. The pike surmounted by the Liberty cap; the two American flags, each with its four rows of three stars, with the thirteenth one stuck in the corner; the motto of "Peace and Amity" on the scroll below, and the pendent laurel branch underneath — all are eloquent of the fact that one hundred-percent-ism is no twentieth-century invention.

HARBESON

In the 1793 edition of the Philadelphia Directory, Benjamin and Joseph Harbeson are listed as "Tin and Coppersmiths" at 44 South Second Street. The next year they name themselves "Copper and Tin Manfrs.," and are found at the same address. By 1797 they appear to have separated; for Benjamin is then located at 239 Arch Street and Joseph at 179 North Third Street; each being down as "Coppersmith and Ironmonger." The same conditions persisted in 1798. But in 1799, Joseph has disappeared and Benjamin, moved to 180 North Third Street, has his name spelled "Harbenson" and is listed simply as "Coppersmith." In 1800, it is "Benjamin Harbeson & Son, Coppersmiths," at 75 Market Street. And after 1803, the style of "Copper Merchants" is taken on and thereafter adhered to. I take it, therefore, that it was somewhere between the years when the Harbesons first came on the Philadelphia scene as "Tin and Coppersmiths" — that is, in 1793 — and the time, ten years later, when Benjamin and his son finally adopted the style of "Copper Merchants," that they indulged in the making and marketing of pewterware. I have therefore assigned to them, as pewterers, the dates 1793–1803. There is nothing in the mark found on surviving pieces of their output to indicate whether it was the two brothers together, one or other of them separately, or the later father-and-son association, that put out the pewter. Nor does it greatly matter. Their pieces contain more lead than those of any other maker of American pewter; and if they had put a little of the copper they dealt in into their pewter alloy, they would have stood higher in the present estimation of their countrymen. Three plates by them are shown in Fig. 106, the middle one being of the seven-and-seven-eighths-inch size and the two flanking ones being eight-and-three-fourths-inch plates. The two impressions of their mark reproduced in Figs. 107 and 108 enable us to see the whole of it after a fashion. An eleven-inch deep plate by them and a six-inch plate, not illustrated, are also in my possession. The middle plate in Fig. 106 is the only one of the size I have seen. I have seen three of the eight-and-three-fourths-inch plates. The Harbesons, therefore, go into the second bracket of comparative rarity — and their rarity is about all they have to commend them.

RICHARD AUSTIN

Richard Austin, 1796 to 1813 in the Boston directories, is next in order. He is, so far as I have been able to discover, no relation to Nathaniel Austin. He bears, however, the same name, "Richard Austin," as the great-grandfather of Nathaniel, who founded that branch of the American family, and it may be that our present Richard is from the same stock. There is one other thing — either a coincidence or a family resemblance — that makes me rather "favor" the idea of this relationship. This is their common habit of signing their pewter with their initials. However, since I had just succeeded in proving that "R.A." really stood for "Richard Austin" when I first came upon an example of the pewter marked "N.A.," and thus got the "hunch" (which proved to be correct) that the latter mark stood for "Nathaniel Austin," my inclination toward relating them is probably less than scientific.

The "R.A. Boston" touch (Fig. 112) has been credited to Richard Austin for many years. But as it was my business, as a would-be investigator of the American pewter field, to find out if possible what authority such traditions as this had back of them, I began questioning the correctness of this one. One day I got hold of a plate that bore on the back the touch shown in Fig. 110. Here, with a most English-looking setting, was the full name of the maker I was so much interested in. But there was nothing (except the fact that no "Richard Austin" figured in the English list and that the plate in question was not hammer-finished) to make me think that the man who applied this touch was an American. The touch, by the way, except for the name, is exactly similar to one of Townsend & Compton's London touches. The whole matter suddenly cleared up, however, in the most convincing way, when another plate, marked as shown in Fig. 111, came into my hands. Here was proof, not only that the Richard Austin of the dove and sheep mark was "R.A.," but that "R.A." was Richard Austin, of Boston.

From 1796 to 1800, "R.A." figures in the city directories as "Pewterer." After the latter date he is also down as "Sealer of weights and measures." He made excellent pewter, although, as yet, nothing by him except seven-

and-three-fourths-inch and eight-inch plates and eight-inch basins have, to my knowledge, been found. An original set of six of the seven-and-three-fourths-inch size, in almost mint condition, and marked with the owner's initials, "S. R." (one of the set is shown at the left in Fig. 109), was turned up for me some time ago and offers an excellent opportunity for calling the reader's attention to a fact that frequently puzzles collectors. How is it possible, they often ask, that half a dozen plates, so old and so easily marred, should have come down in such condition? The answer is that the age-old habit of using part of one's possessions in pewter as a "garnish" — the habit of putting half of a dozen in the dresser and using the rest — persisted as long as did the use of pewter. It is, naturally, more apt to be the plates thus used for ornament than the plates habitually used to eat from that have survived, and that now turn up from attics and other places of stowage. One must also remember that, for the past twenty years or more, there has been still another influence at work, sorting out for preservation the pieces in good condition, and relegating those that were cut and defaced to the melting-pot. This has been the habit of the small dealers, already referred to, of exposing their finds for sale on their way to the junk dealer; with the result that the good pieces were salvaged and the others melted up. The process is somewhat similar, both in method and results, to that by which stray dogs spend a few days at the pound on their way to oblivion.

This wonderful set of "R.A" plates, no doubt once graced the dresser shelves of Mrs. "S. R." and — a piece of luck which their quality and rarity fully deserve — they still continue to do so. They are now the property of Mrs. Stanley Resor, of New York and Greenwich.

Outside of this, only ten pieces by this maker are on my list. He therefore takes a place in the third category as to rarity. It is, however, only fair to collectors to add that, for one thing, this half-dozen plates really represent a single item, having always been together and still being so; and, further, that it appears that Richard Austin's pewter never traveled very far afield. And it would seem that my agents were early in the field where it did, originally, find its market. The result is that the last year has led me to believe that this maker's rarity is much greater than is indicated by his rating in my lists.

SAMUEL GREEN

Samuel Green, who figures in the Boston directories as a pewterer from 1798 till 1810, is included in this list of the makers whose pewter survives, solely because the fine thirteen-and-one-half-inch plate illustrated in Fig. 113, and marked with the touch shown in Fig. 114, is thought to belong to him.

There are other men, silversmiths mostly and of much earlier date, to whom these initials might belong; and there is Samuel Grame, pewterer of Boston, said to have lived in the seventeenth century. But, as the marking of pewter with the initials of the maker and town name seems to have been a local custom during precisely the years when Samuel Green lived and worked in Boston (compare the "R.A. Boston" just dealt with, and the "N.A." touch of Nathaniel of the same name) the crediting of this piece to Samuel Green seems the obvious ascription to make. Samuel Green had a shop on Milk Street from 1798 till 1804. Thereafter, for three years he was in Sweetser's Alley; and later both in Washington and in Mason Streets. He — or, at any rate, the maker whose touch was "S.G. Boston," since he is as yet represented by nothing but this one fine example — is ranked as of the first order of rarity among the early American makers.

PARKS BOYD

Our more or less chronological spotlight now moves to Philadelphia and singles out Parks Boyd, whose name appears for the first time in that city's directory of 1798 — the year after the name of William Will figures there for the last time. Like Colonel Will, and unlike the Harbesons, Boyd was a maker of fine pewter, and there is both quality and finish to everything that I have seen bearing his touch. His career was a long one — twenty-one years — and the course of pewter as an accepted tableware was about run when he disappears from view in 1819. In 1798 he figures in the directory as "Pewterer and Brassfounder" — another of the now familiar examples of the connection of these metal-working trades in the America of the day. In another edition a few years later he is down as "Brassfounder &c." It is not till 1813 that he begins, and thereafter continues, to be listed simply as "pewterer." In 1814 his name is spelled "Parkes." His name will be found among those in the second grade of comparative rarity; for, in spite of his twenty-one years of pewtering, mighty little of his pewter has come down to us. An eleven-inch deep plate, a pint mug, and six-and-a-quarter-inch small plate — all illustrated in Fig. 115 — and three eight-inch plates, of which one is there shown, constitute my bag of this maker's output. The touch shown in Fig. 116 is one of the early appearances of the type of mark that came to be characteristic of the American habit during the final years of pewter-making. It was, indeed, the Philadelphia custom, apparently, during the "teens" of the nineteenth century, to use both an eagle touch and a name touch of this later type. B. Barns did it. So did Thomas Danforth (3). Parks Boyd does not seem to have conformed to this double-touch custom. I have seen the mark we are discussing but once, and then it appeared alone. On the other hand, the touch shown in Fig. 117, which appears on most of his plates, eight-inch and over, is used by itself, as is the smaller eagle touch shown in Fig. 118. The latter appears on the six-inch plate illustrated, and also on the inside bottom of the pint mug.

WILLIAM DANFORTH

I can offer nothing but a surmise as to the place of residence of William Danforth, specimens of whose work are shown in Fig. 119. It seems likely, since Taunton, Norwich, Middletown, Hartford, and Rocky Hill, Connecticut, have all been homes of pewter-making Danforths, that William Danforth also worked in that State. Neither can I offer any facts as to his dates, beyond pointing out that the William Danforth eagle is very much of a piece with the general character of the eagles found on Samuel Danforth's many touches; and Samuel worked about 1810.

The two impressions reproduced in Figs. 120 and 121, however, do about as well as any. They show four things clearly, and these four things are the things that really matter. They show (1) that the owner of the mark was a Danforth, and (2) was named William. And they enable the student to form a clear picture in his mind of (3) the unmistakable tail of the William Danforth bird, and (4) of the way in which the same creature's bill is silhouetted against its wing. It is of the utmost importance that the student, in the case of so habitually blind a "marker" as William Danforth, should have pointed out to him details that can thus easily be used for identification.

The mark upon a piece of William Danforth's pewter is illustrated in Edward J. Gale's "Pewter and the Amateur Collector," Plate XXXVIII, but is ascribed to Samuel Danforth, of Hartford. This particular impression almost duplicates the one shown in Fig. 121, and the mistaken ascription illustrates very aptly the extreme likelihood of such an error, if the several peculiarities just referred to have not been noted and learned.

Specimens of William Danforth's pewter are shown in Fig. 119. I also have had in my possession an eight-and-three-quarters-inch plate that is not here shown. My check list of his pieces includes two eight-inch plates; three eight-inch basins; and three thirteen-inch deep plates. He could, with equal justice, be ranked toward the lower end of the second grade, or near the head of the third grade, of comparative rarity. I have put him in the second.

THE HERO-HERA FAMILY

The name of Hero — or Hera — has no doubt before now driven many a pewter student distracted. One never saw any two lists that contained the same Hero–Hera names; that gave the same dates for them; or that succeeded in doing more than conveying, in an indecisive, hinting sort of way, the impression that there was something mysterious about the family. And on none of the several occasions when I have had an afternoon to devote to the Philadelphia directories have I succeeded, until quite the other day, in doing anything but increase my own sense of muddle with regard to the tribe. The further fact that, while they all seemed to have been pewterers at some stage of their careers, no pewter ever seemed to turn up by any of them, added to the general asylum atmosphere of the matter. Finally, in desperation, the day for going to press with this volume being almost upon me, I took a day off, settled myself with a large sheet of paper, ruled off into separate sections for each of the Hero-Hera family, and systematically put down under the proper heading every mention that any Philadelphia directory, from 1785 to 1822, inclusive, made of any one of the connection. And here, duly arranged in such order as I can achieve, is the whole matter, for the use of future students of the Heroic.

In 1785, and in that directory only, appears one Christiana Herroe (never before now, I believe, included in any published list). She lived between Second and Front Streets, on Callowhill, and was a "Pewtherer."

There was no further issue of the Philadelphia Directory until 1791; and by then Christiana Herroe had passed. But Charlotte Hero, as well as Christian Hero, have appeared, each of these being listed as a "Pewterer," and both of them being located at 170 North Second Street. The next directory appeared in 1793 (the yellow fever having, meanwhile, devastated the city), and in this issue Charlotte is listed, at the same address, but simply as "Widow." Christian, on the other hand, is gone; and one naturally assumes that Christian had been Charlotte's husband, and had died during the epidemic.

And maybe he was and did; although a good case could be made out against both ideas. For why, in that case, or in the pre-feminist days of 1791, did

Charlotte figure as a pewterer in her own right when her pewterer-husband was living, and become a mere non-pewter-making widow after his death? And if they were not married and raising a family of pewterers-to-be in 1785 — and they are not hinted at in that volume of the directory — how does it come that a Christian Hero comes back and starts pewtering at the family address in 1799? But we are getting ahead of the drum major. Charlotte, who was "Widow" in 1793, also, like Christian, disappears from the records in the 1794 and 1795 issues. For these two years there are no Heros in Philadelphia. But, in 1796, Charlotte reappears as "Widow and pewterer," this time at 230 North Second Street — destined, thenceforth, to be the Hero-Hera home for twenty-three years. In 1797, she resumes her title of "Widow"; preserves it in the 1798 issue; and then disappears in real earnest.

Meanwhile in 1797 and 1798, and also at 230 North Second Street, a new member of the family, Christopher Hero, makes his appearance. He also is down as a "Pewterer." And he is never again heard of for certain.

But, in 1799 (every one else in the connection being, for the moment, absent), "Christian I. Heavo" appears at 230 North Second Street as a "Pewterer," and appears, similarly spelled, in the 1800 issue. He then, at least in that spelling, also disappears for good.

In the same 1800 directory, however, "Christian and John Hera" — the first appearance of the later spelling of this family's name — are listed as living at 230 North Second Street, and as being "Plaisterers." And in the 1801 edition the same pair are down as "Pewterers" at the same address. And that is the last appearance, at any rate with names fully spelled out, of "Christian and John."

In 1802, 1803, and 1804, John Hera holds the fort alone at 230 North Second Street and is put down as a pewterer.

In 1805, "C. & J. Hera" appear, or, if they are Christian and John, reappear, at the family home as pewterers. Of course they *might* be Christopher and John. At any rate, they continue to be so listed until 1812, barring the fact that a couple of times the address is printed as 232 North Second Street.

In 1813 and until 1818 inclusive, Christian Hero is the only member of the family in the directories; being listed in all these issues as a pewterer and as living at the family house.

In the 1819 issue, Christian has disappeared and John Hera has taken his place. John, however, only occupied 230 North Second Street for that one year. He then moved to 61 Walnut Street, where he carried on his craft of pewterer until, upon the issue of the 1823 directory, his name — and the family name with him — disappears finally from the Philadelphia records.

They appear to have been a hide-and-seeky sort of family, and seem to have put in so much time playing pussy-wants-a-corner that they had little time to make pewter. For, so far as I know, four nine-inch plates — three in the Princeton Theological Seminary collection, as part of an early New Jersey Presbyterian Church communion service, and the one illustrated in Fig. 122 — are the only pieces that have as yet turned up to represent the family's labors. These pieces, as shown by the marks illustrated in Figs. 123, 124, and 125, are all the work of C. & J. Hera.

I knew that three plates by C. & J. Hera were in the Princeton Museum, because Mr. Arthur Dyer speaks of their being there in his volume upon "American Craftsmen." But because Princeton is less than an hour's run from me, I had put off going over to get permission to photograph these Hera marks. Meanwhile, a plate marked, as shown in Fig. 124, was offered to me and I bought it. I had, of course, no idea who might have made it; but I knew that it was by a Philadelphia maker whose marks I had never seen. So it was listed among my unidentified marks. And then, as one of the clean-up jobs involved in closing the considerable labors of assembling the illustrations for this volume, I took my camera over to Princeton and came, at last, face to face with the three Hera plates. I need tell no collector of the thrill I got when I examined the marks on them.

Moral: Don't fail to buy pieces of American pewter because the marks are not fully identifiable. Not only may the piece turn out a rarity, but it may furnish valuable information, when studied in conjunction with other, only partially decipherable, marks. Note that my C. & J. Hera plate gives the only complete impression of the lower part of its makers' touch.

THOMAS DANFORTH (2) AND THOMAS DANFORTH (3)

We now come to a couple of Thomas Danforths — (2) and (3) in our system of designation — whose tangled identities, thanks to what is no doubt a short circuit somewhere in our information, are almost as brain-racking as the Hero muddle. Indeed, since the family relationships of the pewterless Heros form a purely academic puzzle, the Danforth mix-up is much more practically disturbing. Here are the elements of the tangle:

According to the Danforth records, one of these Thomases was the grandson of the originator of the line, and was born in 1756, at Middletown, Connecticut. In 1778 he is said to have moved to Rocky Hill in that State, and there to have established a sizable business as a tin and copper smith and a maker of britannia and pewterware. He is also said to have founded a branch in Philadelphia and to have lived there during the winter months. In the "Bulletin" of the Wadsworth Athenæum, he is credited with being the Thomas Danforth who is listed in the Philadelphia directories between 1807 and 1813, and whose pewter is illustrated in Fig. 128, and whose marks are shown in Figs. 129, 130, 131, 132, and 132a.

The other Thomas Danforth figures in these records as his son, said to have been born in 1792, and to have died, at Rocky Hill, Connecticut, in 1836. He is credited with having been connected with the Philadelphia establishment of his father, and with having also been connected with a branch in Augusta, Georgia. Fig. 126 shows specimens of the pewter that is said, by the Wadsworth Athenæum "Bulletin," to be his, and in Fig. 127 are reproduced fine impressions of the marks there attributed to him.

Now this last-named youngster would have been but fifteen years of age when his father founded his Philadelphia establishment — the Danforth name appears in the Philadelphia city directories of 1807 to 1813 inclusive — and but twenty-one years old when the Philadelphia place was discontinued. If, after that, he made pewter either at Rocky Hill or elsewhere, it is scarcely likely that he would have used the typically eighteenth-century marks attributed to him. It is worth noting that the individual elements of the hall marks shown in

Fig. 119

WILLIAM DANFORTH

13 inch deep plate
8 inch basin

11¼ inch deep plate
8 inch plate

Fig. 120   Fig. 121

MARK USED BY WILLIAM DANFORTH

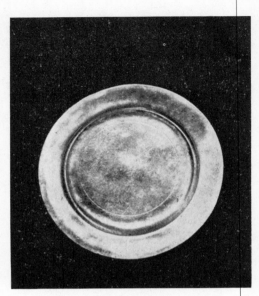

Fig. 122

C. AND J. HERA, 1805–1811

9 inch plate

Fig. 123   Fig. 124   Fig. 125

MARK USED BY C. AND J. HERA

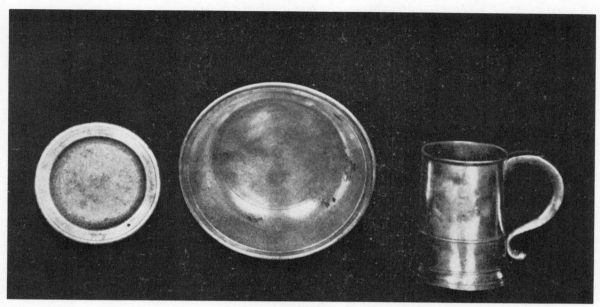

Fig. 126

THOMAS DANFORTH (2)

6¼ inch plate   9 inch basin   Quart mug

Fig. 127

MARKS USED BY THOMAS DANFORTH (2)

Fig. 128

THOMAS DANFORTH (3), 1807–1813

12 inch basin

13 inch deep plate
11 inch deep plate
 9 inch plate
7½ inch plate
6¼ inch plate

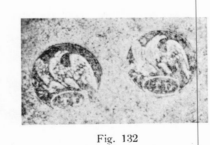

Fig. 130

Fig. 131

Fig. 129

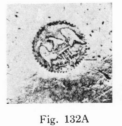

Fig. 132

Fig. 132A

MARKS USED BY THOMAS DANFORTH (3)

Fig. 133

Fig. 134

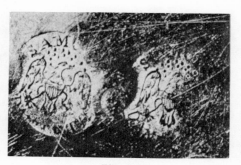

Fig. 135

Fig. 136

Fig. 137

Fig. 138

Fig. 139

MARKS USED BY SAMUEL DANFORTH

Fig. 140

SAMUEL DANFORTH, CIRCA 1810

12 inch plate
8 inch plate
4½ inch porringer

Quart mug

13 inch deep plate
6¼ inch basin
3 inch beaker

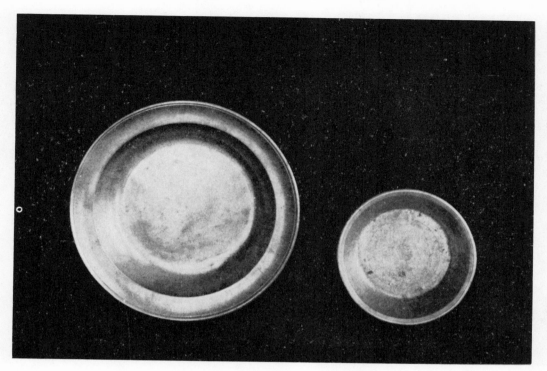

Fig. 141

GEORGE LIGHTNER, 1810–1812

13 inch deep plate   8 inch basin

Fig. 142   Fig. 142A   Fig. 143

MARKS USED BY GEORGE LIGHTNER

Fig. 144

B. BARNS, 1812-1817

13 inch deep plate
8 inch basin

11 inch deep plate
8 inch plate

Fig. 145

Fig. 146

Fig. 147

Fig. 148

Fig. 149

Fig. 150

MARKS USED BY B. BARNS

Fig. 151

SAMUEL KILBOURN, 1814–1824

7¾ inch plate   13 inch deep plate   7¾ inch plate

Fig. 152

MARK USED BY SAMUEL KILBOURN

Fig. 153

R. PALETHORP, Jr., 1817–1822

13½ inch plate
8 inch plate

9 inch plate
4 inch beaker

Fig. 154

Fig. 155

Fig. 156

Fig. 157

MARKS USED BY R. PALETHORP, Jr

Fig. 158

SAMUEL HAMLIN, 1824

5¼ inch porringer   11½ inch deep plate   4 inch porringer
Pint mug

Fig. 159

SAMUEL HAMLIN, 1824

14¾ inch deep plate   13 inch plate
8 inch basin   5½ inch basin

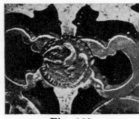

Fig. 160

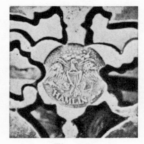

Fig. 161

Fig. 162

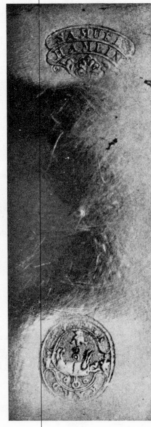

Fig. 163

Fig. 164

MARKS USED BY SAMUEL HAMLIN

Fig. 165

S. STAFFORD

8 inch plate   13½ inch deep plate   8 inch plate
                           Pint tankard

Fig. 166

Fig. 167

Fig. 167A

MARKS USED BY S. STAFFORD

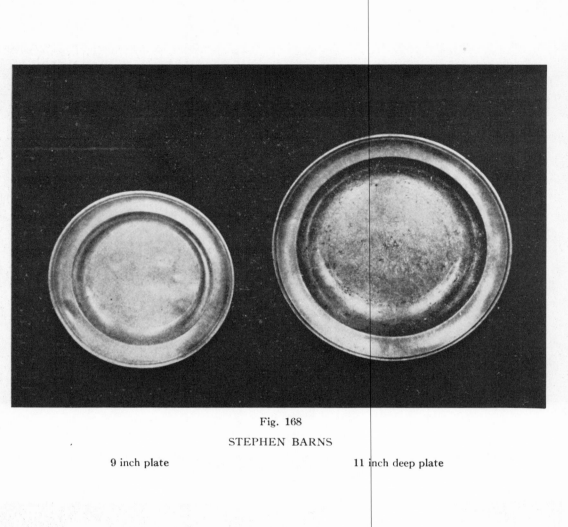

Fig. 168

STEPHEN BARNS

9 inch plate   11 inch deep plate

Fig. 169

MARK USED BY STEPHEN BARNS

Fig. 170

——N BRIGH——

8 inch plate

Fig. 171

MARK USED BY ——N BRIGH ——

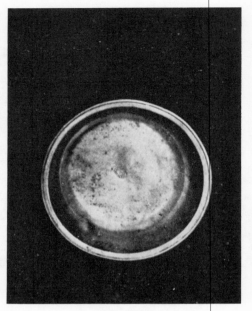

Fig. 172

UNIDENTIFIED EAGLE NUMBER ONE

8 inch basin

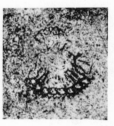

Fig. 173

UNIDENTIFIED EAGLE MARK NUMBER ONE

Fig. 127 are identical with those (Fig. 39) used by Thomas Danforth (1), but that the order of the figure of Britannia and of the leopard's head is transposed. Moreover, the size of the marks is greatly reduced in the later series. These two marks will be conveniently compared by turning to Fig. 347.

Specimens of the pewter marked "T. Danforth Phila." are comparatively common. Specimens by the user of the small hall marks and the snappy, circular lion touch with the initials "T.D." are markedly rare. Of course this rarity, joined to the early character of the specimens bearing it, and the equally early character of the marks themselves, would lead us to imagine that their maker had worked early, and that his pewter had for the most part disappeared.

Yet it is quite humanly possible that while the old man, past fifty when he opened his Philadelphia branch, was not only using the eagle mark of the times, but adopting the new business-like name-touch that was to become almost universal on the work of the next generation, his young son was gazing backward, enamoured of family tradition, and planning to stamp his own pewter when the time came with English hall marks and Danforth lions.

Only, somehow, I can't quite make myself believe it.

I doubt the ascription of this small lion touch to the Thomas Danforth born in 1792; and I would like to know what marks his father put on pewter between the years 1778, when he opened his Rocky Hill shop, and the year 1807, when he began marking his Philadelphia-made articles with his eagle touches and his very modern name and address touch. It is at least as probable that the occasionally found pieces marked with the touches shown in Fig. 127 are the early work of the father, as that they are the late work of the son. And I, for one, prefer, until we get a brighter light upon the matter, to "reserve decision," as the judges so conveniently put it.

The real state of the case is this: We have American-made pewter, marked in three different manners, by makers who were called Thomas Danforth. These three kinds of marked pewter may be the work of three men, or of two. We cannot, for the moment, be sure. But what we can be certain of is that collectors of the eight-inch-plate period Danforths will want all three marks represented in their collections; and that, until we learn the genealogical facts, we need some practical way of differentiating the three kinds of pewter.

I have therefore chosen to speak of them in this book as Thomas Danforth (1),(2), and (3). And I have so far reflected my own belief in the priority of the lion-marked pewter over the eagle-marked variety as to give the figure (2) to that. If it turns out that the Thomas born in 1756 made and marked both of the later groups, my figures will still reflect the correct order.

My own conviction is that as yet we have no marked pewter by the young Thomas Danforth who was born in 1792 and died in 1836.

In Fig. 126 are shown a quart mug — or "open tankard" as the English call the form; an example of the always rare small plate (the "saucer" of the early invoices and inventories) that measures six and one fourth inches in diameter; and a wonderful nine-inch basin in beautiful condition; all bearing the marks of the maker we are calling Thomas Danforth (2). I have, besides these pieces, seen an eleven-inch deep plate bearing the same marks. There is nothing in these forms that would preclude the pieces having been made by the younger Danforth at any time during the eighteen-twenties, provided always that he was, at twenty-five or thirty, a confirmed reactionary, enamoured not only of the disappearing mode in forms, but of the long out-moded family marks; and so much so that he was willing to risk ruin by hanging back on the trend of business in his chosen line instead of pushing ahead along the opening road. Samuel Hamlin would seem to have followed some such course as this along about the same time. Thomas (2) belongs in the second grade for rarity, while Thomas (3) goes into the third grade.

The work of the man we call Thomas Danforth (3) is shown in Fig. 128. It was good work. His metal is excellent, and his form and finish are good. His specialty would seem to have been a full line of flatware and basins. I have never seen anything else bearing his marks. Here we see a thirteen- and an eleven-inch deep plate; and flat plates of nine-, seven-and-three-quarters-, and six-and-one-quarter-inch sizes. The basin pictured measures twelve inches in diameter, and is by far the largest basin of American make that I have ever seen. The nearest approach to it is a ten-inch one by this same maker, shown in Fig. 16 among the graded samples of American-made basins. The few specimens of (3)'s basins that I have examined have all been marked as is this twelve-inch one, on the inside. The nine-inch example of (2)'s work is marked quite abnormally, according to the usual American custom — on the bottom. This fact is stated for whatever it may be worth as a straw for the wind to blow at.

Thomas Danforth (3) used but five touches, shown in Figs. 129, 130, 131, 132 and 132a. I have never seen the name-plate touch (Fig. 130) used alone. It invariably, when present, accompanies one or other of the eagle marks. Of these latter, the larger is usually reserved for large pieces. Thus it occurs on the twelve-inch basin here shown. On all other basins by this maker that I have seen, one of the smaller eagles is used. I have never seen the name-plate touch on a basin.

SAMUEL DANFORTH

No date has as yet been authoritatively assigned to the working period of Samuel Danforth, who lived in Hartford and was a contemporary of the last-mentioned member of his family, at least in the latter's later, Philadelphia, manifestation. It is interesting, too, to note that the articles attributable to Samuel are about the same as the combined product of the two Thomases, except that Samuel is here shown to have made porringers, and that as yet the Thomases are not thus represented. However, the porringer seems to have been pretty much a New England specialty. I have never seen a Philadelphia one, and the only allegedly New York specimens I have seen bear the Boardman touch, and were therefore in all probability made in Hartford, Connecticut. Samuel Danforth, as a study of his marks (Figs. 133 to 139) will show, was an enthusiastic eagle-user. Moreover, his search for a prize specimen of the bird seems never to have ceased — or been rewarded. The eagle on the porringer handle is one of the most amusing of birds.

This porringer, as well as the eagle it bears, are great rarities. I have only once seen this mark on another piece — an eight-inch basin. The small eagle, with the sunburst round its head and the initials outside the wings at the side, shown in Fig. 136, is a very attractive design. It is the mark on the quart mug, on the three-inch high beaker, and on the seven-inch basin illustrated in

Fig. 140. The separate "Hartford" touch (Fig. 139) is found only on rare occasions. Indeed, it was years before I succeeded in finding an impression of it worth reproducing — and even then had to forgo the initial "H." The hall marks are by no means always found on this maker's pieces, either; and the smaller form with only two shields is uncommon. Samuel Danforth's pewter is good, but not of the best quality; although its quality differs more in different pieces than that of most American makers.

I have him credited on my lists with the following types and sizes of pewter pieces: seven-and-seven-eighths-inch plate, nine-inch plate, eleven-and-a-quarter-inch deep plate, twelve-inch plate, and thirteen-inch deep plate; six-and-three-eighths-inch and eight-inch basins; quart mug and porringer. He belongs in the third grade as to rarity.

GEORGE LIGHTNER

George Lightner appears in the Baltimore directories as a pewterer from 1810 to 1812 inclusive. His shop was on High Street, "near Mr. Miller's blacksmith Shop." I have seen a thirteen-inch and an eleven-inch deep plate by him; also a couple of eight-inch basins and an eight-and-three-quarters-inch plate. A thirteen-inch deep plate and an eight-inch basin of his are shown in Fig. 141, and Figs. 142, 142a, and 143 show impressions of his two forms of touch. The touch shown in Fig. 143 is the one used on the basin illustrated. The other touch is usually found on his plates. Both his metal and his workmanship are good. He belongs in the second grade as to rarity.

B. BARNS

B. Barns, who worked in Philadelphia from 1812 to 1817 inclusive, was either the most prolific maker of pewter in this country during the eight-inch-plate period, or else his pieces were somehow endowed by him with charmed lives. I have seen, I should say, fully twice as many plates by him as by any other American maker. He was the Townsend & Compton of the New World. And, as the last-named firm of London makers appear to have supplied about ninety per cent of all the flatware imported into the Central States after the Revolution, one cannot well say more for B. Barns's business activities.

It is only fair to the Londoners to state, however, that there was a huge gulf fixed, in the latter part of the eighteenth century, between the pewter primacies of London and Philadelphia. The most casual glancer-over of the pewter gathered from the farms of Pennsylvania and neighboring States must have seen hundreds of "T&C" pieces. I am sure that I have looked at the bottoms of a thousand. My check list on B. Barns, on the other hand, is as follows:

13-inch deep plates	3
11-inch deep plates	5
9¼-inch plate	1
9-inch basin	1
8¾-inch plates	5
8-inch basins	3
8-inch plates	27

Fig. 144 shows one thirteen-inch deep plate and one eleven-inch one, an eight-inch plate and an eight-inch basin. Metal and workmanship are good in Barns's ware. I have never seen any hollow ware bearing his mark.

Please note, in passing, the light that Barns's success as a maker of pewter throws on the attitude of his territory toward this ware in his day. He retired only a few years before the sale of pewter plates for table use became impossible. Yet he was able, during the five years following 1812, to work up one of the largest trades ever, until then, carried on by any American pewtersmith. It is quite evident that the eight-inch-plate period, when its time came, did not die a lingering death.

Six touches are shown in Figs. 145 to 150 that were used at various times by Barns. On his large pieces, his usual marks are those shown in Figs. 146 and 149: on his small pieces, those shown in Figs. 146 and 148. On occasion, the name-and-address touch is omitted, and only the small eagle with the initials below used. This fact is a good illustration of the importance of knowing the various eagles at sight. A great many makers used a small mark, often with only initials, or with no lettering at all, when marking very small pieces. This matter is dealt with fully in the chapter on "Marks."

The script "B. Barns, Philada." touch, shown in Fig. 145, would appear to be one used toward the end of Barns's business career.

I have come across it only two or three times. Its letters are intaglio, instead of being in relief — a device found on American pieces only in the eighteen-forties usually. The name-and-address touch shown in Fig. 147 was probably an error of the engraver's (the name is spelled "Barnes"), and was no doubt discarded as soon as the mistake was noticed. I know of but one piece — an eight-inch plate — that shows it. The small eagle touch shown in Fig. 150 also seems to have been very little used. I know of but two examples of it — both on eight-inch plates also. Barns is, of course, the chief figure in the fourth grade of comparative rarities.

SAMUEL KILBOURN

Samuel Kilbourn shares with George Lightner the distinction of representing Baltimore during the early period with which we are dealing. He worked, according to the directories, for a full decade — from 1814 to 1824 inclusive. But, for all that, his pewter is of very great rarity. Two thirteen-inch deep plates, an eleven-inch deep plate, and three eight-inch plates are all that he is credited with on my list. Two of these eight-inch plates give us another glimpse at the mysterious ways of Providence in preserving, unmarred and in practically "mint" condition, pewterware of these distant days. When I found these two pieces, they were embellished with oil paintings of winter snow scenes and provided with small rings, soldered to their backs, by which these pictures could be hung upon the wall. And then we meet philistines who question the value of æsthetics! Personally, I am deeply grateful, both to the painter of these pictures and to the cherishers of them. A fairly strong solution of lye restored the plates to their original condition overnight.

Fig. 151 shows one thirteen-inch deep plate and both of the rescued snow-scene holders. Fig. 152 shows Kilbourn's (so far as I know) invariable mark. His pewter and workmanship are excellent. His comparative rarity is grade two.

ROBERT PALETHORP, JR.

For twenty-eight years — from 1817 to 1845 — the name of Palethorp was connected with pewter-making in Philadelphia. The family business back of 1817, and, indeed, after that also for a full twenty years, was the manufacture of "Ink Powder." Oddly enough, looked at from this distance, the end of the early pewter era was followed by a very decided boom in the pewter-making business. All sorts of men who had been engaged in all sorts of little manufacturing trades and businesses seem to have gone into pewter-making. The Palethorps are among the most able and successful of these newcomers.

Robert Palethorp, Jr., however, with whose work we now come to deal, became a pewterer some time before the end of the old era, and disappears from the records about the time that the old era was definitely ending. His father seems to have been the original Palethorp, "Ink Powder Manufacturer," and did business at 444 North Second Street. Here, in 1817, Robert, Jr., began the making of pewter, and continued in that work at that address until 1822. He never, if one may judge from the scarcity of examples of his work, did a large business; but his ware was of fine quality and good workmanship. Fig. 153 shows a specimen of each article that I know to have been made by him — a thirteen-inch plate, a nine- and an eight-inch plate, and a beaker. The beaker is the only one I have seen with Robert's own mark (the touch on this beaker is shown in Fig. 157). Another beaker by one of the later Palethorps is in my collection. Of the other pieces, I have seen three each of thirteen-and-a-half-inch, the nine-inch plates, and two of the eight-inch plates.

It is worth noting that these three thirteen-and-a-half-inch plates and the two large, pre-Revolutionary plates by Frederick Bassett already described, are the only instances I know of dishes of this size, made by pewterers south of New England, that are not of the deep-plate type. I have seen no other Philadelphia or Baltimore flat plates larger than nine inches. They are, then, not only very rare on account of their maker, but also, territorially speaking, on account of their type.

The eagle, without any identifying lettering, shown in Fig. 154, was occasionally used as the sole touch on this maker's smaller plates. It is, however, of unmistakable design, and I was convinced of its identity some years before I found it, alongside of the name-touch shown in Fig. 155, on the back of one of his larger plates. The touch shown in Fig. 156 was, I believe, the usual one placed upon his larger pieces, where it was usually accompanied by the name-and-address mark in Fig. 155. R. Palethorp, Jr., is of the second grade of rarity. As we shall see when we come to J. H. Palethorp among the later workers, he and Robert, Jr., seem to have been associated in business at 50 North Second Street, Philadelphia, from 1820 to 1825 or so. This connection, whatever its nature, does not appear to have registered itself in any marks on pewterware; or, at any rate, in any marks that are distinguishable from those employed by J. H. Palethorp working alone. It will, therefore, be dealt with under the latter's name.

SAMUEL HAMLIN

Samuel Hamlin was a member of that small but influential band of craftsmen who worked in Providence, Rhode Island, pretty well throughout the eight-inch-plate period. His name appears in the Providence Directory for 1824. And he alone of all the pewterers of the period we are dealing with shares with George Coldwell, of New York, the peculiarity of never having made eight-inch plates. For the rest, everything that he did make was characteristic of the best output of the pewterers trained in the old traditions of the craft. He did excellent work in good metal. And, oddly enough, his normal mark is a name-touch reminiscent of the late eighteenth-century fashion, and he affected the use of hall marks. In short, if we knew nothing about him, and found his marks upon a few eight-inch plates, we should unhesitatingly place him at or near 1800. His specialty seems to have been porringers and basins. Both of these forms, marked by American makers, are rare. But I would say that about half of the American marked pieces of both varieties that I have seen have been by him. In Fig. 158 may be seen two of his porringers, one of the four-inch and one of the five-inch size. Also a pint mug and an eleven-inch deep plate. In Fig. 159 are shown a fifteen-inch deep plate, a thirteen-inch plate, and two basins — one eight inches in diameter and the other six and a half. Outside of these forms I have seen nothing bearing his marks except a pair of nine-inch plates of a superior quality of britannia metal, which bore, in addition to Hamlin's normal name-touch, a special touch with the words "Hard Metal." The marks on one of these plates are reproduced in Fig. 163. These two impressions are the only examples I have seen of this "Hard Metal" touch of Hamlin's, as, indeed, the pieces themselves are the only examples I have seen of this alloy from his workshop. The name-touch that is shown in this photograph is the mark habitually used by him on all flatware and on his basins. The hall marks (Fig. 164) I have never seen used except on his large plates and dishes. The three eagle touches shown in Figs. 160, 161, and 162, on the other hand, are found on his porringers. The mug shown in Fig. 158 bears the normal name-touch impressed near the lip, alongside the handle. Of the three eagle touches, that shown in Fig. 162 is the most frequently met with; that shown in Fig. 160 being also quite common. The touch shown in Fig. 161, on the other hand, is distinctly rare. I have, I believe, seen only three or four impressions of it — all on porringer handles.

It should be said, here, that another Hamlin, whose name is given as possibly William, and whose dates are given as 1772–1869, is included in the Hartford Athenæum list as having lived in Providence, and is there apparently credited with the marks shown in Figs. 160 and 161, and so, by inference, with the making of porringers so marked.

My own belief, based upon the similarity of workmanship and design between all these Hamlin porringers, is that one man made them all. On the other hand, I know of no way of determining whether they came from the workshop of Samuel or of the possible William. As they have, with the single exception of the list above quoted, always been credited to Samuel, I have so listed them, subject, of course, to correction.

We are now approaching the end of the old era, or, at any rate, will soon reach the work of that group of makers who, since they followed, to a greater or less extent, the fashions of both periods, are here given separate rating as "Transition Workers." And I look upon it as a happy accident that, as we began the consideration of the eight-inch-plate period with Thomas Danforth (1), the founder of one of the two great pewter-making families of America, we find ourselves logically led to finish our consideration of this important era with the founder of the other of these pewter-making families of the New World, Thomas D. Boardman, of Hartford. But, either before taking up the work of this Last of the Romans, or else after dealing with him and before passing on to the next chapter, it remains for us to consider a few as yet undated, unlocated, or unidentified makers whose work apparently belongs to this period. And I have elected to take these up now.

S. STAFFORD

The first of these slightly known makers, and very possibly the earliest of them, is S. Stafford, of Albany, New York. Some time ago I came into possession of four eight-inch plates by him, all marked with his name-plate (Fig. 167a) and with the separate "Albany" touch shown in Fig. 166. Later on a thirteen-and-a-half-inch deep plate by him was reported to me by a New York State collector. And, until very recently, this was all that I knew of the man or his output. It so happened, however, that a pint tankard (shown in Fig. 165) was also in my collection, where it had been allowed to remain in the hope that some day its mark (Fig. 167) might turn out to be that of an American. And at the very last minute before going to press with this volume a thirteen-and-a-half-inch deep plate by Stafford has come into my hands with the further marks shown in Fig. 167a. It rather adds to the mystery than solves it, but it is very far from detracting from Stafford's interest; and it suggests that he may well have been one of the earliest group of American makers. Who, or what, "P.Y." was, remains to be discovered, and why these letters are thus associated with S. Stafford. Meanwhile they and the pewter that bears them are here shown in company.

STEPHEN BARNS

I know nothing of the residence or, except in a general way, of the dates of Stephen Barns, whose pewter is shown in Fig. 168. The touch he used so carelessly (Fig. 169) places him pretty certainly as a worker of the second decade of the nineteenth century; and one would say, judging from the fact that he made eleven- and thirteen-inch deep dishes, that he probably worked south of the upper border of Connecticut, and very probably in Pennsylvania or Maryland. I thought it likely, for a time, that he hailed from Philadelphia, and was a relative of B. Barns of that city. But his name is not to be found in any Philadelphia Directory, or, at any rate, I have failed to find it there. So we must wait for definite data concerning him until some one turns up a record of him.

Fig. 168 shows an eleven-inch deep plate and a nine-inch ordinary plate by him. And Fig. 169 shows an impression of his touch. He is listed in the second grade of comparative rarity.

——N BRIGH——

In Fig. 170 is shown an eight-inch plate of apparent American origin. The maker's touch on the back of this plate is only partly legible, and is shown in Fig. 171. Personally, I regard these pieces by as yet unidentified makers as important inclusions in any treatise intended, as this one is, to place before its readers all the information at the command of the writer. And I strongly advise all collectors and students of American pewter to add to their collections any pieces of apparent American origin, the marks on which are not to be made out entirely. Failing the possibility of this course, I suggest that they at least add to their notes rubbings of the marks on any such pieces as they may have a chance to examine. It is impossible to tell at what moment such a piece (or rubbing) may supply the information needed for the identification of the maker in question. For, to take this eight-inch plate of Fig. 170 as an example, it is evident that it needs only another, in itself illegible, impression of this maker's touch to give us the letters missing in this example, and thus to supply us with the maker's entire name. And not only, by this conjunction, would the interests of all students of American pewter be served, but the owners of both plates would reap their individual rewards by the turning of their unidentifiable specimens into listed and recognized rarities. Judging from the type of the lettering in this touch, and the position of the dot between the first and last names, the maker worked fairly early — back of 1800, probably. The fact that I have seen no other example of this mark naturally persuades me that the maker, when and if identified, will take his position among the rarities.

The next four specimens have been known to me as "Unidentified Eagle Number One," "Unidentified Eagle Number Two," and so on; being numbered in the order in which they have come into my hands during the last decade. As it will be convenient for us to have a name for them, and as I see no reason for inventing new ones, I shall list them, and refer to them when necessary, in this way.

UNIDENTIFIED EAGLE NUMBER ONE

In Fig. 172 is shown an eight-inch basin, bearing on the inside the eagle mark shown in Fig. 173. The impression of this touch in the illustration is very poor. But then the maker who used the touch seems to have been a mighty poor impressor. For while I have three eight-inch basins bearing this touch, this is the best impression of the lot. I have never seen any other article than a basin thus marked, and have, naturally, no idea as to the identity of the maker. It is of course certain that he worked this side of, say, 1790; and it is almost certain that he worked back of 1825 — the practical limits of the eagle-mark vogue. It should be noted in passing that three out of the five pieces here shown as bearing unknown marks are basins. Also that the only basins known by Nathaniel Austin bear no mark except his eagle touch without any lettering. If we happened not to know his eagle, his basins would also figure in this list. It should be borne in mind that T. Danforth, of Philadelphia, Samuel Danforth, of Hartford, and B. Barns, of Philadelphia, all use their small eagle touches (although these include their initials) in marking their basins. In other words, it seems to have been the habit of the men of the eight-inch-plate period to mark their basins by their lesser touches, where they had a choice. This explains the preponderance of basins in this list. It follows that the only hope of identifying the users of these eagles lies in finding pieces of their pewter where these eagle touches have been struck along with a recognizable touch.

UNIDENTIFIED EAGLE NUMBER TWO *

In Fig. 174 we have another eight-inch basin bearing on the inside the touch shown in Fig. 175, which I have been accustomed to call "Unidentified Eagle Number Two." It is the only example of the mark I have ever seen. Of course you will note that I do not say about these eagle-marked pieces, as I said about the maker of the plate whose last name begins "Brigh——," that their makers will probably, when identified, turn out to belong among the rarities. For we have no way of knowing that the user of any one of these eagle touches may not be represented by many specimens of his surviving work on which this eagle touch was not impressed. I give, as a case illustrating this point, the eagle touch of William Will, illustrated in Fig. 79. It appears upon an eight-inch plate bearing his normal name-touch. And on no other piece made and marked by him that I have ever seen has this eagle touch appeared. William Will disappeared from the records of the Philadelphia directories in 1793 — very soon after the fashion for eagle touches first came in. It is likely that he used the touch for only a short time. And while specimens of his work are scarce and valuable, they are by no means such ultra-rarities as we might conclude if that single impression of his eagle touch had been found, all sole alone, on an eight-inch basin.

*There has come into my possession, too late to have its marks illustrated, an eight-inch plate bearing the normal name-plate mark (Fig. 130) of Thomas Danforth (3) and two very fine impressions of this small eagle. It is probable that the unidentified eagles here numbered " one " and " four " will also turn out to be touches by makers we know well.

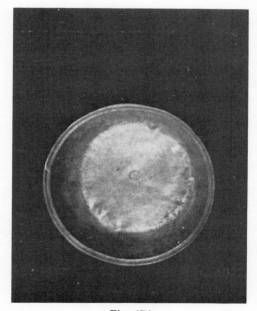

Fig. 174

UNIDENTIFIED EAGLE NUMBER TWO

8 inch basin

Fig. 175

UNIDENTIFIED EAGLE MARK NUMBER TWO

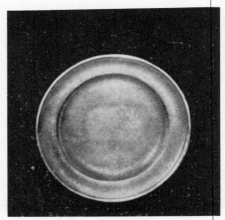

Fig. 176

UNIDENTIFIED EAGLE NUMBER THREE

8 inch plate

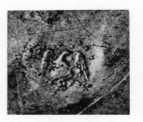

Fig. 177

UNIDENTIFIED EAGLE MARK NUMBER THREE

Fig. 180

UNIDENTIFIED EAGLE NUMBER FOUR

11 inch deep plate

Fig. 181

UNIDENTIFIED EAGLE MARK NUMBER FOUR

Fig. 182

THOMAS DANFORTH BOARDMAN, BEFORE 1825

12¼ inch plate	Ladle	13¼ inch deep plate
7¾ inch plate	6½ inch basin	5¼ inch porringer
4 inch porringer		

Fig. 183

Fig. 184

Fig. 185

Fig. 186

Fig. 187

Fig. 188

MARKS USED BY THOMAS DANFORTH BOARDMAN

Fig. 189

D. CURTISS

8 inch basin   11 inch deep plate   8 inch plate
                         8 inch pitcher

Fig. 190   Fig. 191   Fig. 192

MARKS USED BY D. CURTISS

Fig. 193

ASHBIL GRISWOLD

8 inch plate

13 inch deep plate
11 inch coffee-pot

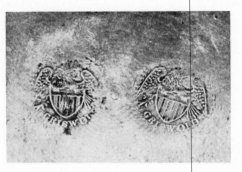

Fig. 194

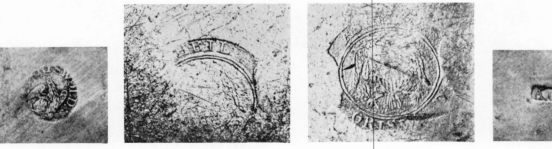

Fig. 195   Fig. 196   Fig. 197   Fig. 198

MARKS USED BY ASHBIL GRISWOLD

Fig. 199

J. DANFORTH

8¼ inch tea-pot   Ladle   10½ inch coffee-pot   Quart mug

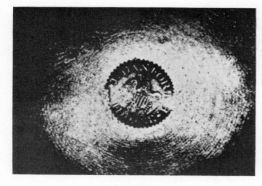

Fig. 200

Fig. 201

MARKS USED BY J. DANFORTH

Fig. 202

WILLIAM CALDER, 1824

4¼ inch porringer   8 inch plate   5 inch porringer

Fig. 203

Fig. 204

MARKS USED BY WILLIAM CALDER

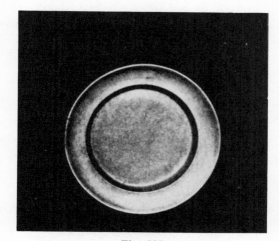

Fig. 205

I. CURTIS

8 inch plate

Fig. 206

MARKS USED FOR I. CURTIS

Fig. 207

HENRY S. BOARDMAN, 1845

$5\frac{1}{2}$ inch britannia beaker

Fig. 208

MARK USED BY HENRY S. BOARDMAN IN PHILADELPHIA

UNIDENTIFIED EAGLE NUMBER THREE

The maker to whom the touch I have called "Unidentified Eagle Number Three" belonged is in a somewhat different category. This touch, as a careful examination of Fig. 177 will disclose, is not an eagle touch without lettering, but an imperfect impression of a touch which, if shown entire, would carry the maker's name, certainly, and quite possibly the town of his residence. And this being so, and the touch being, nevertheless, impossible to identify, we could assume rarity on the part of its maker with more logic than in the preceding cases. However, this mark may well prove to be simply a rare touch belonging to a maker whose normal marks are more frequently seen. The fact that it is on an eight-inch plate (Fig. 176) of normal 1800 to 1825 type, together with the character of the touch itself, suggests that the maker who used it worked about 1810 to 1815.

UNIDENTIFIED EAGLE NUMBER FOUR

The eleven-inch deep plate shown in Fig. 180, which bears the half-obliterated touch marks illustrated in Fig. 181 ("Unidentified Eagle Number Four"), is better calculated, I think, to excite our curiosity than any of the marks we have been considering. The fact that this is the touch of a Boston pewterer — and presumably of one of the Boston pewterers whose names we know, but whose pewter has not yet turned up — is what makes one especially anxious to solve the puzzle of its identity. For it is always more of a satisfaction successfully to fill an interior gap in a series, already nearly complete, than it is to be able to extend the series in either direction.

It is evident that the name of the maker appears in the design of this touch, above the oval containing the eagle. And the balance of the whole, as well as the character of the eagle itself; the quality of the metal and the workmanship on the plate, all suggest a fairly early date for the maker's activities. One wonders whether the piece may turn out to be by Andrew Green, or Mary Jackson, or John Skinner? Whoever proves to have made it, it is the only eleven-inch deep plate that I have ever seen made by a Boston pewterer. Which fact induces me to warn my readers once more against mistaking for dogmatic assertions any arguments from analogy that they find scattered through these pages. There was an unquestionable fondness, on the part of the Boston pewterers (fostered, one supposes, by the preferences of their customers), for the shallow as against the deep-plate type in the larger sizes of these dishes. And this being so, one naturally assumes that, say, a thirteen-and-a-half-inch deep plate by Stephen Barns was not made in Boston. Yet one must advance such deductions as this only as an indication of likelihood; and it is only in this sense that they are advanced in this volume. It is as impossible to carry on an investigation without these tentative deductions, working hypotheses, and experimental "rules," as it is to think without words.

I often like to recall, in this connection, the forgotten meaning of the old saying that "the exceptions prove the rule." Mostly, these days, this saying is regarded as a mystic utterance, the truth of which is by no means apparent, but the authority behind which is too great to be argued with. As a matter of fact, of course, the word "prove" is here used in its meaning of "to test." So that exceptions "prove" the rule very much in the same manner as the men with long-handled hammers "prove" the wheels of Pullman coaches at division points by tapping them. It is thus made evident that the word "rule" itself is here used rather with the meaning we attach to it when we say "as a rule" than with the sterner significance we invoke when we say "that is the rule." In other words, it is only by having our "as-a-rule" judgments put to the proof as to their continued value by the exceptions that turn up that we are kept from forgetting their real nature, or are induced to discard them when, by chance, the rush of exceptions destroys their serviceableness.

THOMAS D. BOARDMAN

The Danforth family hold the American record for long-distance pewter-making. From old Thomas (1), who heads the list of pewterers in the eight-inch-plate period, and presumably began the practice of his craft in the second quarter of the eighteenth century, to the J. Danforth, of Middletown, Connecticut, who worked well into the last quarter-century of American pewter-making, and whom we shall meet in the next chapter but one, the active craftsmanship of the family extended over a full hundred years.

In 1781, Sarah Danforth, said to have been the daughter of Thomas (1), but who was, probably, that patriarch's granddaughter, married Oliver Boardman, of Hartford, Connecticut. Their son, Thomas Danforth Boardman, born in 1784, was the first of the Boardman group of pewterers — a family that established another American record, developing as many craftsmen in one generation as the Danforths had developed in four. But the group activities of the Boardmans belong in the next chapter; and here we have to do only with the individual activities of Thomas Danforth Boardman himself; a maker who stands out as the last pure representative of that period of pewter-making according to the ancient traditions of the craft which had been opened in America by his great-grandfather.

Investigations as to the dates of American pewterers outside of the larger cities are much complicated by the fact that nothing in the way of city directories existed in these smaller towns until after the end of the first period of American pewtering. Thus there is still much confusion with regard to the dates of Thomas D. Boardman. It seems to have been assumed by the compilers of the early lists that he worked "after 1825." In the most complete and valuable of all these lists — that published in the March, 1923, issue of the "Bulletin" of the Wadsworth Athenæum at Hartford, the date of this maker is thus given. Yet, in the notes in the same issue of the "Bulletin," it is stated that Thomas D. Boardman was born in 1784, and that he and his brother Sherman Boardman were pioneers in block tin and britannia-making in Hartford, and carried on "a successful business for fifty years on North Main Street." Now, of course, it is quite evident that these several statements were never correlated by the compiler of this list. For if Thomas D. Boardman was born in 1784, did not start in business as a pewterer until after 1825, and then carried on a successful business in partnership with his brother for fifty years, it follows that they were still successful pewterers in 1875 and that the senior partner was then a bit over ninety!

We shall see in the next chapter that the touches used by the brothers Boardman, in their far-flung enterprises as pewter manufacturers and merchants, cover the whole field of transitional fashions between the eight-inch plate and the coffee-pot eras; but I submit as at least a significant and probably indicative fact that I have seen no specimen of pewter marked by Thomas D. Boardman individually that would not lead one to place him before and not after 1825. And since this is the conclusion to which one is inevitably led by a study of his output, one inclines all the more to regard the facts as to his age and his antecedents as confirming this deduction. He was, remember, born in 1784 and he came of a long line of pewterers. By 1800, he was sixteen, and there were a number of his kin who were practicing the traditional craft of their family in his neighborhood, and from whom no doubt he could have learned the craft. I do not for a moment, myself, believe that he waited until he was thirty-nine to begin his life-work. Nor that he who, after it became evident that "business" was due to succeed "craft" in the new century, helped develop that so thoroughly up-to-the-minute "chain of pewter shops" in Hartford, New York, and Philadelphia, was ever busy making 1815 pewter types "after 1825."

An examination of Fig. 182 will show the types of pewterware that bear his individual touch. In flatware I have by him the following: thirteen-inch deep plates; twelve-inch plate; eleven-inch deep plate; eight-and-three-eighths-inch and seven-and-three-quarters-inch plates. As a proof that this last size was not a freak output of his, made after the end of the period that called for them, but that he worked during the real vogue of the pewter eating-plate, I have seven of the seven-and-three-quarters-inch and one of the eight-and-three-eighths-inch size. In addition to these plate forms, I list two porringers, shown in Fig. 182. One is a four-inch one bearing the touch reproduced in Fig. 185 — a touch, by the way, that I have not seen duplicated — and one is a five-inch one bearing the touch illustrated in Fig. 183. As the extreme bottom part of this impression is not quite plain, I have also reproduced, in Fig. 184, another impression of the same touch which shows this missing part. I have also two basins by Thomas D. Boardman, one of which is shown in Fig. 182. One of these basins is six and a half and the other five and a half inches in diameter. And I have seen, I think, three such ladles as the one here shown. The mark on this ladle is reproduced in Fig. 187, together with an excellent example of this maker's use of the "X" mark so reminiscent of the early English habit of using this mark to indicate extra fine quality. The metal in this ladle deserves the "X." But as, of course, there was no central authority in America to enforce the proper use of such an indicative marking, it follows that, where it was used here, it was entirely as a personal whim. Moreover, one may be allowed to doubt as to whether, after 1800, the public were sufficiently aware of the English meaning of this impressed letter to be influenced by its presence on local pewter. And we shall see, when we come to study the American marks, that its use in this country was practically a family habit of the Danforths and Boardmans. The eagle mark, shown in its entirety by a comparison of Figs. 186 and 188, was the normal touch of this maker on his flatware. The eagle touch with the initials only, shown in Figs. 183 and 184, was his normal small touch, made to be used on such articles as basins, porringers, and so on. If a mug or a tankard or a beaker by "T.D.B." should turn up, one would expect to find this touch on it. As already noted, the "T.D.B." touch on the smaller porringer is the only impression I have seen. Judging from the handle of the porringer, I would take this to have been a very early touch of his. The mark on the ladle is also found on other pieces by this maker. In Fig. 27 is shown a very fine pewter communion flagon that bears this touch, as well as the "X." It also bears, however, the "T.D. & S.B." touch used by Thomas D. and Sherman Boardman during their later joint activities; so that I take this fine flagon to be a piece made by Thomas D., in reality "after 1825"; and very likely shortly before he abandoned the personal making and marking of pewter and branched out into the later business methods that he and his brother introduced. This flagon, by the way, is, as previously indicated, an almost ideal example of the alloy that is at once the ultimate attainment of pewter quality, and the initial point of departure of the britannia decadence. It is now the property of Mr. C. Kaufman of Nutley, New Jersey.

CHAPTER VII

THE TRANSITION WORKERS

IF man's preferences had been consulted, the world would have been neatly divided into clean-cut categories whose edges never overlapped. Just think what a blessing this would have been to the modelers of philosophic systems, the expounders of scientific theories, the students of history, and the investigators of the development of American pewter! For one thing, this chapter would have been entirely superfluous. For the trade would have passed from the eight-inch-plate period to the period of the coffee-pot as swiftly and smoothly as we now pass from Eastern Standard to Daylight-Saving time. Our great-grandparents would have gone to bed pewter-plate fans, and have awakened coffee-pot fiends, and there would have been no trouble whatever except among the farmers.

But, alas, the world was made before the idea of categories was stumbled on; and the chances are, now, that we shall have to struggle on to the end trying to make fact conform to our ideas of neatness and always having something left over that didn't get placed.

The purpose of this chapter is to take up the slack.

TRANSITION WORKERS, OR AMERICAN PEWTERERS WHOSE WORK INCLUDED SPECIMENS CHARACTERISTIC OF BOTH THE EIGHT-INCH-PLATE AND THE COFFEE-POT PERIODS

D. Curtiss			
Ashbil Griswold			
J. Danforth	Middletown, Connecticut		
William Calder	Providence, Rhode Island	(D) 1824	
I. Curtis			
Henry S. Boardman	Hartford, Connecticut, and Philadelphia	1841	1857
Boardman (Lion Mark)	Hartford (?)		
Boardman & Co.	New York City	(D) 1825	1827 (D)
Boardman & Hart	New York City	(D) 1828	1850 (D)
Boardman & Hall	Philadelphia, Pennsylvania	(D) 1844 (D)	
T. D. & S. Boardman	Hartford, Connecticut	c. 1825	1854

It is quite evident that pewterers in various stages of their careers must have been overtaken by the complete and fairly rapid changes in fashion with which we are now dealing. In most cases the character of their average output discloses the character of their relation to the transition.

D. CURTISS

The first maker on our list is D. Curtiss. So far as the few surviving specimens of his pewter can be relied upon for guidance, he was a maker of the
earlier tradition whose sole yielding to the new fashions was the making of
graceful water pitchers of the type shown in Fig. 189. Outside of these (of
which, I think, I have seen three), my lists include only a couple of eight-inch
plates, the eight-inch basin illustrated, and the eleven-inch deep plate shown
behind the pitcher in the illustration. If it were not, therefore, for the existence of these pitchers (definitely, I believe, a type that belonged to the latter
era), this maker would be listed among the eight-inch-plate men and rated (as
he is, anyway) as of the first order of rarity; although among the late, not the
early, holders of that distinction. He used, so far as I know, but two touches:
one, the very attractive one shown complete in the two cuts numbered 190
and 192; and the other reproduced in Fig. 191. The latter is found on the
bottoms of his pitchers. It is ascribed to the same maker as the user of the
other (and much earlier-looking) touch, because of the unusual spelling of the
name "Curtiss" on both. It is, of course, possible that the maker of the pitcher
may turn out to have been a son or a namesake of the maker of the other
pieces. In that case the apparent discrepancy in type between the two
touches would be explained. For the present, however, we shall have to leave
them together, even if they don't agree.

Some of the earlier lists give New York as the location of this maker's
workshop. I have failed to verify the ascription. As will be seen by the
general list in this volume, several makers by the more ordinary name of
"Curtis" worked in New York City during the coffee-pot era. But I have
nowhere, between 1786 and 1840, found trace of D. Curtiss in the city directories.

ASHBIL GRISWOLD

Our next maker, Ashbil Griswold, is an excellent example of the complete straddler type. He made enough eight-inch plates to relegate him, on that score alone, to the third, if not to the fourth, grade of comparative rarities. And he made, perhaps, more coffee-pots than any other exploiter of the new era's specialty. At the very least, he made more coffee-pots marked with an eagle mark than any other maker. And in addition to all this he managed to conceal from us both his habitat and his dates. Which is some record.

I have heard A. Griswold repeatedly referred to by dealers in Philadelphia and Pennsylvania as a Philadelphia maker. And in my experience almost all of his pieces turn up in the territory tributary, in the old days, to that city.

But I have failed to find his name anywhere at all in the Philadelphia records; and I see nothing for it but to adopt the good old Mother Goose method and "leave him alone," confident that in good time he'll come home with his address and dates trailing behind. He was a one-hundred-per-cent eagle fan. The wretched double impression of his large, sprawling birds with his full name above and below, shown in Figs. 196 and 197, is the touch he habitually used on his flatware. Moreover, he habitually used it even less carefully than here shown. The small eagle, with "A. Griswold" above, shown in Fig. 195, is the touch he used on his coffee-pots. The "A. G." touch reproduced in Fig. 198 is found on beakers and lidded "spice-boxes," and is here shown on the chance (which I regard as a strong probability) that it was used by this maker. Remains the eagle touch shown in Fig. 194. This is on the bottom of an eight-inch plate, and is the only impression of the touch I have ever seen. Examples of this touch of Griswold's I should be inclined to regard as real rarities, worthy of inclusion in any collection, no matter how "choosey."

It is, I think, impossible to study the matter of American pewter very much, or to handle any variety of examples of it, without being more and more persuaded that the collecting of it resolves itself into the collecting of makers. One may, of course, and collectors unquestionably will, specialize in certain periods. But such confinings of activity can but make more definite and conscious the confiner's interest in the men who worked in the period chosen. This being of the essence of the American pewter situation, it follows, I think, that the very rare marks of the more prolific makers will come to be regarded as themselves of the elect.

Take this man Griswold as an example. Whatever his dates may turn out to be — and he apparently worked for some years — he was essentially late. And, moreover, he was unquestionably prolific. So that, so far as the more exclusive type of collector and collection is concerned — out he goes. And yet, even if one had been reveling in a feast of Bassetts and Wills, Austins and Jones's, and others of the Olympians, would not a sight of the rare eagle of Ashbil Griswold's, in actual being on the back of a real plate, excite the interest and rouse the envy of any student and collector?

J. DANFORTH

J. Danforth, of Middletown, Connecticut — where it will be recalled that Thomas (3), the grandson of the first Thomas Danforth, was born in 1756 — may stand here as a fitting example of a maker whose work lay mostly in the final period, yet who at the beginning of his career paid his respects to the old order. The exact dates when this maker worked are yet to be discovered, although they are no doubt discoverable from the records of Middletown. On the other hand, it would seem to be a safe guess that he started the practice of his craft in the eighteen-twenties; for it would otherwise be hard to understand his having made the quart mug illustrated in Fig. 199, and marked, on the inside bottom, with the eagle mark reproduced in Fig. 200. Especially is this true because of the fact that at least two eight-inch plates by him, also marked with this eagle touch, are in existence. One of these is in my possession, although not here illustrated. For the rest, the specimens of this Danforth's work are mostly tea- and coffee-pots, some of which bear the eagle touch, but most of which are marked by the typical final period touch shown in Fig. 201. On the score of his eight-inch plates — carefully qualified for his late date — J. Danforth is rated as of the first order of rarity.

WILLIAM CALDER

William Calder, of Providence, like Samuel Hamlin, of the same town, worked toward the close of the earlier period. His name, like Hamlin's, appears in the local directory for 1824. While scarcely figuring as a maker of eight-inch plates (the example illustrated in Fig. 202 is one of the only pair that have come to my hands), he nevertheless confined himself mostly to other types of continuing popularity. His porringer output is second only to that of Hamlin. Most Calder porringers measure from four and seven-eighths to five and a quarter inches in diameter. One of these is shown at the right in Fig. 202. The porringer at the left is one of two measuring four and a quarter inches in diameter that I have found. These and the eight-inch plates referred to are all pewter. I note ten-and-a-quarter-inch plates (presumably patens) in britannia of rather inferior quality, and a britannia communion flagon by Calder, as well as two small "courting" lamps. All of these pieces, except the porringers, bear the name-touch illustrated (natural size) in Fig. 204. The eagle touch shown in Fig. 203 is found — so far as my experience goes — on all porringers. I understand, although no example of such use has come to my own notice, that this eagle touch is also found on other pieces besides his porringers.

Not only are Calder *pewter* pieces scarce, but a somewhat mysterious vogue for his work has been developed in New England that makes specimens of his handicraft harder to come by than they otherwise would be. The same thing has happened in the case of Israel Trask, a maker of the last period who has been collected quite extensively and without, an unbiased observer would say, any relation to his intrinsic worth. With Calder the case is different, since his affiliations are distinctly with the old tradition; and since, too, he comes in among the Rhode Island makers, who have already shown unmistakable signs of being collected as a class. It is likely, too, that family tradition has added its influence to local association in fostering these individual cults. However, in spite of his lateness, and on the score of his eight-inch-plate standing, Calder must be placed in the second rating for rarity. He is also, as will be noted in due course, one of the very few makers of the so-called "courting" or "sparking" lamps, by whom marked examples exist.

THE BOARDMAN GROUP

We come now to the overwhelmingly dominant composite figure of the whole transition period — the Boardman group. So catholic were their tastes and so tenacious were they of the old forms, while at the same time so ready were they to meet the coming fashions with a warm and experimental welcome, that it may almost be said that a collector, who confined himself to the work of this family and the men intimately associated with them as partners, could gather a nearly complete exhibit of the forms taken by American pewter in its normal manifestations. And in spite of its being something of a fashion just now to look with scanty respect upon fine specimens bearing the Boardman eagle, I make no doubt whatever that the group will yet come to be collected by itself, and that pieces by some of the rare members of it will be bitterly fought for before much water has passed under the local pewter mill. For, as we shall see presently, there is a fascinating mix-up among these variously affiliated Boardmans and non-Boardmans; and not only did the group turn out some really exquisite things, but Sherlock Holmes himself would enjoy solving some of the puzzles presented by the subject. The more I have studied the family records and marks, the more certain have I become that "Little Mary Mix-up" must have been a Boardman.

That there were several American Boardmans engaged in the making of pewter has been well known for many years. The earliest lists give us the names of Thomas D. Boardman, of Hartford; of Timothy Boardman & Co., of New York; and of Boardman & Hart, of New York. Boardman & Hall, of Philadelphia, do not seem to have been noted so early. And while there has been a growing feeling that there was a relationship and possibly even a business affiliation between these various firms, this has apparently been merely one of those feelings that reside, as the say is, "in the air."

Now, "having a feeling" may be very convincing to the possessor of the hunch — a "hunch" being a super-heteradyned conclusion, arrived at without either aerial or ground. I have even known several men whose hunches it was distinctly unsafe to ignore.

But one hesitates to offer one's beliefs of this order for general acceptance until one is able to add at least a few brass tacks to the mixture. During the last year or so I have come across numerous indications, both in the pages of the New York and Philadelphia city directories, and in the markings of the various specimens of Boardman pewter, that make out at least a strong circumstantial case for the belief that most, if not all, of the wares sold by the firms above named were made in Hartford, Connecticut; were there marked according to their intended destination; and were thence shipped to the Boardman branch, or agency, or whatever the various firms really were, for disposal to the public.

The earliest directory reference to any pewter-making Boardman in this country, so far as I know, is the listing in the New York City Directory of 1822 of the firm of Timothy Boardman & Co. The offices of this firm were at 178 Water Street, and the name was listed in the New York directories up to and including 1824. In 1825 the firm of "Boardman & Co." at the same address appears, and in 1828 this listing is abandoned and "Boardman & Hart," still at the same address, appears in its place. Please note, however, that although the firm of Boardman & Hart continues to be listed in the New York directories until 1850, and although the name of Lucius Hart appears in all these issues of the directory, *no Boardman is listed in any of these volumes as a member of this firm or as residing in New York.* Moreover, in 1850, four years before the end of the activities of the two Hartford brothers, Thomas D. and Sherman Boardman, Lucius Hart dropped the name of "Boardman" from his business title, and continued thenceforth, first as "Lucius Hart, Britannia Ware Manufacturer," and, after 1863, as "Lucius Hart and Company" at the old address.

In 1841, the name of Henry S. Boardman appears as a pewterer in the Hartford Directory at 67 Trumbull Street. In 1844, the Philadelphia Directory lists the firm of "Boardman & Hall, Britannia Ware Manufacturers," at 436 High Street; and gives the members of this firm as being Henry S. Boardman and F. D. Hall.

This is the only year in which the name of "Boardman & Hall" appears in the Philadelphia Directory.

In 1845, Henry S. Boardman is listed as "Manufacturer" at the same address on North Third Street where "Hall, Boardman & Co., Drygoods," are listed as doing business. In 1846, "Hall, Boardman & Co." have apparently given up the drygoods business and become "Britannia Ware Manufacturers"; and so continue during 1847 and 1848. In 1849, the firm name becomes "Hall & Boardman," and so continues until, in 1857, just three years after the two Boardman brothers have ceased operations in Hartford, it disappears for good and all.

It seems odd that the pewter marked with the name of "Boardman & Hall," a firm that existed but for a single year, should be fairly common to-day, while apparently the entire output of the firm of "Hall, Boardman & Co." and of "Hall & Boardman" — firms that, between them, continued in business for twelve years, should have disappeared.

Yet suppose, just for fun, that these successive forms of the firm name used by Henry S. Boardman and F. D. Hall in their business of agents for the britannia and pewterware made in Hartford by the brothers Boardman were ignored by the Hartford factory which did the marking of the ware shipped to them. Suppose, for instance, that, having had dies made for the first of these firm names, they did not care to go to the expense of altering them; or that they did not share Mr. Hall's preference for having his name come first on the sign over their warehouse in Philadelphia.

If we examine the touch of Boardman & Hart shown in Fig. 222, we see that two dies have been used separately to impress the whole inscription of "Boardman & Hart N-YORK." If we examine the touch of Boardman & Hall shown in Fig. 224, we see that two dies have been used separately to impress the whole inscription of "Boardman & Hall Philada." And if, finally, we examine the particular impressions of the touch of Boardman & Hall reproduced in Figs. 226 and 226a, we can, upon close examination, satisfy ourselves that, on the first, the "N-YORK" touch, characteristic of the marks on Boardman & Hart pieces, has been struck here under the name of Boardman & Hall; *and that afterward the error has been corrected by striking the (Boardman & Hall) "Philada" touch over the (Boardman & Hart)*

"*N–YORK*" *impression;* while on the other the complete "Boardman &
Hart N–YORK" mark has first been impressed on the piece, and then the
"Boardman & Hall Philada" marks struck over them.

This could not conceivably have happened except at a central shop, where
the touch dies of both Boardman & Hart and Boardman & Hall were present
and in use.

Again, in Figs. 215 and 217 will be found the impressions of two very fine
eagle touches, neither of which bears any lettering or other inscription that
would enable us to identify it unless it were found in connection with other,
known, touches. Of course, both of these eagle touches are so found in these
two cases. The normal eagle mark of Boardman & Co., New York, accompanies each of them. But in Fig. 225, one of these eagles is found impressed twice
on a nine-inch Boardman & Hall, Philadelphia, plate; and it happens that I
have a set of these plates and that this eagle appears upon them all. And so,
again, we get the strongest kind of a suggestion that these New York and
Philadelphia pieces have somehow had a more material relationship to each
other than the mere presence of the Boardman name in their respective mer-
chandisers' firm titles.

Again, in Figs. 228, 229, and 230 we have the touch used by the brothers
Boardman, of Hartford — the "T.D.&S.B." mark that stands for Thomas
D. and Sherman Boardman — impressed on the handle of one of their own
porringers; impressed upon the bottom of a communion flagon that is marked
with Thomas D. Boardman's individual touch; and, finally, stamped under
the eagle touch of Boardman & Co., New York, on the bottom of a characteristic communion flagon of their habitual make — or at least marking. The
inference is again strong that all of these pieces came from the same factory.

Finally, in Fig. 206 we see the same Boardman eagle that we have found
in conjunction with the name-touches of Boardman & Co., New York, and of
Boardman & Hall, Philadelphia, keeping company with a heretofore unknown
maker's touch — that of one "I. Curtis" — on the back of the eight-inch plate
shown in Fig. 205. So far as I know but two examples of this Curtis eight-inch
plate have turned up. And its turning up at all in this form suggests a pos-

sible explanation of the use of these unsigned eagle touches by the Hartford Boardmans. They may have been regarded by them as their own secret hall mark, impressed upon goods that they were making and marking with the names of other firms for these other firms to sell as their own manufacture.

This general assumption, moreover, of the essential concentration of the manufacturing activities of the Boardmans in the hands of the Hartford representatives of the name gives us the only satisfactory explanation of two Boardman touches not otherwise accounted for.

One of these is the "Boardman and Lion" touch shown in Fig. 210, which there is no valid reason for assigning to either the New York or the Philadelphia firms, and for which no other sponsors have been found; but which would be quite logically accounted for as a touch used by the home office in Hartford, whose managers and founders were the sons of Sarah Danforth, of that lion-bearing line of Connecticut and Massachusetts pewterers. The touch, which reads simply "Boardman Warranted," and which is here shown with those of Boardman & Co., New York, which it closely resembles in character (see Fig. 216), would also explain itself as a special touch placed, in Hartford, upon pieces of especially fine pewter or of a special grade of hard metal.

All of these considerations taken together have led me to adopt as the most likely explanation the theory that the real captains of the Boardman pewter industry lived in Hartford. This belief is greatly strengthened, too, by the slight importance apparently borne by the actual Boardman members of these New York and Philadelphia concerns. During most of its business life the Boardman & Hart concern appears to have had no resident Boardman partner. And Henry S. Boardman would appear to have been rather a partner of Mr. Hall's in the drygoods business, who persuaded him to start an agency for the wares of his Hartford relatives, than the leading spirit of the Philadelphia partnership.

Of course, this is all merely an attempt to deduce the most likely facts from a mass of circumstantial evidence. And one's conclusions in such a case are colored and influenced by many small observations that never get themselves stated in such an explanation as this. But I add one such straw here as an example. For a single year, 1845, this Henry S. Boardman figures in

Fig. 209

BOARDMAN (LION MARK)

8 inch plate   11¼ inch coffee-pot   8 inch plate

Fig. 210

LION MARK USED BY BOARDMAN

Fig. 211

THE BOARDMAN LION MARK SURCHARGED
"WHITLOCK, TROY, N.Y."

Fig. 211A

TIMOTHY BOARDMAN & COMPANY, 1822–1824

5¼ inch beaker   3¼ inch beaker

Fig. 211B

MARK USED BY TIMOTHY BOARDMAN & COMPANY

Fig. 212

BOARDMAN & COMPANY, 1825–1827

Three fine types of communion flagons

Fig. 213

BOARDMAN & COMPANY'S USUAL MARK

Fig. 214

BOARDMAN & COMPANY, 1825–1827

10¾ inch plate   12 inch coffee-pot   9 inch plate
7½ inch tea-pot   5 inch porringer

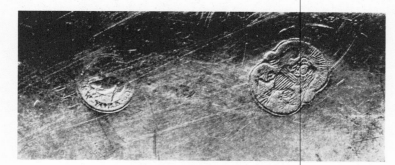

Fig. 215

Fig. 216

Fig. 217

OTHER MARKS FOUND ON BOARDMAN & COMPANY'S PIECES

Fig. 218

BOARDMAN & HART, 1828–1850

9¾ inch plate   5½ inch slop bowl   7¾ inch plate

Fig. 219   Fig. 220

A VERY EARLY MARK OF BOARDMAN & HART

Fig. 221

BOARDMAN & HART, 1828–1850

Half-pint mug   7 inch lamp   7¾ inch water pitcher   7 inch lamp   Pint mug

Fig. 222

USUAL MARKS USED BY BOARDMAN & HART

Fig. 223

BOARDMAN & HALL, 1844

9 inch plate   11 inch coffee-pot   9 inch plate

Fig. 224   Fig. 226   Fig. 225   Fig. 226A

MARKS USED BY BOARDMAN & HALL

Fig. 227

T. D. & S. B.
(THOMAS D. AND SHERMAN BOARDMAN, 1825–1854)

5 inch porringer

Quart mug

3¼ inch porringer

8½ inch tea-pot (britannia)

4½ inch porringer

Fig. 228

Fig. 229

Fig. 230

MARK USED BY T. D. & S. B.

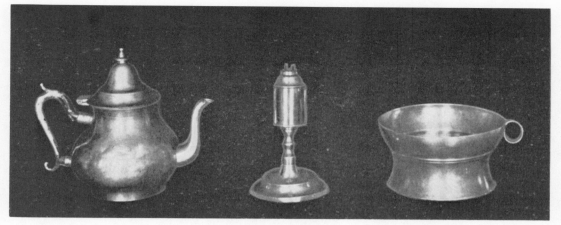

Fig. 231

ROSWELL GLEASON, 1830

7½ inch tea-pot 6 inch lamp 6 inch cuspidor

Fig. 232

ROSWELL GLEASON, 1830

11 inch covered pitcher 6 inch baptismal bowl 12 inch flagon

  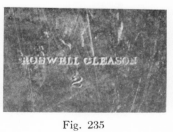 

Fig. 233 Fig. 234 Fig. 235 Fig. 236

MARKS USED BY ROSWELL GLEASON

Fig. 237

ISRAEL TRASK, 1825–1842

10½ inch coffee-pot   9 inch britannia coffee-pot   12 inch coffee-pot

Fig. 238

ISRAEL TRASK, 1825–1842

7½ inch lamp   11¼ inch communion flagon   7½ inch lamp

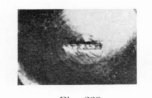

Fig. 239

MARK USED BY ISRAEL TRASK

Fig. 240

OLIVER TRASK, 1792–1874

12 inch britannia communion flagon

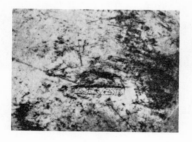

Fig. 241

MARK USED BY OLIVER TRASK

Fig. 242

EBEN SMITH, CIRCA 1840

7½ inch tea-pot   8¾ inch britannia coffee-pot

Fig. 243

EBEN SMITH, CIRCA 1840

6 inch pewter lamp   10½ inch britannia communion flagon   6 inch pewter lamp

Fig. 244

MARK USED BY EBEN SMITH

Fig. 245

BABBITT, CROSSMAN & COMPANY, 1824
CROSSMAN, WEST & LEONARD, 1827

7¼ inch britannia sugar bowl
by Crossman, West & Leonard

10½ inch britannia coffee-pot
by Babbitt, Crossman & Company

Fig. 246

MARK USED BY
CROSSMAN, WEST & LEONARD

Fig. 247

MARK USED BY
BABBITT, CROSSMAN & COMPANY

Fig. 248

BAILEY & PUTNAM

7 inch tea-pot   11 inch coffee-pot

Fig. 249

BAILEY & PUTNAM AND PUTNAM

6¾ inch lamp   11inch coffee-pot   6¾ inch lamp
by Bailey & Putnam   by Putnam   by Bailey & Putnam

Fig. 250   Fig. 251   Fig. 252

MARKS USED BY BAILEY & PUTNAM AND PUTNAM

Fig. 253

L. BOARDMAN

8 inch tea-pot

Fig. 254

MARK USED BY L. BOARDMAN

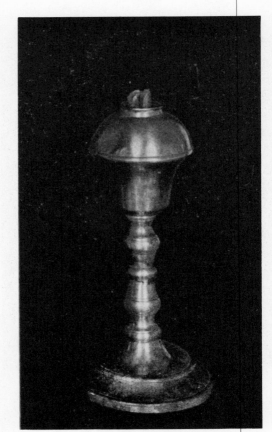

Fig. 255

BROOK FARM, 1841–1847

$7\frac{1}{4}$ inch lamp

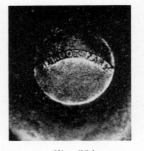

Fig. 256

MARK USED AT BROOK FARM

Fig. 257

CAPEN & MOLINEUX, 1848–1853

Various sizes of lamps

Fig. 258

CAPEN & MOLINEUX, 1848–1853

Various sizes of lamps from $2\frac{1}{2}$ inches to $7\frac{1}{2}$ inches

Fig. 259   Fig. 260

MARKS USED BY CAPEN & MOLINEUX

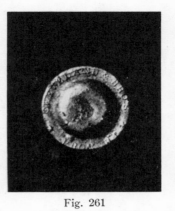

Fig. 261

MARK USED BY CLEVELAND & BROTHERS

Fig. 262

T. S. DERBY

9¼ inch tea-pot   Cuspidor   11 inch coffee-pot

Fig. 263

MARK USED BY T. S. DERBY

the Philadelphia Directory as a "Manufacturer" on his own hook. Awhile back I found the beaker — if that is its proper name — illustrated in Fig. 207 and bearing on its under side the touch illustrated in Fig. 208. I ascribe it, perforce, to the activities of Henry S. during his one year of solo manufacturing. And since it is a poor, thin, badly designed example of the most tinpanish of mid-Victorian "Britannia," it has not greatly increased my belief that Henry S. was personally responsible for the really excellent wares that were sold by his firm, marked "Boardman & Hall."

BOARDMAN (LION MARK)

Having thus set forth the evidence, so far as I know it, in the matter of the Boardman mystery, I shall proceed to take up in turn the wares bearing the respective touches of the several Boardman firms.

On the assumption that the "Boardman and Lion" mark is a touch used by the Hartford factory; and also because this is the only Boardman mark except that of Thomas D. Boardman "himself," that I have seen on enough eight-inch plates to suggest that, during its use, a small trade in these vanishing table plates might still have been carried on, I place this touch at the head of the line. Fig. 209 shows two of the three eight-inch plates with this mark (Fig. 210) that I have come across, and a coffee-pot similar in design to those that we assume to have been sent out from the Hartford factory, marked "Boardman & Co." and "Boardman & Hart." I also have a communion flagon and a nine-and-a-half-inch deep plate bearing this touch; and have seen fine covered water pitchers and a large basin with domed cover thus marked. The touch shown in Fig. 211 is from one of the fine covered water pitchers of the Boardman type with what I take to be the stamp of a Troy, New York, dealer impressed over the name of Boardman. This at first I supposed to have been done by Whitlock after the piece had come into his hands. But in view of the readiness of the Hartford Boardmans to mark their wares with the ultimate sellers' names, it may well be that the Whitlock touch was thus applied in Hartford before the piece was shipped. The pitcher from which this mark was photographed is the property of Mr. Louis Guerineau Myers, of New York.

TIMOTHY BOARDMAN & COMPANY

Just what position Timothy Boardman occupied in the Boardman connection I do not know. According to the New York City directories he lived in New York from 1822 to 1824. Coincidentally with the change of the name of the Boardman agency from "Timothy Boardman & Co." to plain "Boardman & Co.," his name disappears from the directory, and I have not found trace of him either before or since these happenings. After his disappearance, no Boardman resident in New York seems ever to have been connected with either Boardman & Co. or with the succeeding firm of Boardman & Hart. The work made, or at any rate sold, by Timothy Boardman & Co., and marked with their initials as shown in Fig. 211b, is very seldom met with. In all my experience I have seen only two specimens of it. Both of these happen to be beakers, one five and a quarter inches high, the other three and a quarter. Both are shown in Fig. 211a. It seems only to be expected, however, that a general line of the then Boardman output was marked with his touch and sent to his shop for sale.

BOARDMAN & COMPANY

As we have already seen, the firm name of Timothy Boardman & Co. was, in 1825, replaced in the New York City Directory by that of Boardman & Co. Pewter bearing the marks shown in Figs. 213, 215, and 217 was manifestly sold from this office, and on the whole does credit to its makers and sponsors. The output was in an excellent sense typical of the transition period that it represents; and it would by no means surprise me if articles bearing the Boardman & Co., New York, touch (Fig. 213) were in reality sold for some time after the firm name of Boardman & Hart went up on the Water Street store. I have, for instance, never seen a communion flagon bearing the Boardman & Hart touch. Yet I doubt if this handsomest of all the Boardman shapes was discontinued after 1828; or, to put it another way, was only made for three years. A group of three variations of this form, all marked with the Boardman & Co. eagle mark, is shown in Fig. 212. These are all fine britannia metal, only a trifle less entitled to be classed as good pewter than the flagon by Thomas D. Boardman shown in Fig. 27, and already discussed. In Fig. 214 are shown a pewter coffee-pot and a pewter tea-pot, both bearing the normal Boardman & Co., New York, touch; also a five-inch porringer, with the same touch on the handle; also a ten-and-a-half-inch plate marked as shown in Fig. 215, and a nine-inch plate marked "Boardman Warranted" (see Fig. 216).

In addition to the pieces here shown, I have the ten-and-one-half-inch basin with the "Boardman Warranted" touch already described; a sugar bowl with the eagle mark (Fig. 213), and a nine-and-three-quarters-inch deep plate (see Fig. 218) that carries both the Boardman & Co. touch and the, presumably very early, Boardman & Hart touch shown in Figs. 219 and 220. This combination proves, if the matter needed proof, that Boardman & Hart were successors to Boardman & Co., and not a newly formed partnership. I mention this because I have seen this fact stated as a mere probability. The combination of marks shown in Fig. 217 is from another ten-inch plate. These ten-inch plates are — all that I have seen — made of a very fine grade of hard metal. The other pieces shown are all normal pewter.

BOARDMAN & HART

Fig. 218 shows, at the left, the nine-and-three-quarters-inch deep plate with both the Boardman & Co. and the early Boardman & Hart marks on it. Both impressions of the latter are reproduced (Figs. 219 and 220) in order to give as complete a picture of this very rare touch as possible.

This illustration also shows at the right an eight-inch plate with the normal Boardman & Hart touch (see Fig. 222); this being the only eight-inch plate I have ever seen bearing the imprint of any of the transitional Boardman agencies, except, of course, the three plates already illustrated and referred to that are marked with the "Boardman and Lion" touch, and the "I. Curtis" plate shown in Fig. 205. This fact is rather remarkable, I think, and shows how extremely clean-cut must have been the end of the old fashion, and how unusually well the facts of the actual development lend themselves to our convenient "classification by categories."

The central specimen in Fig. 218 is the slop bowl of a tea-set, and is also marked on the bottom (outside) with the ordinary Boardman & Hart touch. It is astonishing how scarce good marked slop bowls are. One meets occasionally with a monstrosity in thin britannia, tortured into the convolutions that the eighteen-forties looked upon as beautiful. But *pewter* bowls, of simple form and good sheen, marked even by coffee-pot period makers, are scarce, indeed. This is one of the finest I have seen. In Fig. 221 are grouped some of the characteristic forms that bear the Boardman & Hart imprint. Of lamps they appear to have made extremely few. This pair, and another single one, are all my notes make mention of. And as no other maker, whose marked lamps have come to my notice, started business as early as the Boardman & Hart date of 1828, I take it that these lamps were not among Boardman & Hart's earlier output. Attention has already been called to the fact that the "N-York" touch usually found accompanying the "Boardman & Hart" touch is a separate die. The "Boardman & Hart" touch is therefore found without the "N-York" touch on occasion, especially on smaller pieces. Two mugs are shown in Fig. 221. One is four and a quarter inches high, and of an early shape. The other is three and three quarters inches high, and of the typical nineteenth-century design. Water pitchers of several designs and in sizes up to a gallon were made with the Boardman & Hart imprint. A medium-sized example is here shown.

BOARDMAN & HALL

Two eight-and-seven-eighths-inch plates and a coffee-pot by Boardman & Hall are illustrated in Fig. 223. The marking of these plates, already discussed, is shown in Fig. 225. A fine coffee-pot, of normal Boardman form, but decorated with gouged foliated designs, is also shown in Fig. 34. Attention is called to the resemblance between the tops of the Boardman & Hall coffee-pot in Fig. 223 and of the "Boardman and Lion" one in Fig. 209. Also to the resemblances between the spouts and handles of these two pieces. Taken alone, one would hesitate to base much of an argument on these resemblances. But added to what we have already discussed, they tend to convince one of the common origin of these variously marked pieces. I have also seen a very fine covered pitcher marked "Boardman & Hall," and a very indifferent britannia slop bowl — indifferent both in design and in metal. Almost the latter persuaded me that Henry S. Boardman, who presumably is responsible for the beaker in Fig. 207 above, did some slop-bowl work for the firm later on! Boardman & Hall pieces are by no means common. A much larger business appears to have been done at the New York store; although, of course, the Philadelphia concern started only in 1844. At any rate, specimens of Boardman & Hall pewter that are pewter, and that are of good shape, are decidedly worth picking up.

T.D.&S.B.

In Fig. 227 are shown five articles, all of which bear the initialed touch (Fig. 230) of the brothers Boardman, of Hartford. They seem to have marked most of the porringers made by them with this touch of their own rather than with that of any of their southerly agencies or branches. I have, I think, seen but one or two porringers — one is shown in Fig. 214 — bearing the Boardman & Co., New York, touch. I have seen two marked with the personal touches of Thomas D. Boardman. And that is all. But only Samuel Hamlin and William Calder appear to have made as many porringers as bear the "T.D.&S.B." touch. At the left of Fig. 227 is a five-inch specimen with the once fashionable English type of handle. At the right is a four-inch, and in the center a three-inch, specimen. The mug shown is a quart size; and this again is a form that seems not to have been put out by the Boardmans except with this initialed touch. The tea-pot — a late, badly designed shape and made of a poor quality of britannia — is a type of vessel that seems, on the other hand, to have been seldom marked with this touch by these makers. A good average impression of this touch is shown in Fig. 230. It is an impression from a porringer handle. The other impressions shown in Figs. 228 and 229 are taken from the bottoms of communion flagons. I also have a twelve-inch plate with the "T.D.&S.B." mark.

CHAPTER VIII

THE COFFEE-POT ERA

WE have now reached totally different *terrain* from the country that we have been traversing. Heretofore there have, it is true, been differences in quality, in character, and in collectibility between the various craftsmen with whose work we have been dealing; but in the entire list of forty-seven names with which we have dealt, there has not been a single maker that was really negligible. No collector, I take it, who elects to make a general collection of American pewter will be likely deliberately to exclude any pewterer whose name is there set down.

But in the period that we are about to consider, these conditions no longer hold good. Here is a land where, for the most part, names in themselves are devoid of magic, and acquire interest only through their connection with forms that, because of their intrinsic beauty, or their decorative qualities, or their distinctively American origin, are destined to represent their period on the shelves of collectors.

Again, small as the early list is, when regarded as comprising all the craftsmen of the best period of American pewter-making, it nevertheless invites subdivision by specialists. But whether your specialist elects to devote himself to a particular region (like Rhode Island), or to a particular period (like the Revolution-spanning generation), or to a particular marking fashion (like the eagle touches), the ultimate units of specialization will be the names of the eligible makers, and not the forms of the eligible articles. Not, of course, that forms will not figure. It is, for instance, unthinkable that the eight-inch plate should not be collected. But it is almost a foregone conclusion that the specimens in such a collection would be shown *with their backs to the front*.

Broadly speaking, however, specialization doesn't flourish in the climate of the "Coffee-Pot Country." It is, rather, a happy hunting-ground for eclectics. Not only are some of its forms very fine, but the simple truth is that no general collection of American pewter can be complete, representative, *or at its decorative best*, without examples of these types. A glance at the two panels of the author's pewter room, shown in Figs. 1 and 358, will illustrate the decorative value of some of these late forms. And surely a covered water pitcher such as that shown in Fig. 32, a coffee-urn such as that shown in Fig. 35, or a sugar bowl like that shown in the frontispiece, need not apologize for their presence in any collection of American pewter. But the sugar bowl is G. Richardson's only claim to be individually remembered. It matters little whether the coffee-urn be by Roswell Gleason or another. And it is of far more moment to a collection that the covered and open-topped pitchers be shown in their several sizes and shapes than that McQuilkin, Dunham, Porter, and the others be individually represented.

Again, we have now to do with a period that comprises but twenty-odd years between its start and its finish; so that anything like a chronological consideration of it would be meaningless. I have therefore elected to deal separately with the few makers entitled, because of their output or for some other reason, to special consideration; and then to combine text and pictures into an alphabetical, illustrated glossary of the period.

The pewterers of this later division who require special mention are Roswell Gleason and Israel Trask and his group.

ROSWELL GLEASON

Roswell Gleason, of Dorchester, Massachusetts, is said to have begun work about 1830. And, like the Boardmans in Hartford, he must have carried on the making of pewter and britannia ware more after the manner of a modern business than after that of an earlier craft. Lamps, candlesticks, communion sets (including flagons, patens, and baptismal bowls, but so far as I know, no chalices), tea-pots, coffee-pots, coffee-urns, water pitchers (with covers), mugs, syrup jugs, and cuspidors, are all found bearing his marks. These exhibit all degrees of taste, from the beautiful to the hideous; and all qualities of metal, from fine pewter to britannia that deserves the worst that was ever said of this much-abused alloy. His fine pieces are so fine that examples of them have in several cases been selected to illustrate their type in the general part of this volume. Thus, one of his coffee-urns is shown in Fig. 35. One of his huge covered pitchers is shown in Fig. 32. And in Fig. 3 is shown a "close-up" of an interesting tankard that is, I imagine, a device of his own invention. As the picture shows, this tankard has a top that *screws* on, instead of being hinged. I take its purpose to have been an ecclesiastical one, enabling the priest to carry the sacramental wine to the sick without danger of accident.

In Fig. 231 are shown other Gleason pieces. An attractive tea-pot, reminiscent of the days of Queen Anne; a lamp, and a graceful handled dish that, at the time of its original bow to the public, had a movable cuspidor top fitted over its present rim. All three of these pieces are excellent pewter. In Fig. 232 are shown a fine covered pitcher, a baptismal bowl, and a communion flagon, all of which are britannia — the pitcher of fine quality, the baptismal bowl of excellent grade, and the flagon of good but less commendable metal.

In Fig. 235 is shown the incised mark that Gleason used on most of his large pieces, such as urns, pitchers, patens, and the like. On the bottoms of his earlier lamps, candlesticks, and so on, he used the touch shown in Fig. 236, in which, as in most touches of the period, the letters are in relief upon a sunken panel. The similar mark shown in Fig. 234 I take, from its associations, to be a later edition of the one just discussed. The mark bearing the eagle and stars, shown in Fig. 233, is comparatively rare, and found, so far as I know, only on lamps and candlesticks. The design, oddly enough, is exactly similar to one of the touch designs of J. B. Woodbury, Philadelphia. (Compare Fig. 338.)

THE BEVERLY GROUP
ISRAEL TRASK   OLIVER TRASK   EBEN SMITH

A few moments ago, like the Psalmist, I said in my haste that specialists would not thrive in the "Coffee-Pot Country." But, of course, I assume that no one took me too literally. Like the sick gambler who said, "I'll lay you three to one on it," when the doctor told him he was dying, the born specializer is not too easily discouraged. And, indeed, the whale-oil lamp is, as we shall see in due course, almost a specialty in itself. But one maker, or a little group of makers, the specialists have already, for no reason visible to the non-specializing eye, cut out of the coffee-pot herd and branded for their own. These are Israel Trask, of Beverly, Massachusetts; Oliver Trask, his brother; and Eben Smith, an employee of Israel's, who, later on, seems to have made quite a success on his own account in this little Massachusetts town.

The data assembled by the Boston Art Museum give the dates of Israel Trask's activities in pewter-making as 1825–1842. Local tradition assigns much earlier dates to his work — as early, for instance, as 1812. I have personally seen nothing bearing his mark that does not fit in exactly with the Museum's dates. Figs. 237 and 238 give examples of his characteristic output. The high-shouldered, or pigeon-breasted, tea-pot in the middle position in Fig. 237 would appear to have been a design of his own. And no one in America ever equaled him in his handling of the type of coffee-pot shown at the right of this same group. He is one of the few workers in this country who used chiseled decoration on his pewter pieces. To those who are unacquainted with the horrors of Continental "decorated" pewter, the few beginnings of this work of supererogation in this country have a certain quaint and naïve attractiveness. And, indeed, the matter was never carried here to the point of hiding the line of the piece or destroying the surface of the metal. So that one can safely, in the American ware, indulge such liking for the vogue as comes to one. The same thing is true in England. But beyond the Channel, beware. "Hitting the pipe" a few times just to see what it's like, and buying a little "decorated pewter" just as a variety, are equally dangerous. The left-hand coffee-pot in Fig. 237 shows a band of this tooling about the upper body of the piece. Fig. 239 shows (far more legibly than the mark can usually be seen with the eye) Israel Trask's invariable touch.

For a time, Israel's brother Oliver and another brother, George, worked under him in Beverly. George soon gave up the craft of the pewterer to enter the ministry; but Oliver set up in business for himself in Beverly.

If one may judge from the rarity of pieces bearing his touch, he was never a prolific workman. Fig. 240 shows a vessel of a distinctly unusual shape; undoubtedly a communion flagon. It is twelve inches high; is made of a fairly good grade of britannia, and bears the touch shown in Fig. 241. It is the only piece of Oliver's making that has ever come into my possession. He also made coffee-pots, however.

The maker whose mark is shown in Fig. 244 also belongs in this little group. In such of the earlier lists as gave the name of E. Smith, he is tentatively assigned either to Connecticut or to Albany, New York. For the data that make this E. Smith's identity certain, I am indebted to Mr. John Whiting Webber, whose article on Israel Trask in the January, 1924, issue of "Antiques" is one of what I hope will be a long line of monographs on individual American pewterers. Eben Smith, who was born in 1773 and who died in 1849, worked under Israel Trask in Beverly and later set up for himself. His son, Eben, who was born in 1802, was in business with him. They made britannia and pewter, and seem to have made quite a fortune out of brass hose nozzles. A tea-pot, made by them and still in the possession of the family, bears the E. Smith mark. Even if this latter bit of evidence as to the identity of E. Smith with Eben Smith were lacking, one would only need to examine the tea-pot at the right of Fig. 242 to satisfy one's self that the E. Smith who marked it and the Eben Smith who worked under Israel Trask were the same. For here is the Trask pigeon-breasted model to the life. A tea-pot by J. B. Woodbury, of Philadelphia, shown in Fig. 334, is the only thing at all like these that I have seen by any other maker. Woodbury, it will be recalled, is the only other user of the eagle touch used by Gleason, of Dorchester, Massachusetts. One wonders where Woodbury came from when he appeared in Philadelphia in 1837. Unlike Oliver Trask, the Smiths were decidedly prolific. Tea- and coffee-pots, flagons and lamps seem to have been their chief standbys. The little tea-pot on general Queen Anne lines, shown at the left of Fig. 242, reminds us of the one by Gleason in Fig. 231. It is also similar to the one marked "B.&P." shown in Fig. 248. In Fig. 243 are shown a pair of E. Smith lamps and a britannia flagon of the same make.

And now before proceeding with our pictorial summing-up of the balance of the men of this division and their work, I shall insert the alphabetical list of those makers of the period of whose make, so far, pewter specimens have been found. The list follows:

AMERICAN PEWTERERS OF THE COFFEE-POT PERIOD, SPECIMENS OF WHOSE WORK ARE KNOWN, ARRANGED ALPHABETICALLY

Babbitt, Crossman & Co.	Taunton, Massachusetts
Bailey & Putnam	
Henry S. Boardman	Hartford, Connecticut, Philadelphia, Pennsylvania
L. Boardman	
"Brook Farm"	West Roxbury, Massachusetts
Capen & Molineux	New York City
Cleveland & Bros.	Providence, Rhode Island
Crossman, West & Leonard	Taunton, Massachusetts
T. S. Derby	
R. Dunham	Portland, Maine (?)
R. Dunham & Sons	Portland, Maine
Endicott & Sumner	New York City
Fenn	New York City
Fuller & Smith	Connecticut (?)
Roswell Gleason	Dorchester, Massachusetts
Henry Graves	Middletown, Connecticut
J. B. & H. Graves	Middletown, Connecticut
Hall & Cotton	
Holmes & Sons	Baltimore, Maryland
Homans & Co.	Cincinnati, Ohio
Henry Hopper	New York City
Houghton & Wallace	
M. Hyde	
L. Kruiger	Philadelphia, Pennsylvania
Leonard, Reed & Barton	Taunton, Massachusetts
J. D. Locke	New York City
William McQuilkin	Philadelphia, Pennsylvania
Morey & Ober	Boston, Massachusetts
Morey & Smith	Boston, Massachusetts
J. Munson	
J. H. Palethorp	Philadelphia, Pennsylvania
Palethorp & Connell	Philadelphia, Pennsylvania
C. Parker & Co.	New York City (?)
A. Porter	Southington, Connecticut
F. Porter	Westbrook, Connecticut
Putnam	
Reed & Barton	Taunton, Massachusetts
G. Richardson	Cranston, Rhode Island
Samuel Rust	New York City
Sage & Beebe	
Savage	Middletown, Connecticut
Savage & Graham	Middletown, Connecticut
Samuel Simpson	New York City
Sellews & Co.	Cincinnati, Ohio
Sheldon & Feltman	Albany, New York
E. Smith	Beverly, Massachusetts
Smith & Co.	Albany (?), Connecticut (?)

Smith & Feltman	Albany, New York
H. Snyder	Philadelphia, Pennsylvania
Taunton Britannia Manufacturing Company	Taunton, Massachusetts
Israel Trask	Beverly, Massachusetts
Oliver Trask	Beverly, Massachusetts
H. B. Ward & Co.	Guilford, Connecticut
J. Weekes	New York
Weekes & Co.	New York
Thomas Wildes	New York City
Lorenzo L. Williams	Philadelphia, Pennsylvania
J. B. Woodbury	Philadelphia, Pennsylvania
Woodbury & Colton	Philadelphia, Pennsylvania
Woodman, Cook & Co.	Portland, Maine
Charles Yale	New York City
H. Yale & Co.	Wallingford, Connecticut
W. & S. Yale	Wallingford, Connecticut
Yale & Curtis	New York City

BABBITT, CROSSMAN & CO.
CROSSMAN, WEST & LEONARD

Babbitt, Crossman & Co. started business in Taunton, Massachusetts, in 1824 as britannia manufacturers. The present firm of Reed & Barton derives from this beginning. The coffee-pot at the right of Fig. 245 is by this firm and is britannia ware. Fig. 247 shows their mark. In 1827 the firm name became Crossman, West & Leonard. The sugar bowl to the left of Fig. 245 is a britannia piece by the latter makers. Their mark is shown in Fig. 246. The next year, 1828, Henry C. Reed and Charles E. Barton began work with the firm as apprentices. These two, with Gustavus Leonard, formed the firm of Leonard, Reed & Barton (of which more later) in 1835. Such pieces as are here shown are of no interest to pewter collectors as such.

BAILEY & PUTNAM
"B&P"
PUTNAM

Figs. 248 and 249 illustrate the work of two — or it may be three — makers whose addresses and exact dates are not known. The firm of Bailey & Putnam made the coffee-pot illustrated in Fig. 248 and the pair of lamps shown in Fig. 249. Both are pewter. The small tea-pot (of similar shape to those shown by Gleason and E. Smith) is marked as shown in Fig. 252, which suggests that it may be by this same Bailey & Putnam. Of course it may not be. The coffee-pot in Fig. 249 is marked "Putnam," as shown in Fig. 251. The two makers are here shown together to emphasize the probability of their being found to be different stages of one firm name. The Bailey & Putnam mark is shown in Fig. 250. All five pieces shown are of good pewter.

L. BOARDMAN

I know nothing of the family connection, the dates, or the town of residence of the next maker shown. He marks the one piece of pewter I have ever seen or heard of by him, "L. Boardman, Warranted." The name, plus his use of the term "Warranted," almost induces one to say "Hartford" and to assign him to THE Boardmans. But we mustn't go too fast. The tea-pot shown in Fig. 253 is of good metal and workmanship. The mark on it is shown in Fig. 254.

BROOK FARM

On the bottom of the handsome lamp illustrated in Fig. 255 appears the mark shown in the next illustration. One naturally assumes that this "Brook Farm" touch indicates that one of the activities engaged in at the famous Brook Farm Community of the eighteen-forties was the making of the then fashionable whale-oil lamps. It has, however, been suggested that this is not a maker's touch, but a trade name. But, while it would not have been at all surprising had a lamp been named for the Brook Farm group during the concurrent fashions for whale-oil lamps and Transcendental Philosophy, the mark here under discussion seems too conventional a maker's "touch" of the time to be twisted into anything else. It seems superfluous to remind the reader that the Brook Farm Community was an experiment carried on at West Roxbury, Massachusetts, between 1841 and 1847, by a group of men and women, including such celebrated names as those of Nathaniel Hawthorne, Charles A. Dana, George W. Curtis, Margaret Fuller, and so on. I know of only two lamps thus marked, and have heard of no other types of pewter bearing this touch.

CAPEN & MOLINEUX

Capen & Molineux appear to have been the leading specialists in pewter lamps. It seems likely that their surviving output, added to that of Roswell Gleason, would make up nearly half the known marked specimens of this type of article. But while Gleason was a general manufacturer, Capen & Molineux appear to have made nothing but lamps. I have never, at any rate, seen either of their marks on anything else. Figs. 257 and 258 show a selection of their lamps. Note the raised decoration on the pair of lamps in the middle of Fig. 257. Note, also, that the second lamp from the left in Fig. 258 is somewhat similarly treated. No other American maker whose work I have come across has shown any such treatment.

The firm of Capen & Molineux was composed of Ephraim Capen and George Molineux. They were located at 132 Williams Street, New York City; and worked from 1848 to 1853. They used two similar marks, shown in Figs. 259 and 260. I take that shown in Fig. 259 to have been the earlier of the two. That in Fig. 260 is less commonly met with.

Fig. 264

R. DUNHAM
R. DUNHAM & SONS

| 6 inch candlestick by R. Dunham | 6½ inch lamp by R. Dunham | 8 inch britannia tea-pot by R. Dunham & Sons | 6½ inch lamp by R. Dunham | 6 inch candlestick by R. Dunham |

Fig. 265

R. DUNHAM

11¼ inch flagon   6½ inch pitcher

Fig. 266   Fig. 267   Fig. 268

MARKS USED BY R. DUNHAM AND R. DUNHAM & SONS

Fig. 269

ENDICOTT & SUMNER, 1846–1851

4½ inch lamp   8¾ inch lamp   4½ inch lamp

Fig. 270

MARK USED BY ENDICOTT & SUMNER

Fig. 270A

GAIUS AND JASON FENN

Inkwell 1½ inches high

Fig. 270B

MARK USED BY FENN, NEW YORK

Fig. 271

HENRY GRAVES, 1849
J. B. & H. GRAVES
FULLER & SMITH

| 5¼ inch lamp
by Fuller & Smith | 9 inch candlestick
by J. B. & H. Graves | 11 inch coffee-pot
by Henry Graves | 9 inch candlestick
by J. B. & H. Graves | 5¼ inch lamp
by Fuller & Smith |

Fig. 272

MARK USED BY HENRY GRAVES

Fig. 272A

MARK USED BY J. B. & H. GRAVES

Fig. 273

MARK USED BY FULLER & SMITH

Fig. 274

HALL & COTTON

1⅞ inch inkwell

Fig. 275

MARK USED BY HALL & COTTON

Fig. 276

HOLMES & SONS

2¼ inch lamp   10¼ inch coffee-pot

Fig. 277

MARK USED BY HOLMES & SONS

Fig. 278

HENRY HOPPER, 1842–1847

12 inch candlestick   4¼ inch candlestick   8¼ inch pitcher   12 inch candlestick

Fig. 279

MARK USED BY HENRY HOPPER

Fig. 280

M. HYDE

3¼ inch lamp

Fig. 282

L. KRUIGER, 1833

10⅛ inch ladle

Fig. 281

MARK USED BY M. HYDE

Fig. 283

MARK USED BY L. KRUIGER

Fig. 284

LEONARD, REED & BARTON, 1835–1845

Communion service

7 inch chalice   12 inch plate   7 inch chalice
10¾ inch flagon

Fig. 285

MARK USED BY LEONARD, REED & BARTON

Fig. 286

J. D. LOCKE, 1835–1860

8 inch tea-pot

Fig. 287

MARK USED BY J. D. LOCKE

CLEVELAND & BROS.

The pewter button shown in Fig. 261, with the inscription "Cleveland & Bros. Prov. R. I." around its edge, is from the head of a screw which fastens the bowl of a dipper made out of a cocoanut shell to its very gracefully turned wooden handle. There is a pewter rim to the cocoanut-shell bowl. I know nothing beyond these facts as to Cleveland & Bros., or the nature of their business. It is possible that they worked in pewter. It is also possible that they put these cocoanut-shell dippers on the market and had their names put on the pewter fittings.

T. S. DERBY

T. S. Derby is another of those makers whom we know only through the presence of their names on the bottoms of pewter articles. In Fig. 262 are shown the types of vessels on which the touch is found. Taken all in all, I should say that he is of greater importance to the completeness of the record than to the beauty of our shelves.

R. DUNHAM
R. DUNHAM & SONS

Somewhere I once saw R. Dunham put down as having worked in Boston. I failed to find his name in the Boston directories, but on the bottom of the britannia coffee-pot shown in Fig. 264, I found the mark — "R. Dunham & Sons, Portland, Me." — illustrated in Fig. 268, and I therefore assume that R. Dunham made pewter in Portland, Maine, before he and his sons took to making britannia there. R. Dunham has three claims on our interest. He made quite a good many open-topped pitchers of the type shown in Fig. 265. He also made some of the nicest lamps and candlesticks of his day. The design of both of these articles, as shown in Fig. 264, is characteristic of his work, and not only his workmanship, but his metal, is good. The communion flagon shown in Fig. 265 is to be classed as britannia rather than pewter, although the quality is good. Of course, the design of this piece is characterless and uninteresting. One would say that it was about halfway down the road toward the unspeakable coffee-pot in Fig. 264.

For the most part, Dunham used the touch shown in Fig. 266. I have seen a few of his later pieces marked with the incised "R. Dunham" shown in Fig. 267. I take these articles, like the flagon we were just discussing, to be about halfway between those marked as in Fig. 266 and those marked with the touch shown in Fig. 268. Dunham's pitchers and candlesticks rank with the best of his period.

ENDICOTT & SUMNER

Endicott & Sumner seem to have specialized in lamps and candlesticks. They were situated at 106 Elm and 195 Williams Streets, New York City, between 1846 and 1851. "Edm. Endicott" and William F. Sumner made up the firm. In spite of having worked for five years, they do not seem to have produced a very large amount of pewterware. At any rate, comparatively little of it has survived. A candlestick by them is in the Essex Museum, at Salem, Massachusetts. Fig. 269 shows the only specimens of their work that I have found. It is worth noting, however, that the marks shown in Fig. 270 include the number "30." If this, as is often supposed, is the number of the maker's mould, it would appear that Endicott & Sumner were fairly busy people after all. Of course, we do not really know the meaning of these numbers so common on the pewter pieces of the coffee-pot era. Even if they are mould numbers, some of the pewterers may have been like the men who number the first check on a new bank account "1001." Careful examination of Endicott & Sumner's touch will show that it is more reminiscent of the eighteenth-century name-plate type than any other coffee-pot-era mark. There is a faint suggestion of the decorative methods employed by William Will. And these æsthetic leanings are reflected in their lamps. Such specimens of the latter as turn up should be eagerly sought for by collectors of American lights.

FENN

In the early eighteen-twenties, G. Fenn figures in the New York City directories as a "grocer" at 35 Peck Slip. His name, it develops, was Gaius, and soon he was joined in the grocery business by Jason Fenn, perhaps a brother. By 1830, they had ceased to be listed as grocers and had become "Merchants." They then began to specialize in "faucets" and by the middle eighteen-thirties were down as dealers in hardware. By 1840, they claimed "Metals" as their field. And after 1845 they seem to have assumed that they were too well known to need any description, and are simply listed as "Gaius Fenn, 35 Peck Slip," and "Jason Fenn, 35 Peck Slip." Soon after this they moved to 39 Spruce Street, where the same listing was persisted in. I left them, still going strong, in the early eighteen-fifties. There are a few other Fenns in the New York directories; a whipmaker, a manufacturer of bellows; a school teacher, and, for a year or two, a plumber. But I take it that some time during the twenty years following 1830, when this pair of presumable brothers were dealing in "faucets," hardware, and metals, they made, or had made for them, the pewter inkwells of which the one shown in Fig. 270a is a survival. The mark on the bottom of this piece is shown in Fig. 270b.

FULLER & SMITH

Fuller & Smith seem likewise to have specialized in lamps and candlesticks. It has been intimated in certain early lists that they worked in Connecticut. There seems to have been a tendency to refer the unidentified Smiths to Connecticut; just why I have never discovered. The only pewter-making Smiths whose habitat we know are Eben Smith, of Beverly, Massachusetts, and the Albany Smith of Smith & Feltman. The work of Fuller & Smith is not common, nor is it especially distinguished. A pair of their lamps is shown in Fig. 271, and an impression of their touch is reproduced in Fig. 273.

HENRY GRAVES

Henry Graves worked in Middletown, Connecticut, about 1849. The coffee-pot shown in Fig. 271 is the only piece of his work that I happen to have seen. It has not whetted my appetite for more. The partial impression of his touch shown in Fig. 272 is from the bottom of this same coffee-pot.

J. B. & H. GRAVES

The pair of nine-inch candlesticks shown in Fig. 271 are marked "J.B. & H. Graves" as illustrated in Fig. 272a, and I take the "H. Graves" of this apparently family partnership to be the Henry Graves just referred to. This pair of sticks were in the George Ives collection, and it was only by accident, during the sale and while they were being carried up and down the aisles, that I happened to discover that they were marked.

HALL & COTTON

I am forced, in the case of Hall & Cotton, to illustrate another imperfect mark impression. The necessity is due to the same cause; the fact that the mark is on the only piece by these makers that I have run across. This is the inkwell illustrated in Fig. 274. Marked American inkwells are great rarities. I have seen but two, the one now under discussion, and the one by Fenn, New York, already described. I think I know of the existence of another, marked by Ashbil Griswold. I pursued it for some time without ever catching up with it, although I had descriptions of it meanwhile from two different sources. My experience, therefore, leads me to regard the inkwell shown in Fig. 274 as a fairly rare piece of its period; since it is an example of an unusual type, bearing a mark that is hard to find.

HOLMES & SONS

Baltimore was rather well represented during the eight-inch-plate period. It appears to have bred but one representative of the coffee-pot era. And he, like quite a few of his fellows, is here present more for the sake of the record than for what he made. The coffee-pot illustrated in Fig. 276 is a rather terrible example of what the "decorators" of pewter could do when they really turned themselves loose. The little lamp alongside of it is almost classic by comparison. When one looks at the lettering of the Holmes & Sons touch in Fig. 277, one understands why the Baltimore bootleggers get so wealthy.

HENRY HOPPER

Henry Hopper has come quite deservedly to have a reputation for making fine candlesticks. He was a New York pewterer who worked at 234 Second Street from 1842 to 1847. That he did not confine himself to "lights" is shown by the open-topped pitcher illustrated in Fig. 278. I have, however, seen no other pieces of the same nature bearing his mark. The tall candlesticks shown in the same illustration share with the other twelve-inch pair by the Taunton Britannia Manufacturing Company, illustrated in Fig. 323, the distinction of being the finest examples of American candlesticks that I know of. Hopper candlesticks are neither scarce nor plenty. I know of but one example of a lamp by him. His mark is shown in Fig. 279.

M. HYDE

The only thing that I know about M. Hyde is that his name, with a presumable mould number "20," is stamped as shown in Fig. 281 on a small lamp in my possession. The latter is illustrated in Fig. 280. There is, of course, no question about this piece being of American origin. The dates and address of its maker, one hopes, will turn up in due time.

LEWIS KRUIGER

Lewis Kruiger worked at 119 Callowhill, Philadelphia, during the single year 1833. He is listed in the city directory as a pewterer, but his name is there spelled "Kruger." Naturally one accepts his own spelling of his own name as shown in the pewter ladles which, so far as I know, alone represent his work. One of these ladles is shown in Fig. 282. The incised mark on the back of its handle is shown in Fig. 283. This is the earliest instance so far noted by me of the use of this incised type of mark by any American pewterer. It indicates, I should say, that all sense of craft pride had disappeared from the consciousness of its user.

LEONARD, REED & BARTON

It has already been noted, under the heading of "Crossman, West & Leonard," that Henry C. Reed and Charles E. Barton entered the employ of this firm as apprentices in 1828. In 1835 the firm name was changed to Leonard, Reed & Barton, these two young men having been taken into partnership by Mr. Gustavus Leonard. In Fig. 284 is shown a britannia communion set by this firm. Their mark is shown in Fig. 285. On the death of Mr. Leonard in 1845, the present firm name of Reed & Barton came into use. Leonard, Reed & Barton are supposed to have made nothing in pewter.

J. D. LOCKE

An occasional tea-pot turns up bearing the touch of this maker. The fact that one sees few such pieces, while it in no wise grieves one, constitutes something of a puzzle when taken in connection with the New York City Directory records. J. D. Locke is there set down as having been located at 241 Water Street from 1835 to 1841; as having been at 193 Water Street from 1842 to 1860; and as having then removed to 47 Cliff Street. His career at the latter location I did not pursue. Just what he did at these various places of business during more than twenty-five years is something of a mystery. He couldn't have put in much of the time making tea-pots. His mark is shown in Fig. 287.

WILLIAM McQUILKIN

William McQuilkin was much less long-winded but much more industrious than Mr. Locke. He is listed as a "manufacturer of britannia ware" at 91 North Second Street, Philadelphia, from 1845 to 1853. He first appears in the Philadelphia records as a clerk in 1839. He figures as a dealer in "Fancy Hardware" until 1845. After 1853 he disappears. His output, so far as I know, consists of covered and open-topped pitchers, coffee-pots and tea-pots, mostly of pewter. His open-topped pitchers, a pair of which is shown in Fig. 289, are what make him important to the American pewter collector. The tea-pot shown between them was a normal article of the day, as a comparison with the Locke tea-pot just mentioned will show. The two pieces shown in Fig. 288 have been chosen from among a number of McQuilkin examples because their designs are apparently original with him. His mark is shown in Fig. 290. Very occasionally he added a separate touch, reading "Philadelphia."

MOREY & OBER
MOREY & SMITH

These makers appear to have been the only lamp specialists developed in
Boston. David B. Morey and R. H. Ober started the business in 1852 at 5
and 7 Haverhill Street. Their association continued through 1855, the firm
name during this latter year being "Morey, Ober & Co." The middle lamp in
Fig. 293 and the one at the right of the picture bear their mark as shown in
Fig. 295. For the one year, 1857, Morey & Smith succeeded the firm of Morey,
Ober & Co. Specimens of their work are rare. The lamp at the left of Fig. 293
is by them. The mark on it is shown in Fig. 294. So far as I know, these firms
made nothing but lamps. It is, however, never safe to assume that candlesticks were not also, even if infrequently, put out by the lamp-maker of this
period.

J. MUNSON

The coffee-pot shown in Fig. 291 carries on its bottom the mark of J.
Munson; and I take both the pot and the touch to indicate American origin.
I have seen one or two other coffee-pots with this mark. I know nothing
further about their maker. In this case, as in all similar ones, I will greatly
appreciate it if any one discovering either the dates or the place of residence
of undated and unplaced makers will share their new information with me.

J. H. PALETHORP

We now come to the later portion of the history of the Philadelphia Palethorps. J. H. Palethorp was quite evidently a relative of Robert Palethorp, Jr., whose pewtering activities toward the end of the eight-inch-plate period we have already discussed. J. H. was also an "Ink Powder Manufacturer." From 1820 to 1845 he is listed in the city directory as "Ink Powder and Pewter Manufacturer." In spite of the early beginning of his activities in pewter-making, I have seen nothing bearing his mark that was not distinctively of the coffee-pot period; unless one excepts the ladles shown in Fig. 296. For some years after 1820 "Robert, Jr., and J. H. Palethorp" are listed in the Philadelphia Directory as pewterers at 50 North Second Street. This is the same address at which, during these same years, John H. Palethorp was carrying on his own ink powder and pewter manufacturing business. Some of the Palethorp ladles are marked as shown in Fig. 297 — "Palethorp's." I have sometimes wondered whether this was the touch used by these two men during their association. John H. Palethorp, by himself, worked at 50 North Second Street from 1820 to 1836. In 1837 he was at 55 North Sixth Street. After that, and until 1845, he was at 144 High Street. I have seen a three-inch beaker marked by him; also tea-pots and ladles. His personal mark is shown in Fig. 298. The Philadelphia touch does not always accompany it.

PALETHORP & CONNELL

From 1839 to 1841, inclusive, "J. H. Palethorp & Co." are also listed in the Philadelphia Directory as doing business at 144 High Street. The members of this firm appear to have been John H. Palethorp and Thomas Connell. The only echo of this business connection that I have gotten from the pewter, as against the record, side of our sources of information is the mark shown in Fig. 300, which is impressed on the bottoms of the graceful pair of tea-pots shown in Fig. 299.

C. PARKER & CO.

I have several times come across pewter spoons of mid-nineteenth-century type, bearing the touch "C. Parker & Co.," as shown in Fig. 301. In the New York City Directory for 1849 appears the name of Caleb Parker, "White-smith," Twenty-Ninth Street near Seventh Avenue. Whether or not he is the C. Parker of the spoons, I am unable to say. I give the facts, however, for what they may prove to be worth.

A. PORTER

A. Porter is said to have worked in Southington, Connecticut. As he made pewter lamps he must have worked somewhere between 1830 and 1855. Fig. 302 shows his mark. It is photographed from the bottom of a lamp belonging to Mr. Louis Guerineau Myers, of New York; the only piece by this maker that I have ever seen.

F. PORTER

F. Porter, of Westbrook, Connecticut, shares with R. Dunham and William McQuilkin the task of keeping American collectors supplied with open-topped pitchers such as the one shown in Fig. 304. Porter, whose exact dates in the coffee-pot period I cannot give, seems to have been a prolific worker. He made many lamps, quite a few candlesticks, at least a third of the surviving water pitchers, and some very unprepossessing coffee-pots. One of the latter is shown in Fig. 303. A pitcher and a lamp of his are shown in Fig. 304. A good impression of his mark appears in Fig. 305. This mark appears with various numbers, as, " No. 1," " No. 2 "; and I have heard it intimated that these should be regarded as variations of the mark. It is, of course, possible that collectors will elect so to regard them. To me, personally, the differences seem unimportant.

Fig. 288

WILLIAM McQUILKIN, 1845–1853

12½ inch coffee-pot   10⅛ inch water pitcher

Fig. 289

WILLIAM McQUILKIN

6⅝ inch water pitcher   8 inch tea-pot   6⅝ inch water pitcher

Fig. 290

MARK USED BY WILLIAM McQUILKIN

Fig. 291

J. MUNSON

10¾ inch coffee-pot

Fig. 292

MARK USED BY J. MUNSON

Fig. 293

MOREY & OBER, 1852–1854
MOREY & SMITH, 1857

4½ inch lamp
by Morey & Ober

6¼ inch lamp
by Morey & Ober

3⅞ inch lamp
by Morey & Smith

Fig. 294

Fig. 295

MARKS USED BY MOREY & OBER AND MOREY & SMITH

Fig. 296

J. H. PALETHORP, 1820–1845

10¼ inch ladle   10 inch coffee-pot   10½ inch ladle

Fig. 297

Fig. 298

MARKS USED BY J. H. PALETHORP

Fig. 299

PALETHORP & CONNELL, 1839–1841

Pair of 7½ inch tea-pots

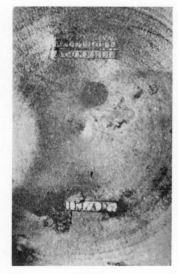

Fig. 300

MARK USED BY PALETHORP & CONNELL

Fig. 301

MARK USED BY C. PARKER & COMPANY, 1849

Fig. 302

MARK USED BY A. PORTER

Fig. 303

F. PORTER, AFTER 1825

12 inch coffee-pot

Fig. 304

F. PORTER

6¼ inch water pitcher   8¼ inch lamp

Fig. 305

MARK USED BY F. PORTER

Fig. 306

G. RICHARDSON, 1824

10 inch coffee-pot   6½ inch sugar bowl   7 inch tea-pot

Fig. 307

MARK USED BY G. RICHARDSON

See also Frontispiece

Fig. 308

SAMUEL RUST, 1837–1842

$6\frac{3}{4}$ inch lamp

Fig. 309

MARK USED BY SAMUEL RUST

Fig. 310

SAGE & BEEBE

8 inch tea-pot   10¾ inch coffee-pot

Fig. 311

MARK USED BY SAGE & BEEBE

Fig. 312

SAVAGE
SAVAGE & GRAHAM

11 inch coffee-pot
by Savage & Graham

10¾ inch coffee-pot
by Savage

Fig. 313

Fig. 314

MARKS USED BY SAVAGE & GRAHAM AND SAVAGE

Fig. 315

SAMUEL SIMPSON, 1843–1845

7½ inch tea-pot   8 inch tea-pot

Fig. 316

MARK USED BY SAMUEL SIMPSON

Fig. 316A

SELLEW & COMPANY

9 inch lamp   8 inch plate

Fig. 316B

MARK USED BY SELLEW & COMPANY

Fig. 317

SHELDON & FELTMAN
SMITH & FELTMAN

10⅝ inch flagon
by Smith & Feltman

11 inch coffee-pot
by Sheldon & Feltman

10¼ inch flagon
by Sheldon & Feltman

Fig. 318

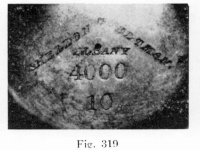

Fig. 319

Fig. 320

MARKS USED BY SHELDON & FELTMAN AND SMITH & FELTMAN

Fig. 321

SMITH & COMPANY

Pair of 8¼ inch lamps   8 inch tea-pot   6 inch lamp

Fig. 322

MARK USED BY SMITH & COMPANY

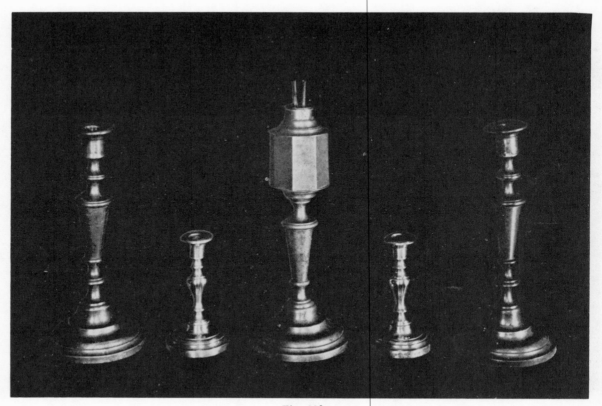

Fig. 323

TAUNTON BRITANNIA MANUFACTURING COMPANY, 1830

12¼ inch candlestick
marked "T.B.M. Co."

13¼ inch lamp
marked "T.B.M. Co."

12¼ inch candlestick
marked "T.B.M. Co."

6¼ inch candlestick
marked "T.B.M. Co."

6¼ inch candlestick
marked "T.B.M. Co."

Fig. 324

Fig. 325

MARKS USED BY THE TAUNTON BRITANNIA MANUFACTURING COMPANY

Fig. 326

MARK USED BY VOSE & COMPANY

Fig. 327

J. WEEKES
WEEKES & COMPANY

6 inch candlestick by J. Weekes   Pair of 7 inch lamps by Weekes & Company   6 inch candlestick by J. Weekes

Fig. 328   Fig. 329

MARKS USED BY J. WEEKES AND WEEKES & COMPANY

Fig. 330

THOMAS WILDES, 1833–1840

7 inch lamp

Fig. 331

MARK USED BY THOMAS WILDES

Fig. 332

L. L. WILLIAMS, 1838–1842

4 inch creamer   9 inch coffee-pot   7 inch sugar bowl

Fig. 333

MARK USED BY L. L. WILLIAMS

Fig. 334

J. B. WOODBURY, 1837–1838
WOODBURY & COLTON, 1835–1836

10¾ inch coffee-pot
by J. B. Woodbury

8 inch lamp
by J. B. Woodbury

9½ inch tea-pot
by Woodbury & Colton

Fig. 335

Fig. 337

Fig. 338

Fig. 336

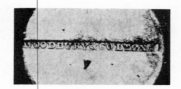

Fig. 339

MARKS USED BY J. B. WOODBURY AND WOODBURY & COLTON

GEORGE RICHARDSON

George Richardson worked at Cranston, Rhode Island, about 1824. He seems to have confined his efforts to tea-set pieces, and coffee-pots, tea-pots, and sugar bowls are the only specimens of his work that have come to my knowledge. Fig. 306 shows one of each of these types; the mark on the coffee- and tea-pots being that shown in Fig. 307, with, occasionally, the addition of the small eagle shown in connection with the marks on the covered sugar bowl which, together with a picture of its bottom, forms the frontispiece to this volume. These bowls are very beautiful, and I know of but three examples of the type, although others doubtless exist. I take the name of "Glenmore Company" to be a business name assumed by Richardson at some stage of his career. The beauty of this bowl, together with its extreme lateness — for it was assuredly made well after the coffee-pot era had established itself — induced me to select it for the place of honor it holds among the illustrations of this book. For it seemed fitting, considering the patronizing attitude assumed on occasions in the past toward American pewter as a collectible, because of its lateness and lack of beauty, that the aristocratic rarities of the pre-Revolutionary period should stand modestly aside while a plebeian sugar bowl of the eighteen-thirties took the part of "Miss America" and sat on the throne of the Queen of the May. The piece thus honored is now the property of Mr. A. B. A. Bradley, of New York.

SAMUEL RUST

For some years back of 1837, a man by the name of Samuel Rust had been listed in the New York directories as a "Printing Press Maker." In 1837 he appears at 125 Fulton Street as a "Lamp Maker"; taking care to have himself put down as "Formerly printing press maker." His name continues to figure in the directories at the same address until 1842. From 1842 to 1845 John N. and Samuel Rust appear in the directories at 77 Williams Street and later at 38 Gold Street, with the single word "Lamps" after their names. In 1849 Leonard M. Rust is listed at 8 Dominick Street as "Lamp Maker." I am led to put the whole of these Rust data down under the name of Samuel Rust, because, in addition to three lamps marked "Samuel Rust's Patent," one of which is shown in Fig. 308 and its incised mark illustrated in Fig. 309, I have also seen a fine pewter lamp, unmarked as to its bottom, but bearing on its brass burner the inscription "S. Rust New York, pat. 1844." As this date is toward the end of Samuel's association with John N., it would look as though both of these lamp-makers might be represented, as far as touches go, by Samuel's marks. After 1845, when Samuel evidently retired from business, he is listed in the New York Directory as "Formerly Lamp Maker." If all of our pewterers had been as careful to keep their record clear as Samuel Rust, looking up their histories would be an easy matter.

SAGE & BEEBE

Figs. 310 and 311, the one showing a tea-pot of no great distinction and a coffee-pot of distinctly plebeian appearance, and the other illustrating the mark on the bottom of both pieces, will give the reader all the information that I have concerning these makers. The tea-pot is pewter. The coffee-pot is britannia of fairly good quality. The mark, as can easily be seen, is impressed or incised or intaglio, or whatever you want to call it. For the sake of a clean record, one hopes that the dates and the location of these makers will be supplied by whoever runs across the information.

SAVAGE & GRAHAM
SAVAGE

Savage & Graham made coffee-pots at Middletown, Connecticut, during this period. Fig. 312 shows one of their pieces at the left and Fig. 313 shows the mark from the bottom of it. The coffee-pot is well formed, graceful, and made of good metal. The mould number "1" would indicate that it is a piece of their early make. It would seem that Graham disappeared from the firm later on. For occasional pieces of a later type appear with the mark "Savage, Midd. Ct." without the Graham. The right-hand pot illustrated in Fig. 312 is one of these. Its mark is shown in Fig. 314. And it will be noted that the mould number is "35."

S. SIMPSON

Samuel Simpson worked at 272½ Pearl Street, New York City, from 1843 to 1845 inclusive. I have seen tea-pots and coffee-pots bearing his mark, which is shown in Fig. 316. Two tea-pots by him are illustrated in Fig. 315. In 1846, Simpson and Benham are listed in the directory at the same address. I have seen a tea-pot bearing their mark, but am unable to illustrate either the touch or the piece itself. It is, however, on the strength of this marked piece of theirs that I have credited them in the summaries with surviving specimens.

SELLEW & CO.

In the now celebrated list of American pewterers published in the "Bulletin" of the Wadsworth Athenæum of Hartford, Connecticut, in the spring of 1923, there appeared the name of "Sellers & Co. Cincinnati." It was one of some twenty-five names that did not figure at that time on my list as then compiled (at the same time my list contained some forty names not on the Athenæum list). I had never seen a piece of this maker's pewter and for more than a year I continued to be ignorant of what they had made. Recently, however, I have acquired two specimens of what I suppose to be the makers referred to, although the name proves to be slightly different from the form given to it in the Athenæum list. It seems to have been "Sellew" instead of "Sellers." These two pieces are illustrated in Fig. 316 and consist of a very graceful whale-oil lamp and a very much battered eight-inch plate. This latter, made by a firm which one supposes was in business during the coffee-pot era, is rather surprising. But, of course, we have no definite knowledge as yet as to the true dates assignable to the firm. The lamp also differs from any other I have ever seen in that the thread onto which the burner was meant to screw is on the outside of the little neck at the top of the oil well, instead of inside, as seems to have been the universal habit. One would naturally place the makers of this lamp this side of 1830; and the character of their mark would indicate the eighteen-forties at least. All of which makes the eight-inch plate even more surprising.

SHELDON & FELTMAN
SMITH & FELTMAN

Both Sheldon & Feltman and Smith & Feltman worked in Albany, New York. I do not know their dates, but they must have been fairly late to judge by their output. The britannia pieces illustrated in Fig. 317 are a fair representation of their work as far as I have seen it. It has, as a glance at this group of articles will show, little to commend it to collectors even of britannia. The communion flagon at the left of this group bears the Sheldon & Feltman touch shown in Fig. 318. The coffee-pot is marked on the bottom as shown in Fig. 319. The right-hand flagon bears the Smith & Feltman mark reproduced in Fig. 320. The similarity of these two flagons and the presence of the Feltman name in both marks, together with the identical mould numbers, lead me to assume these to be successive names of one business organization.

SMITH & CO.

Wherever Smith & Co. may have carried on their business of pewter-making, and whatever may have been their dates, they did uniformly tasteful and craftsmanlike work. Their designs are simple and clean-cut. Their metal is of the best. And they deserve, better than most makers of their day, the respect and the patronage of modern collectors. Lamps, candlesticks, and tea-pots are the only articles that I happen to have seen by them; and their lamps are by far more numerous than either of the other forms. Fig. 321 shows a fine and typical pair of their lamps. I have a pair of candlesticks by them, six and three-quarter inches high, the bases and stems of which are identical with those of the pair of lamps here illustrated. Their invariable mark is shown in Fig. 322. Several lists hint that they probably worked in Connecticut. The Wadsworth Athenæum "Bulletin" assigns them tentatively to Philadelphia. I have never gotten any clue to their real address.

TAUNTON BRITANNIA MANUFACTURING COMPANY
("T.B.M.CO.")

The mark of the Taunton Britannia Manufacturing Company, shown in Fig. 324 ("T.B.M.Co."), has long been regarded as one of the unidentified American marks. I take it that the reason for this is that this initialed touch of theirs has never happened to come, in the hands of an observant collector, into juxtaposition with their name mark as shown in Fig. 325. This latter mark is from the bottom of a britannia slop bowl which came into my hands a few months ago. It was the first specimen of that mark that I had seen. On the other hand, I have owned candlesticks bearing the abbreviated mark for fifteen years, and have seen quite a number of pieces so marked. Fig. 323 shows a characteristic group of the "lights" made by this organization. The pair of tall candlesticks have already been referred to as the only peers of Henry Hopper's tall sticks that ever came to my notice. The lamp with similar base and stem, but with the octagonal bowl at the top, is without any exception the handsomest example of a whale-oil lamp that I have ever seen. It is now the property of Mr. John S. McDaniel, of Easton, Maryland. This lamp and these candlesticks are all good pewter.

VOSE & CO.

Vose & Co. made britannia articles of inferior grade in Albany, New York. I have never seen anything by them worthy of the interest or attention of the collector of American pewter. However, I include a reproduction of their mark in Fig. 326.

WEEKES & CO.
J. WEEKES

I believe that a glance at Fig. 327 will convince the most skeptical that Weekes & Co. and J. Weekes were different names of the same makers. I take Weekes & Co. (Fig. 329) to have been the earlier because this mark shows the raised letters in an engrailed rectangle that are typical of the early years of the coffee-pot era. This mark is from the bottom of the lamps shown in Fig. 327. The "J. Weekes" touch shown in Fig. 328 is from the candlesticks in this illustration. It shows the impressed letters characteristic of the later and more careless habits of the coffee-pot era makers. "Lights" by Weekes are seldom met with, and, as they are of graceful design and exceedingly fine pewter, they deserve a place in the collection of any one lucky enough to find them. I have seen a piece by J. Weekes marked "N.Y." James Weekes is in the New York City directories of 1856, 1857, and 1858 as "tinware and tinman" at 32 Platt Street. After 1859 he dealt in toys.

THOMAS WILDES

Fig. 330 shows a whale-oil lamp with a candlestick base made by Thomas Wildes. The mark from the bottom of it is shown in Fig. 331, and it will be noticed that it carries an impressed "X" in addition to the name touch. Wildes worked in New York City from 1833 to 1840, at Hester and Second Streets. This lamp is the only specimen of his work that has ever come into my hands.

LORENZO L. WILLIAMS

An occasional coffee-pot, of no great beauty, turns up bearing the impressed name of this maker. He worked in Philadelphia, at "3rd Street and the R. Road," from 1838 to 1842. As he invariably used an incised mark, it may be interesting to note that this fashion was already well established by 1838. The sugar bowl and cream pitcher shown in Fig. 332 came together. The sugar bowl bears his mark. The cream pitcher is not marked. The coffee-pot came from a different source. It is, of course, marked. I have seen nothing by him except tea-set pieces. His mark is shown in Fig. 333.

WOODBURY & COLTON
J. B. WOODBURY

It is all very well to call attention, as I have just done, to instances where actual dates can be assigned to actual types of marks; but it is equally important to remind one's self that there is nothing conclusive about such matters. I take immediate occasion, therefore, to cite the cases of Woodbury & Colton and J. B. Woodbury whose joint dates run from 1835 to 1838, and whose marks, as shown above, run from the most orthodox coffee-pot period engrailed rectangle touches back to a typical eight-inch-plate period eagle. In 1835 and 1836 Woodbury & Colton worked at 22 Library, Philadelphia. The coffee-pot at the right of Fig. 334 was made by them and bears the mark shown in Fig. 339. The firm consisted of J. B. Woodbury and O. Colton. The next year, 1837, J. B. Woodbury appears alone, as "Japanner and Britannia maker," at 361 Cedar Street. He was similarly listed in 1838, after which his name disappears from the records. The coffee-pot at the left of Fig. 334 is by him. It is made of fine pewter and is a very clean-cut and graceful piece. It carries on the bottom the mark shown in Fig. 337. The lamp between these two coffee-pots is one of a fine pair marked as shown in Fig. 338. The odd coincidence that this type of eagle mark should have been used by J. B. Woodbury in Philadelphia and by Roswell Gleason in Dorchester, Massachusetts, and by no other makers so far as we know, has already been commented upon. Lamps, candlesticks, and coffee-pots are the only articles that I have seen with the Woodbury marks. An interesting combination of lamp and candlestick, however, seems to have been made by Woodbury himself. This consists of a candlestick and what used to be technically known as a "skirt lamp." A specimen of this light is shown in Fig. 357. The lamp is there shown on top of the candlestick where it is held by a circular plug that fits into the candle socket. And, of course, on occasion, both lamp and candlestick could be used. Other forms of Woodbury marks are given in Figs. 335 and 336.

H. YALE & CO.

This firm made britannia ware at Wallingford, Connecticut. They are of little, if any, interest to pewter collectors, but are here included for the sake of the record. The eleven-inch britannia deep plate shown in Fig. 340 was no doubt intended to be used as a collection plate in church. It is quite likely that during its years of service it had a piece of red plush glued to it to keep the coins from chinking as they fell. Many a good pewter plate has thus come down to us in uninjured condition. In Fig. 341 is shown the mark from the bottom of this britannia plate.

YALE & CURTIS

One of the mysterious facts about many of these pewter-makers of not so very long ago is the number of years they seem to have worked, and the few specimens of their handicraft that appear to have survived. Yale and Curtis seem to have specialized in the making of whale-oil lamps in New York City from 1858 to 1867. Yet I have never, in all the years that I have been interested in American pewter, seen but three or four lamps bearing their touch. Fig. 342 shows an extremely interesting specimen of their work. It is a lamp with two burners, apparently intended to work on the student-lamp principle. There was, however, no way to fill the main receptacle of this lamp except to unscrew one of the burners, hold the lamp almost horizontal, pour the oil in where the burner had been removed, and let it run back into the larger bowl. Fig. 342 shows their mark. They were situated at 67 Beeckman Street for a time, and later at both 90 Fulton Street and 45 Gold Street. Henry Yale and Stephen Curtis, Jr., constituted the firm. For one year — 1868 — after the firm of Yale & Curtis had gone out of business, Stephen Curtis, Jr., carried on as "Curtis & Company" at 90 Fulton Street. I've never seen anything marked by him.

CHAPTER IX

THE MARKING OF AMERICAN PEWTER

THE marking of pewterware with the maker's private mark, or "touch," seems to have been a custom of extremely early origin. Moreover, it appears to have derived originally from private initiative and to have been commanded by law and enforced by the authorities only after the custom had become practically universal in the reputable trade. Pride of craftsmanship — mixed with the natural impulse of the worker in less precious material to ape the habits of the gold- and silversmiths — was no doubt responsible for the practice among pewterers in the beginning. But it could not have been long before the need of protection against fraud added the support of practical utility to a custom inaugurated by vanity. At any rate, the habit seems to have been practically universal when the earliest records — along in the thirteenth and fourteenth centuries — begin to give us definite information.

We have already seen that the marking of pewterware was made obligatory by act of Parliament in England in 1503. It is, however, interesting to note, as Mr. Massée points out, that this act only applied to the workers in "ley metal" — an inferior grade of pewter from which salts and pots and other hollowware were made; thus implying that the better grade of pewter, from which it had long been the rule that all plates and chargers should be fashioned, was already habitually marked by its makers. From this time onward there is a constant stream of regulations governing the marking of pewter in England; the Pewterers' Society having apparently been most anxious to keep the official marks from being used in any way that savored of advertising, and the individual makers having been more and more unwilling to restrict themselves to a mere mark of identification. At first (greatly to the confusion of the modern collector) nothing much beyond the maker's initials and an ornamental or heraldic device of some kind, framed in a circle or a scroll, was countenanced.

Fig. 340

H. YALE & COMPANY

11 inch platter

Fig. 341

MARK USED BY H. YALE & COMPANY

Fig. 342

YALE & CURTIS, 1858–1868

$8\frac{1}{4}$ inch lamp

Fig. 343

MARK USED BY YALE & CURTIS

Later — after many changings of the rules pro and con — the maker's full name was allowed. Finally the word "London" or the statement "Made in London" — these latter generally themselves made parts of separate, ornamental touches or marks — was allowed; and some makers even came to stamping their street addresses on their ware.

A pewter "touch plate" was kept at the guild hall of the Pewterers' Society upon which each maker was required to impress his private touch mark. Five of these "touch plates" have been preserved, and they contain parts of the series of marks officially registered from the early seventeenth to the early nineteenth centuries. Not only is the series incomplete, however, but many of the marks have been carelessly struck, or struck one on top of another, so as to be imperfectly legible; and the register of names of the makers whose marks are represented has been lost. So that these records, valuable and interesting as they are, leave much to be desired in the way of a complete guide to understanding.

Much English, and some American, pewter bears, in addition to the touch of the maker, a series of (generally four) smaller marks, struck in a row and commonly called "hall marks." These are, and have always been, even in England, entirely unofficial as used upon pewterware. They are, indeed, either literal copies of, or closely patterned after, the official hall marks demanded from early days by the rules of the Goldsmiths' Company and by the English laws. The rules of the Goldsmiths' Company required that all plate exposed for sale in London be brought to the guild hall, there to be stamped with the company's stamp. Hence the term "hall marks." Copies or colorable imitations of these hall marks as used upon gold and silver pieces were stamped upon pewterware from very early times — no doubt with intent to impress the purchaser, if not, indeed, to deceive him. In 1635 the Goldsmiths' Company protested so strongly against allowing the habit to continue that stringent rules were passed forbidding it. These rules, however, seem to have been very spasmodically enforced, and the unofficial use of pseudo-hall marks upon English pewter continued until the end of the eating-plate period.

It must be remembered that these small stamps were used with method and meaning by the goldsmiths and silversmiths. To the general public they represented an official guarantee. To the initiate they conveyed more detailed information; such, for instance, as the identity of the maker, the place of origin, and the year of manufacture. Back of 1697 these marks consisted of the maker's private mark, the annual letter (the alphabet, with the style of type changed every twenty-six years, was used, seriatim, to indicate the date of the piece), and two official heraldic emblems, the "Leopard's Head" and the "Lion Passant." Between 1697 and 1720 these two heraldic emblems were changed to a "Lion's Head Erased" and a figure of Britannia. After 1784 an additional mark of the "Sovereign's Head" was used to indicate the payment of the tax on plate. On provincially manufactured plate the arms of the town of origin were added to the regular London marks after 1700.

Quite naturally, it was mostly from these official marks that the pewterers selected those that they chose to use unofficially. We shall see presently the relation between these and the "hall marks" used by the ten American makers who followed their English fellow craftsmen in this custom.

Two other special marks, used by the English pewterers with special meanings, also concern us in our study of American pewter marks. One of these is the so-called "Rose and Crown" mark which, by the rules of the Society of Pewterers, was restricted to use upon articles made for sale outside of London. How strictly this rule was adhered to does not concern us; but there was a further rule of the English Society which seems to have been better enforced than most and with which it is important for us to be familiar. This was the regulation that absolutely forbade any users of the "Rose and Crown" mark to add thereto either their initials, or a date, or any other private mark. Now the device of the "Crowned Rose" was a favorite one in the craft, not only in England, but on the Continent. Only, on the Continent, it was customary for its users to include in their die a date mark or their initials or some other distinguishing symbol. This may be kept in mind as one convenient and generally reliable way of distinguishing the Continental marks of this order from the English ones. But because the rule of the Society of Pewterers did not run on this side of the Atlantic, our local craftsmen were also apt to use the "Rose and Crown" design without heeding the restrictions imposed by that Society's regulations. This fact, together with the further one that most Continental pewter, like most American, is *not hammered finished*, is cited here as a warning against jumping at conclusions on insufficient evidence.

The other special mark, used by English pewterers, of which we find examples on American pewter, is the "X." This was used in England, either with or without the addition of a crown, to indicate that the piece so marked contained metal of extraordinary quality. It must, of course, so far as English pewter is concerned, be remembered that all of these rules were broken at times, and that there were periods when they were slackly enforced, if enforced at all, by the authorities. On the other hand, they were never enforced on this side, even when, theoretically, the authority of the Pewterers' Society might have been held to be valid here. They do, however, explain many features of our American pewter marks that would be meaningless without a knowledge of their derivations and former meanings.

We have, in the last few chapters, passed in review, without much comment, the marks of almost all those American makers whose pewter has as yet been found. And it has no doubt been evident that there was a presumably chartable curve of development in the type of these marks; a curve which, roughly plotted, began in English orthodoxy, rose through colonial individualism to a national consciousness, and then quickly fell to a business-as-usual utilitarianism. It is the purpose of this chapter to plot this curve; to indicate the extent to which it is safe to rely upon it as a means of dating pieces by makers otherwise undated; and generally to sum up the bearing of American marks upon American pewter-collecting. Before, however, proceeding to a detailed development of these objects, it is necessary for us to remove from our path a somewhat awkward obstacle to our mutual understanding.

This has to do with the widespread belief that unmarked pewter is, *ipse facto*, American pewter.

So far is this dictum from being reliable, that there is but one article — the pewter whale-oil lamp of the 1830–1850 period — to which it is safe to apply it. These were never made or used elsewhere, and so — not because they are unmarked, but because they are of solely American origin — they are classable at sight as American. For the rest, this rule is a slipshod generalization founded on a misconception.

As a rule such generalized inaccuracies as this come to be accepted in the collecting world because the average collector craves — more than anything else on earth — the boon of ready-made categories and the convenience of easily applied tests of identification. Half knowledge has no charms for him. Upon debatable ground he will never wittingly enter. And once let him become possessed of a convenient conviction and settle down to take his ease in it, it requires more than the discovery that truth resides elsewhere to induce him to move.

An excellent example of this is furnished, in the early history of glass-collecting in this country, by the greedy acceptance, on the part of the collecting public, of the uncritical notion that all clear glass that "rang" when it was struck was Stiegel glass. A few years ago it would have been easier to rob a she-bear of her prize cub than to disabuse the mind of the ordinary glass-collector of this pet theory. The facts, of course, are that this "ring" is an attribute of all "flint" glass, not merely of Stiegel-made flint glass; that for a generation after Stiegel's failure and death small flint-glass works kept springing up in the newborn United States, many of them manned by Stiegel-trained workmen, or by workmen trained by such workmen; that these short-lived enterprises made and attempted to market plain "flips," "measures," decanters, and so on, all fashioned in the late eighteenth-century mode; and that, in the case of most of this output, no one can tell with any certainty whether a specimen is or is not of Stiegel origin. Yet so strong has been the desire to "know," and so powerful the inclination to believe that what one has found is really of the celebrated breed, that this habit of unauthorized ascription has proved nine-lived, like a cat. About eight of this particular cat's lives have by now, let us hope, been snuffed out.

The pewter cat, however, while it promises to have the normal number of lives, appears to possess a different pedigree from the Stiegel one. It was already current when few collectors even knew of the existence of American pewter, and when fewer yet cared anything about it. It seems, therefore, to have been less a thought fathered by a wish than a conclusion born of a fallacy. And the silent syllogism that led to the conclusion seems to have run somewhat thus:

> All English pewter had to be marked.
> No American pewter had to be marked.
> Therefore, all unmarked pewter is American.

Which is about equal to the argument that:

> No intoxicating beverages may any longer be brought into the United States.
> No such beverages may any longer be manufactured in the United States.
> Therefore, all Hooch is Pre-War stuff.

The facts are that unmarked pewter, in spite of the rules of the Pewterers' Society, was always made in England; and that at the time when most unmarked pewter appears to have been actually made in the United States (from 1830 to 1850), the marking of similar pewter articles by the English makers had ceased to be habitual. The marking of nineteenth-century English candlesticks, for instance, is even less usual than of the American. The same is true, too, of the ordinary table-sized "beakers" of this period.

The marking of pewterware by its makers was first made compulsory in England during the reign of Henry VII. Already, during the next reign, there is record of complaints that outlaw pewter was being made by unscrupulous craftsmen, not only in country towns, but "in the woods and forests." And from that time until its power finally dwindled to nothing and was allowed to lapse, toward the close of the eighteenth century, the Pewterers' Society, backed up by successive Acts of Parliament passed at its request, was engaged in an unending struggle with profiteering pewterers who undertook to evade its rules, and with the outlaw tribe of pewterer-tinkers who canvassed the countryside recasting worn vessels, and haunted the country fairs selling wares both legal and illegal. That much of the latter was unmarked goes without saying. And that a good deal of it found its way to America, either in the personal effects of immigrants or through the less regular channels of trade, is by no means to be called unlikely.

This habit of specializing in pewter at country fairs, by the way, was still in full vogue in England fairly late in the nineteenth century. Mr. Massée gives a list of a dozen or so of towns in England where fairs were held less than a century ago and where pewter was among the specialties featured.

Of course, it is only, really, with regard to occasional pieces, unquestionably very old and of doubtful origin because of their showing neither marks nor evidences of hammer-finishing, that this question will greatly interest the serious collector of American pewter. For the possibility certainly exists that such a piece — often a thirteen-inch or a fifteen-inch plate or charger — may actually be of early eighteenth-century, or even of late seventeenth-century, American make. After 1750 the interest of the marked (and therefore undebatably American) pewter is too great to leave much room for concern about the unmarked. Moreover, these marks themselves are so largely determinative of date, sectional origin, and comparative rarity (not to mention the certainty of their coming to be regarded, because of their intrinsic interest, variety, and graded scarcity, as a collectible series in themselves) that the possible American-ness of the unmarked becomes of little moment.

With regard to the dilemma created by the earlier pieces, all that can helpfully be said is to point out the fact that these unmarked pieces may quite as possibly have come from England as have originated here. For the absence of hammer marks can no more be taken as conclusive proof of American origin than the absence of touch marks. Little if any Continental pewter was hammer-finished. And while hammer-finishing was strictly enjoined by the rules of the Pewterers' Society, it is scarcely to be argued that outlaw workmen in England who were side-stepping this onerous rule would have incriminated themselves by obeying the supporting regulations about identifying marks.

With regard to the period after 1750, it may be said that, on the one hand, unmarked plates of this period are so few as to be negligible; and, on the other, that unmarked basins are extremely numerous — marked specimens by American makers being among the decided rarities. If these unmarked basins, or any sizable proportion of them, are to be regarded as American, then there are one or two facts that need explaining. To begin with, every last marked specimen of these vessels that I have seen have been by eight-inch-plate men; and of course it is fairly to be inferred that the unmarked basins belong to the same period as the marked ones. Yet practically all unmarked American pewter — lamps, candlesticks, and beakers, chiefly — belong to the later, or coffee-pot, era. Finally, to make the puzzle complete, it may be added that a majority of the unmarked basins show that they were finished on the lathe, and lathe-finishing is frequently declared to be an absolute sign of American origin. Against this statement, I offer the following considerations: First, the fact that the lathe was used in England as early as the seventeenth century, as is proved by the Pewterers' Society having forbidden its use in 1681; and, second, the fact that it was used in England in the nineteenth century, as is proved by marked pieces of London pewter of that period so finished and in my possession.

The last words on the subject are two. First, the individual collector's decisions, when faced by such conditions as these, are determined, not by judgment, but by temperament. Second, to the collectors for whom this treatise is written the question is largely academic; for except in very special cases only marked specimens will interest them.

To the collector of marked American pewter, on the other hand, there is no single acquirement that will prove so useful as a complete familiarity with the marks of the various makers. The nearer one comes to being able, at a casual glance, to identify the marks on pieces of the ware, the more thoroughly will one become satisfied of the fact that the accomplishment is worth all it costs. To begin with, it constitutes a convincing proof of expertness; and there are times when it is of real and instant value to a collector to be able to give this proof without appearing to do so. And as for more visibly substantial rewards, I need only cite the fact that a collector well enough known to have "followers" at auction sales, can save himself much money and annoyance by being able to go through, say, a pile of pewter plates at an exhibition, without displaying even by a pause any special interest in any one of them.

But quite beyond these considerations, the broad fact remains that the collector and student of American pewter is inescapably a collector and student of makers' touches to a degree that is in no sense true of collectors of the European metal. And expertness in one's particular field is fertilizer to one's enjoyment.

When we come to examine in detail and in series the marks on American pewter, we find that while there were practically no changes in the *styles* and *forms* of pewterware during the seventy-five years of the eight-inch-plate period, there were at least three definite changes in the types of *marks* used by the eight-inch-plate men. And it soon becomes evident that these changes reflect with considerable definiteness the altering political conditions of the day in America.

Thus the marks on the earliest specimens of the American ware are for the most part either typically British in character or else, while displaying a certain freedom in their treatment of hard-and-fast rules, strongly influenced by contemporary English custom. Perhaps it would be nearer the truth as these old craftsmen would themselves have felt it, to say that they used the kind of marks that were *characteristic of their craft* "at home" or "in the old country." For, apparently, it was only certain features of these marks that were later felt to be typically English, or perhaps typically Royalistic, and so due to be discontinued under the Republic. The "Crowned Rose" is the most prominent of these. And one ventures the guess that it was rather the implications of the "Crown" than the associations of the "Rose" that damned the device in democratic eyes. For such marks as Richard Austin's alternative touch (Fig. 110) and those of the two earliest members of the Danforth family (Figs. 38 and 42), while unmistakably English in both origin and design, do not seem to have borne about them any of the stigma of British association. The reason, as suggested above, probably was that these older fashions in marks were looked upon as pewter-makers' fashions and not English fashions. On the other hand, the "Crowned Rose," as used by Frederick Bassett (Fig. 48), by Henry Will (Fig. 52), and by the user of the "Semper Eadem" touch (Fig. 92), if they were used at all after the Revolution, soon gave way to marks of quite another kind.

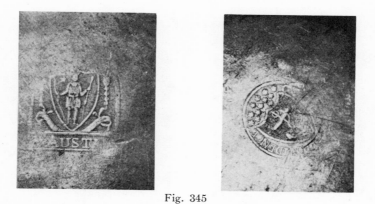

Fig. 345

COLONIAL EMBLEMS REPLACING BRITISH ON POST–REVOLUTIONARY
AMERICAN PEWTERERS' TOUCHES

Fig. 346

TYPICAL NAME-PLATE TOUCHES OF LATE EIGHTEENTH–CENTURY
AMERICAN PEWTERERS

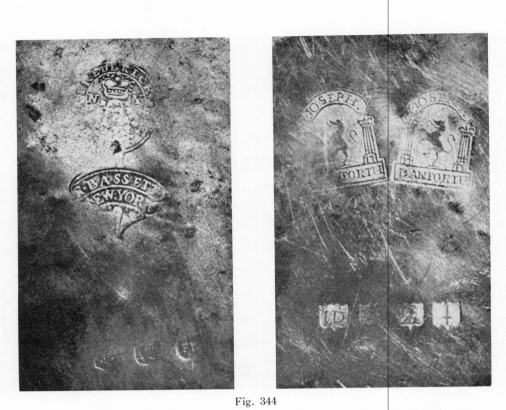

Fig. 344

ENGLISH TYPES OF MARKING USED ON EARLY AMERICAN PEWTER

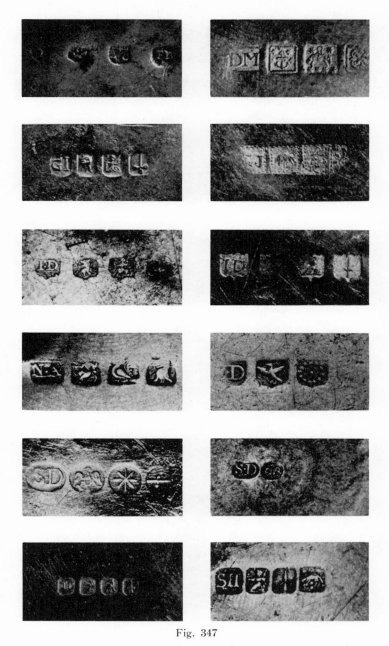

Fig. 347

**"HALL MARKS" OF THE TEN AMERICAN MAKERS WHO AFFECTED THIS
UNAUTHORIZED HABIT OF THE ENGLISH PEWTERERS**

Frederick Bassett	Daniel Melvil
Gershom Jones	Gershom Jones
Thomas Danforth (1)	Joseph Danforth
Nathaniel Austin	Edward Danforth
Samuel Danforth	Samuel Danforth
Thomas Danforth (2)	Samuel Hamlin

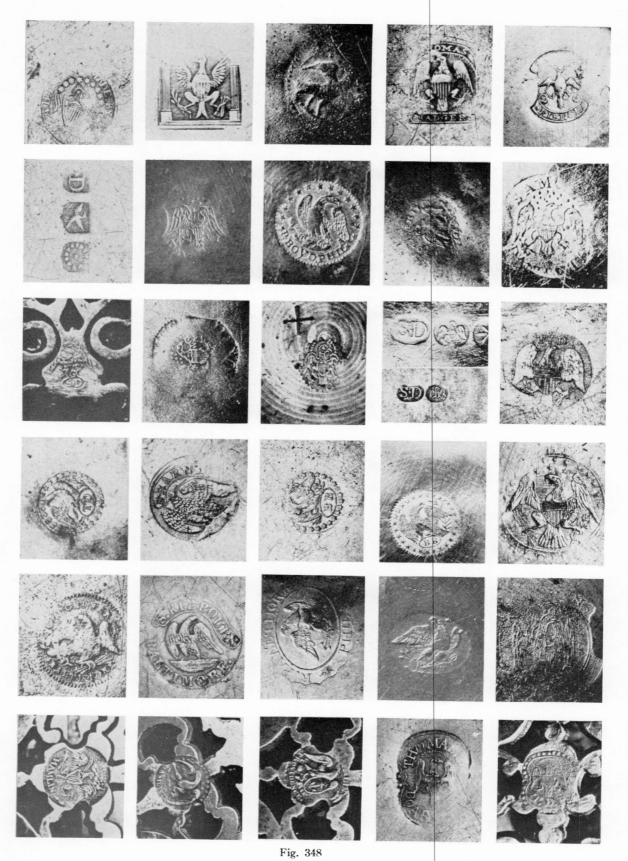

Fig. 348

THIRTY EAGLES USED BY THE EIGHT–INCH–PLATE MEN

As a rule, the marks in this second group took one or other of two forms. A few makers — those, apparently, who were quick on the trigger and of ready resource — substituted for the long-used heraldic emblems with English associations some form of colonial symbolism: as, for example, the adaptations from State coats of arms used by some of the Rhode Island and Massachusetts pewterers (Fig. 345). The majority, however, took to using a more or less ornamental, but always strongly individual type, a name-plate touch (Fig. 346); as though, having ceased to be English and not having yet become anything else, there was nothing for them to do but be individualists.

And then, with the wave of somewhat exuberant patriotism that swept the new nation as the reorganization of the powerless Confederation into the final Union began to promise a real success to the national experiment, the American eagle began to appear — modestly at first, but soon more and more boldly — as the accepted and typical basis of the American pewter mark design. From the early seventeen-nineties until the end of the eight-inch-plate era — and in the case of the transition workers, quite a bit beyond, into coffee-pot time — the eagle reigned all but supreme. The extent to which this fashion prevailed among the pewterers is evidenced by the fact that, out of twenty-three makers who worked between 1790 and 1825, fourteen "said it with eagles."

After 1825, the making of pewter (and, indeed, of pretty much everything else) rapidly ceased to be a handicraft and became a business. And the feeling engendered by this fact is swiftly reflected in the change of marking fashions among the makers of pewterware. Not only did the breed of eagles rapidly die out, but an almost standardized type of plain name, or name-and-address, punch took the place of all the earlier individualization.

The glamour — such as it was — of the old craft-consciousness had departed. It was still the part of wisdom to mark one's coffee-pots for identification. But it was a business necessity, not a personal gesture.

Turning back, now, for a moment to our approximately chronological list of the eight-inch-plate men, we find, if we look into the question, that of the eight men, out of the Revolution-spanning group of eleven, whose pewter we know, six used the English style of marks.

These were:

> Francis Bassett
> Frederick Bassett
> Thomas Danforth
> Joseph Danforth
> Gershom Jones
> Henry Will

Note, however, that Gershom Jones is known to us not only by his earlier, English style of touches, but by later designs that include both Rhode Island' arms elements and a sort of embryo American eagle.

In other words, we can see by his marks, as well as by his dates, that he was a transition worker between these two early subdivisions of the eight-inch-plate period. I cannot but remember, however, that it was several years after I had become acquainted with this maker's later marks before I found a specimen showing his pre-Revolutionary usage. And I think that this fact should give us pause in too quickly assuming that Richard Lee and William Will, both of whom undoubtedly worked before the Revolution, did not have earlier forms of marks as well as those by which, as yet, we alone know them. It is well, on such points as this, to preserve an open mind until a more exhaustive search for specimens shall justify a final decision.

In the next group, Daniel Melvil, Nathaniel Austin, and William Billings are typical users of the fancy individualistic name plate characteristic of the post-Revolutionary time. Melvil also, like Gershom Jones, was one of the prominent users of colonial symbols in his touches. As was Nathaniel Austin, if as seems likely, he turns out to be the maker of the pewter marked with the arms of Massachusetts and with the name of Austin, illustrated in Fig. 68. He is also an eagle-user in his later period, so that, like Gershom Jones, he was evidently one of those quick on the trigger in the way of adapting himself to the changing modes.

Samuel Hamlin, who also used the ornamental name-plate touch, must be spoken of at this point. He worked late — about 1824; nearer, really, to the end of the eagle period than to that of the ornamental name-plate vogue. Yet he used a touch (Fig. 163) that was altogether characteristic of the latter fashion. He is at once a convenient and a striking example of a tendency that must always be taken into account in judging dates from styles — the tendency of certain temperaments to prefer the rear-platform view of life. He was, in his way, a fancier of the antique! — so that we must not be thought to be complaining of him, or of his form of temperament. But he and his like are stumbling-blocks in the path of the lightning date-calculator. We have already met and wrestled with this puzzle in the matter of the identity and date of the maker we have elected to call Thomas Danforth (2). Thank goodness the dilemma is an Irish one, however, and only has one horn. Dead fashions may rise to haunt and puzzle us long years after we think we're through with them. But from unborn fashions we are safe until their day arrives. Richard Austin's lamb-and-dove mark (Fig. 110) may have been used by him before the Revolution, although, as yet, we have no other evidence that he worked so early. Or it may simply have been adopted by him in the seventeen-nineties because he liked it. But the American eagle had to be hatched before his version of it could get onto his pewter pieces.

And so many eagles did, eventually, get onto pewter plates that I have thought the best way to facilitate the reader's study of their types and relationship was to assemble them in something like the sequence of their original employment. This has been done in Fig. 348.

Referring, now, to this pictorial summary, it will be found that, without counting Samuel Danforth's large and small (but otherwise identical) hall-mark eagles as more than one bird; and counting as one, also, B. Barns's two versions of his smaller mark; there are here shown a total of forty-six eagle marks identified and four as yet not identified. Discarding the latter, we see that six of these forty-six come to us from the seventeen-nineties. Twenty-two of them date between 1800 and 1825. The four transition workers are responsible for nine eagle designs. And three makers of the coffee-pot period have given us four eagle marks. These figures offer an interesting commentary upon the completeness with which the impulses that led to this lavish use of

nationalistic emblems on pewterware had passed by, say, 1830. The Boardmans were the leading manufacturers of pewter and britannia between 1825
and the late eighteen-forties. They used eagle marks, in some cases at least,
as late as 1845 (see Boardman & Hall marks in Fig. 225). Yet their example
was followed by none of the opportunist dabblers in the craft that sprang up
like weeds in New York, Connecticut, and points North. J. B. Woodbury, of
Philadelphia, used the eagle rather freely during the two years he worked,
from 1837 to 1838. Roswell Gleason seems to have experimented for a moment with his one scarce eagle touch; and G. Richardson honored a few of
his finest pieces with the diminutive bird shown in the frontispiece.

Proselytes are said to be the greatest bigots. But it must be remembered,
too, that the opposite of the convert — namely, the political exile — can also
be more royalist than ever was the king in the day of his power. And so, it is
no surprise to see that out of this whole aviary of eagles, nine belong to the
four transition workers, who no doubt thus expressed their disdain for the
company they were forced to keep and the degraded age into which they had
lived their way.

We have already noted that Gershom Jones's marks, as well as his dates,
showed that he had been a transition worker between the pre- and post-
Revolutionary divisions of the eight-inch-plate period. We also noted that
Nathaniel Austin's marks thus placed him as working both before and after
the beginning of the eagle time. I now want to call attention to the early indications of the coming plain-name-plate fashion that was to supplant the
eagle type of mark and to characterize the coffee-pot period.

As early as 1807, T. Danforth (3) in Philadelphia was using a name-and-
address die in conjunction with his eagle marks (Fig. 130). B. Barns followed
the same custom in the same town a few years later (Fig. 146). R. Palethorp,
Jr., also in Philadelphia and still later on, followed suit, although he introduced a trifle more of individuality into his design (Fig. 155). These, I take it,
constitute the advance guard of the coming change.

Parks Boyd worked in Philadelphia from 1798 to 1819. He used three
touches so far discovered. Two of these are eagle marks and one (Fig. 116) is

a name-plate mark. It has, please notice, a number "1" made part of it. These numbers — presumably design or mould numbers, were later much in vogue on coffee-pots and so on. But they were then always impressed separately. I have never seen this name-plate touch of Boyd's used in conjunction with either of his eagle marks. It was, perhaps, a late touch. At any rate, it marks another step toward the new era.

It was in 1825 that Timothy Boardman & Co. became "Boardman & Co.," and ceased, for good apparently, to be run, locally, by a Boardman. The Hartford managers of the enterprise used eagle marks of the earlier type for this firm's output. After 1828, however, when the firm name changed to "Boardman & Hart," all the name-touches for the Boardman enterprises — "Boardman & Hart," "Boardman & Hall," "T.D.&S.B.," "I. Curtis" — were plain name-plate touches except the first (and exceedingly rare) circular "Boardman & Hart" mark. When eagles were used by the Boardmans after that, they were beautifully executed, but unsigned, renderings of this patriotic motif; and were, practically without exception, added to the name-plate mark used, either as a private mark or for decoration — it does not really appear which.

There is not, however, so far as I have been able to discover, any reliable guidance to be obtained from the eagle designs themselves, by which one can determine the approximate position in the eagle series of an otherwise unidentified specimen. This appears quite plainly from the fact that it would be rash to date any of the four unidentified eagles here shown by their designs alone.

With the facts just developed still fresh in our minds, I wish to call attention to Fig. 347, where all the examples, known to us so far, of the use of the so-called hall marks on American pewter are shown together for ease of comparison.

There are here, all told, twelve sets of hall marks belonging to ten American makers, and it is striking how many of the influences we have traced above are also operative in these comparatively inconspicuous little marks. Thus

Gershom Jones, it will be noticed, adopted a brand-new set of hall marks after he had abandoned his pre-Revolutionary style of touches and adopted his later, American, style of marking. In his earlier set of hall marks his initials appear in the first shield, the leopard's head in the second, the figure of Britannia in the third, and a dagger in the last. In the first of these shields, too, the "I" is used for the "J.," after the old style of lettering. In the new set we find the initials still in the first shield, but with a real "J." instead of the old "I." In the second shield the anchor and stars of the Rhode Island arms have replaced the leopard's head; and in the third the trussed sheep of the old tin-makers has replaced the figure of Britannia. Both Jones and Melvil — both Rhode Island men — use a conventionalized figure in the last shield (Melvil uses it in his larger touch also) the meaning of which escapes me. There is a striking similarity between Melvil's hall marks and this later set of Jones's.

These two are, however, the only instances of the colonial symbolism being carried into the hall marks. All three of the Danforth sets, belonging to Thomas (1), to Joseph, and to Thomas (2), use the conventional English symbols. The first two use them in identical order, also. The last reverses the leopard's head and Britannia. The inference is inescapable from a study of these hall-mark sets that less significance was attached to the symbols in these small shield marks than to those upon the larger touches used by the same maker. One would imagine that the figure of Britannia (if, indeed, the true nature of this little figurine was still held in mind by the users of it) would have been sternly banished from American ware. But not only do the early men use it, but even Nathaniel Austin retains it. And Samuel Hamlin (his retro-spective complex still active) is found flaunting Britannia in the face of his eagle-loving compatriots. It is, therefore, probably perchance that he happens to prefer the tin-men's sheep to the leopard's head. It was, we are forced to conclude, the liking for this old-time pewterers' trick of sporting a set of gold-smiths' marks on their lesser ware that induced these men to continue the practice; and most of them neither knew or cared what had once been the origin or the significance of the individual stamps. On the other hand, both

Edward and Samuel Danforth were less superficial. Each of them after his own fashion devised appropriate forms of national American symbolism to take the place of the ancient goldsmith signs.

We must own, however, in the case of these eagerly sought hall marks, no less than in that of the touches that are less strikingly associated in our minds with the earliest of pewter traditions and customs, it is unsafe to accept too uncritically indications of date at their face values. At the very least it is necessary to keep an eye out for the Hamlins.

There are, however, other and less conspicuous signs that one comes to look for and, within bounds, to rely on in these matters. For example, let me cite the placing of the dots (both on touches and in hall marks) between the names of makers, or between other words or symbols upon their mark designs. There is a striking and exceptionally clean-cut distinction in custom in this matter between the habits of the engravers of the eighteenth, and those of the nineteenth, century, roughly speaking. In the earlier period it appears to have been the almost invariable custom to place the dots, not on the line, as was done later and as we should do to-day, but about halfway between the bottom and top lines of the lettering. Examples of this can be seen in the touch marks of Francis Bassett (Figs. 44, 45, and 46), Frederick Bassett (Fig. 48), Richard Lee (Fig. 64), Joseph Belcher (Figs. 87 and 88), William Billings (Fig. 103), R.A. Boston (Fig. 112), and S.G. Boston (Fig. 114). Also in the hall marks of Thomas Danforth (1) and (2), Joseph Danforth, Nathaniel Austin, Edward Danforth, and Samuel Danforth (see Fig. 347).

On the other hand, in Frederick Bassett's touch, while the dot between the "F." and the "Bassett" is normal for the time, that between "New" and "York" is placed in the modern fashion. It is the sole example that I have noted until the mark on G. Coldwell's spoons comes along in the seventeen-nineties. The next instance is in P. Boyd's eagle marks (Figs. 117 and 118), after which, with the sole exception of Samuel Danforth's hall marks, the modern custom is always followed.

It is in small matters of this kind — unconscious followings of the customs of the day — rather than in more basic things such as designs or symbols, where personal preferences come in and are specifically indulged, that judgments as to dates may be most safely based upon the internal evidence of style in marks.

It is for this reason — to give a specific instance — that I feel more confidence in assigning the mark "——n Brigh——" (Fig. 171) to the end of the eighteenth century than I should in making any guess as to the date of one of the unidentified eagle marks already referred to. No two men arrive at their judgments in matters of this sort by identical paths of reasoning. Decisions of the kind are both complex and subtle. They do, it is true, include reasoned arguments and conscious deductions. But they also rest in part upon less-than-conscious observation and inferences that follow instinctive rather than logical paths from premise to conclusion. To these regions one can but point.

Mention has been made already of the fact that some of the American makers rather fancied the trick of using the "X" mark which, under the rules of the Pewterers' Society, was reserved for pieces containing extraordinarily fine metal. There is nothing to indicate that it was used here with any such actual significance. Indeed, while so far I have observed its use on pieces by eight, and perhaps nine, American makers, six of these are members of the Boardman family and only two of the lot — Samuel Danforth and Thomas D. Boardman — worked during the eight-inch-plate period. The list of these users is as follows:

> Boardman (Lion)
> Thomas D. Boardman
> Timothy Boardman & Co.
> T. D. & S. Boardman
> Boardman & Hall
> Boardman & Hart
> "B.&P." (If this is truly a mark of Bailey & Putnam)
> Samuel Danforth
> Thomas Wildes

This American use of an old English mark has no meaning and, even to collectors of American pewter varieties, little significance. The facts are here set down simply to make the record as complete as possible.

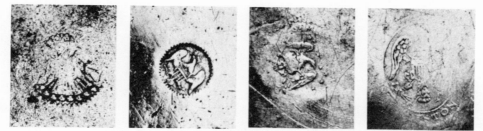

Fig. 349

FOUR UNIDENTIFIED EAGLES

Fig. 350

NINE EAGLES USED BY THE TRANSITION WORKERS

Fig. 351

FOUR EAGLES USED BY PEWTERERS OF THE COFFEE-POT ERA

Fig. 352

TYPES OF UNMARKED AMERICAN WHALE-OIL LAMPS

There is one other series of marks that should here be set down for the same reason. They have been, are, and are likely to remain for some time, a puzzle to the student of American pewter. I refer to the initial-marked porringers so frequently found in the country tributary to Boston and illustrated, with their marks, in Figs. 6 to 12 inclusive. Of these the ones marked "I.G." (Fig. 8) are by far the commonest; with those marked "S.G." letters shown reversed (Fig. 9), and those marked "W.W." (Fig. 12) about tied for second place. Those marked "R.G." (Fig. 10) are rare and, when identified, should prove valuable. The one marked "E.G." (letters shown reversed) and the one marked "C.P." (Figs. 7 and 11) are the only examples of their respective types that I have seen. Much innocent amusement is had by fitting these initials to pewterers who, for the most part, would have died of the horrors at the thought of such die-cutting. I take it, however, that all of these porringers will be collected; although I doubt if any of them, unless it be the "R.G." ones, will keep company with the recognized rarities. I have been unable to run to ground any absolute information as to these pieces.

Before concluding this survey of the classes into which American pewterers, by the types and significance of their marks, thus divide themselves, I want to call attention to the fact that the *end of the eighteenth century* does not coincide with any line of demarcation, major or minor, with which we have had to do. Of course long habit has taught us to look upon centuries as natural "antique" containers and sorting-bins. And it is difficult, at first, not to think of "eighteenth-century" and "nineteenth-century" American pewterers as a deeply meaningful differentiation between them. When, however, we stop to think of our thirty-seven eight-inch-plate men as the compact group they are — the total representation, in American pewter, of the old tradition; and when we remember that not only does this group extend almost as far this side of the century line as it does the other, and that even the minor divisions into which events separated them bear no relation to the century line; it becomes evident that, both as students and collectors, we must either learn to treat this group as an entity, or do violence to a natural, homogeneous, and highly collectible classification.

One other matter it behooves us to keep in mind. It is inevitable, the world being as it is, and the riders of hobbies being conspicuous marks for sharp-shooters, that attempts should be made to counterfeit the marks on American pewter. But the fact should not disturb us any more deeply than the fact that attempts are recurrently made to counterfeit five- and ten-dollar bills.

The only reason that any one ever is fooled by a counterfeit is that he is not sufficiently familiar with the original. And we have to do, in this American pewter-mark field, with originals as material, concrete and examinable as the five- and ten-dollar bills themselves. To the casual glance of the uninitiated, the eagle marks assembled in Fig. 348 are all "coons that look alike." To the student collector, any single one of them may well be recognizable across a room as the touch of the particular maker who used it. Yet there are pos-sibilities of familiarity undreamed of by even this knower of eagles. Pick any ex-ample from the lot and, simple as its design appears, a close study of its details will reveal idiosyncrasies, inaccuracies, divergencies from true symmetry — in short, peculiarities individual to that particular execution of that particular die that, once noted and known, can be recognized at a glance. It is only as a matter of fact, when one has been driven to an intensive study of a mark in order to be able to *know the genuine from any possible fake* that one becomes aware of these inaccuracies and peculiarities in either the design or the lettering of marks. And it is no more to be expected that the ordinary collector will master this knowledge than that the ordinary spender of five- and ten-dollar bills will become an expert on currency. But in spite of the fact that here and there one of us now and then gets taken in by a bad bill, the fact remains that the ability of the experts to distinguish these from the genuine, and to describe them and make their presence known, soon puts them out of circulation. And the same thing would prove true in the other field. Counter-feits are not identical with the originals, no matter how completely so they may appear at first sight. And there are few things better calculated to astonish one than the complete dissimilarity that a counterfeit and an original may take on for one after a few days of seeing them together when, at first meeting, they seemed utterly identical. Even in the field of American glass the attacks of the fakers have failed of success. Yet they had only the indefiniteness of type and quality, of variable form and changeable color, to reproduce. So that even the judgment of the most expert was not demonstrable. *The amateur could not be shown through a magnifying glass.* Indeed, if one but magnified sufficiently a genuine piece of Wistar glass and a fake piece, no one could tell which was which. On the other hand, if one magnifies sufficiently the right portions of a real five-dollar bill, or a real American pewter mark, and the corresponding portions of the false, the very crowd in Times Square could see the difference on the screen.

CHAPTER X

THE PEWTER LAMP

THE pewter whale-oil lamp is often pointed to with pride as the single addition made by the American pewterer to the standard products of his ancient craft.

The statement, in this form, is misleading. It suggests that the American pewterers devised the form. As a matter of fact, they merely hastened, in company with the glass-blowers, the tinsmiths, and the braziers, to exploit the opportunity offered them by the sudden popularity developed for this type of lamp about 1825.

From prehistoric times until close to the middle of the nineteenth century the type of lamp known to us as the "Roman" was in general and more or less universal use all over the world. Here in America "fat lamps" of this general type were made as late as 1848, to my knowledge. And of course the so-called "Betty" lamp was standard in the American Colonies well into the nineteenth century. Whale-oil was burned here from early times. But like all the other illuminants used, it was burned, not in closed, but in open, lamps.

Just when, or by whom, the type of lamp known to us as the "whale-oil lamp" was invented is not, I believe, definitely known. It has been said that Benjamin Franklin invented it, together with his many other inventions. Whether this is true or not, however; and whether the type was really devised and used here and there that early or not; it is quite evident to any one who has had much to do with the glass and pewter manifestations of the lamp, that the invention must have been little known and seldom applied until the second quarter of the nineteenth century. I have, I think, seen something like four or five specimens of hand-blown flint-glass lamps of this kind that might have dated from the eighteenth century. But with these few exceptions (and of course they may just as well have dated from any time before 1830), practically all the glass lamps of the American division of this type are assignable to some stage of the development of the Sandwich enterprise, or of the development of that pioneer factory's rivals and imitators.

In the matter of the pewter specimens of this vogue, the testimony is peculiarly convincing; for here we have makers' names and the dates within which many of these worked to guide us. And it is certainly strongly indicative of the late entry of the craft of pewterers into the lamp game in America to find that no single one of the twenty-eight pewterers by whom marked lamps have so far turned up, and whose dates we know, began to work before 1828; while most of them worked in the late thirties, the forties, and the early fifties.

Again it should be noted that, had the making of these lamps been a part of the pewterer's standard business during the eight-inch-plate period; and had this phase of their activities increased steadily until it took on a really important meaning for the trade during the coffee-pot era, one ought to find the transition workers fairly active in the making of these "lights." As a matter of fact, however, I have seen but one lamp by any of the Boardmans (the pair by Boardman & Hart, shown in Fig. 221). And, of course, while Boardman & Hart started in 1828, they continued in business until after 1850. William Calder is the only other member of this group who is known to have made any lamps, and of these I have seen but one, and have seen pictures of two others; all three being "courting lamps" about three and a half inches high. Calder worked about 1825.

Of the general line makers who included these lamps in their output, the following can be dated:

Roswell Gleason	1830
Henry Hopper	1842–1847
Eben Smith	1840's
T. B. M. Co.	1830's
Israel Trask	1825–1842
J. B. Woodbury	1837–1838

Among those makers who appear to have made lamps only, the following can be dated:

Brook Farm	1841–1847
Capen & Molineux	1848–1853

Morey & Ober	1852–1854
Morey & Smith	1857
Samuel Rust	1837–1842
Thomas Wildes	1832–1840
Yale & Curtis	1858–1867

Add to this the fact that no pewter lamp, marked by any maker of the eight-inch-plate period, has ever to my knowledge turned up; and I think we are warranted in coming to the conclusion that, however long before the beginning of the coffee-pot era this form of lamp may have been devised and occasionally employed, it was not until the seething interest in the development of controlled (and, a bit later, of oxygen-fed) oil lighting, came up in the thirties, forties and fifties, that the American pewterers turned to the making of what we know as "whale-oil lamps."

Mr. Arthur Hayward, in his "Colonial Lighting," illustrates a pewter lamp (Number 172 in Plate 33) of which he says: "Although very unpretentious in its general appearance, [it] is closely connected with some of the most stirring events in the history of our infant republic. This lamp was secured by Dr. Norton in the homestead of Josiah Quincy, of Braintree, now in the town of Quincy, Massachusetts, and the family tradition is that it was made in the workshop of Paul Revere at Boston. Dr. Norton therefore dates this lamp before 1770."

Now I respectfully submit that this sort of family tradition is about as worthless, as a basis for placing dates upon the articles concerned, as any other hearsay evidence that has necessarily passed through several sets of ears and mouths. I have been told in all good faith by a most respected and respectable lady that a Staffordshire plate with the "Landing of Lafayette" on it had been in her family over two hundred years!

The reasons for the unreliability of this sort of tradition are not very hidden. For one thing, stories about the weight of years have the same tendency to grow as they travel that stories about the weight of fish have. Again, articles that have been a century in one family have generally spent a good deal of time in the attic. And when we go "up attic" to identify the article that grandma used to tell us stories about when we were young, we often hit upon the wrong article. And, finally, when we are young, we seldom pay very close attention to what grandma says about the old contraptions she used to hear her own grandmother tell of. Later, when we get nearer her age, we begin to wish we'd listened a bit more carefully. And we go up attic, and pick out what we take to be that old contraption, and fit what we recall of grandma's story to what we've picked out and — lo, a family tradition is born.

To come back to Paul Revere's pewter lamp: it is one of about twenty specimens, no two alike, taken from Dr. Norton's collection. Mr. Hayward figures that "they represent, probably, more than a century and a half." This probability is figured, so far as I can gather, from indications largely of the family tradition type. I quote this, simply to show how radically it is possible for two investigators of such a subject to differ from each other in their honest conclusions. Personally I do not for a moment believe that a single American lamp in these two groups dates earlier than 1830.

In Figs. 352, 353, 354, and 355 are shown some twenty-five lamps, no two of which are quite similar. With one or two exceptions they are all unmarked. In Fig. 356 the right-hand example is by Houghton & Wallace, the name being impressed on a thin brass plate which is soldered to the bowl of the lamp. The left-hand lamp in the same picture is marked on the bottom "Patent," but without name or date. It is apparently intended to force the oil up to the wick by gravity; the long neck being pulled out when the lamp is filled, and sinking gradually as the oil is burned. It works on the same principle as the typical French lamps of the same period.

In Fig. 354 are shown five examples of the rather scarce swinging lamps, intended either to carry in the hand, like a candle, or to hang on the wall like a sconce — the saucer then becoming the reflector. These lamps are sometimes, erroneously, referred to as "ship's lamps." They would serve this purpose excellently on a ship that was guaranteed to pitch without tossing, or to toss without pitching. But (since the lamps swing but one way) they would be only halfway accommodating on the ordinary type of seagoing vessel. I have seen just one lamp that was probably an actual "ship's lamp." This was hung, like a compass, on a double swivel, so that it would swing level no matter how much you corkscrewed the support. Unfortunately I failed to take its photograph while it was in my possession.

It takes only a little study of the various lamps shown to see that the apparently endless variety afforded by the type is, in reality, made up of combinations between a comparatively small number of basic bowl, stem, and base designs. Thus, in the bowls, almost all lamps may be regarded as belonging to one or other of the following design types: the acorn, the urn, the truncated cone, the cylinder, the lemon, and what one may call the lozenge. This last refers to the design shown in Fig. 334. Naturally, these basic designs, besides appearing pure, are frequently found with added decorative mouldings and other modifications.

The marked specimens of the whale-oil lamp belong, by rights, on the collectors' shelves. They are far from plenty; and with the exception of Capen & Molineux, Roswell Gleason, and, to a less degree, Eben Smith, most of them are really rare. On the other hand, the unmarked ones, since they differ materially from the contemporary pewter lamps of France and Spain and Germany, can without fear of error be identified as of American origin. And, like the glass lamps of the same period, they make the most suitable, convenient, and attractive light standards available for many positions. The fact that the pewter alloy absorbs so much more of the light that falls on it than does any other metal that we use is what gives it, in general, the lovely softness of sheen and color that we admire in it. This attribute of the metal is particularly happy when a pewter standard is carrying for us a shaded electric bulb.

The fact that the great majority of pewter whale-oil lamps are unmarked is due, I believe, to the fact that they were made, not to be sold on the premises by the makers, as was the case with the handiwork of the earlier craftsmen; but to be wholesaled to the dealers in lamps — a breed of retailer that had not existed up to the time of the excitement over the revolution in lighting notions that swept the country between the thirties and the sixties.

Making due allowances for the differences in population and in what constituted a stampede, one imagines that the rush to get into the lamp business

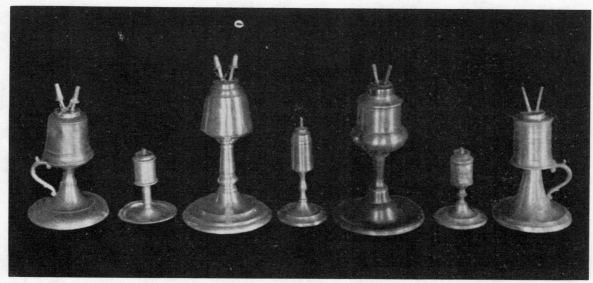

Fig. 353

TYPES OF UNMARKED AMERICAN WHALE-OIL LAMPS

Fig. 354

TYPES OF UNMARKED AMERICAN WHALE-OIL LAMPS INTENDED EITHER TO CARRY OR HANG
ON THE WALL

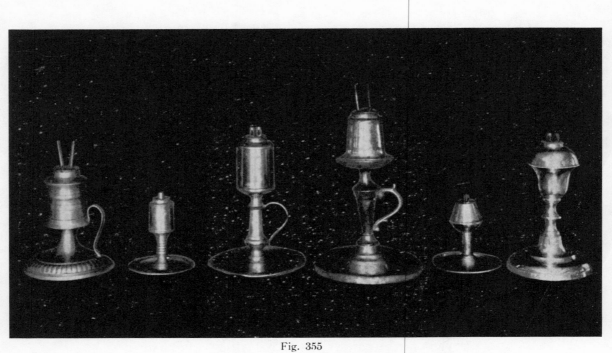

Fig. 355

TYPES OF UNMARKED AMERICAN WHALE–OIL LAMPS

Fig. 356

TYPES OF AMERICAN WHALE–OIL LAMPS, MARKED AND UNMARKED

Fig. 357

COMBINATION OF A CANDLESTICK AND A "SKIRT" OR
"PETTICOAT" LAMP, MADE BY J. B. WOODBURY

Fig. 358

PORTION OF SOUTH WALL IN AUTHOR'S PEWTER ROOM

in the eighteen-forties must have been something like the rush to get into the radio business in the nineteen-twenties. The New York directories of that decade and the next fairly bristle with such designations as "Dealer in Lamps," or merely "Lamps." There is, usually, no indication as to whether glass lamps, or pewter lamps, or what variety of lamps were dealt in; and it would seem that the fair inference is that in many, or perhaps in most cases, the dealer in question handled the various types of lamps being tried out at the moment by the experimenting public. Through the hands of these dealers, then, and in the country districts through the hands of the general-store keepers, must have passed a large proportion of the glass and pewter and tin and brass whale-oil lamps, or camphene or lard-oil lamps (the difference was more often a difference of burner than of lamp), that were sold in such quantities to the public. And since, both here and in England, it seems to have been the habit of this period to leave maker's marks off of any pewter articles such as inkwells, salt and pepper shakers, candlesticks, and, hereabouts and in France, lamps, one can only conclude that these stores were largely supplied by makers who were content to remain anonymous.

The extent of this rush into the new business is also indicated by the fact that, out of eleven New York City makers of pewter who started business there during the coffee-pot era, and who are known to us by examples of their ware, six made lamps. Moreover, four of these six seem to have made nothing but lamps; one of them made candlesticks and lamps; while the remaining one, Henry Hopper, also made pitchers.

CHAPTER XI

AND, FINALLY, BRETHREN—

I DO not suppose that Polonius really expected Laertes to follow much of the advice offered him at parting. Yet no doubt Laertes himself, difficult as it is for him, even now, not to look bored while his father is talking, would have felt cheated had he been allowed to leave without his due allowance of platitudes.

You will therefore bear with me — you will no doubt experience a certain satisfaction in the accomplishment of the expected — if I follow the traditional procedure of all writers upon pewter and tell you solemnly whether or not you ought to clean yours.

Twenty years ago the weight of expert opinion inclined toward the negative. It seems to have been felt that the dirtier a specimen was, the older it was. Perhaps the change of attitude that has recently taken place has in part been brought about by the increase in the number of "masters' bathrooms" and in part by the discoveries of the bacteriologists. It is also possible that an increased sensitiveness to beauty, and a certain alertness toward decorative values, not previously so prevalent as now, have had something to do with the change. At any rate, the weight of opinion now seems to incline toward the affirmative. Indeed, old iron candle-stands are the only things, now, that it is not thought advisable to clean. The seventeenth-century tallow in their grease cups, and the end of the burned match that has always become embedded in it, are still looked upon as too valuable proofs of age to lose — even if one risks infection.

But with pewter, one is now free to follow one's æsthetic and sanitary instincts, if any.

Remember, however, that there is no royal road to a true pewter sheen for pieces that have, through neglect or exposure, become darkened or discolored. For these a preliminary soaking in a bath of a strong solution of lye is most helpful. After this, *repeated* cleanings with some good brass polish, alternated, perhaps, with good rubbings with Bon Ami, will gradually bring the hidden surface back to light through the overlying discoloration. But this is true only of such forms of discoloration or oxidization as have not eaten into the metal itself. There is a form of oxidization that becomes known to habitual handlers of old pewter by its peculiar black color and by the *pebbled* surface that it often takes on in addition. This is said, by some authorities, to be, in effect, a "disease" of the pewter alloy itself. Which is a way of saying that this surface manifestation has really derived from a chemical deterioration of the metal, which has eaten into its surface and, in the process, has "boiled up" into a fluorescence of matter that is, so to say, the ashes of the metal thus consumed. Be the origin of this black oxide what it may, however, no amount of rubbing or home polishing will remove it. Certain treatments with acid or with oil are said to remove it; but they leave the cleaned surface of the metal looking like the surface of the moon as seen through a telescope. Buffing on a lathe, with the abrasives used by the trade, will grind this black oxide away, and also grind down the metal underneath until the eaten surface is removed. But this process leaves a hard, shiny, utterly un-pewter-like and (to a pewter-lover) unattractive surface rather less desirable, to the sensitive, than was the blackened face of the oxidized piece.

One cannot give advice in such matters. One can but place the facts on the table and explain the choices that are open.

One warning may, however, be sounded. Haste is seldom a good counselor. A buffed piece is a buffed piece forever. One cannot undo the damage — if one comes, later, to feel that it has been damage. So it is perhaps the part of wisdom not to be in a hurry to decide how one will deal with badly oxidized pieces. I would not, myself, advise taking on too many of these. On the other hand, I would advise leaving buffed specimens alone as far as possible. One of the unfortunate developments in the pewter field during the past year has been the haste made by many dealers who have had little experience with pewter and who have in consequence developed no sensitiveness toward its essentially delicate charms, to have everything that falls into their hands buffed, with the notion that they are thus "cleaning" it and improving its condition.

Marked American pieces are so rare that one pretty much has to take them as one finds them, oxidized or not, buffed or unbuffed. But, outside this one field, there is scant reason for any one's buying either pieces that suffer from black oxide, or pieces that have been "cured" of this disease by either the acid or the buffer treatment.

For my own part, I have never had a piece buffed in my life; nor treated with acid; nor dealt with in any way whatever except by the good old formula of some home polish, plus abundant "elbow grease." Of course I own a number of pieces that buffing would improve in the eyes of many. And of course I own a number of marked pieces that had been buffed before I got to them. And I own a couple of pieces that I allowed a man to have "cleaned" for me at his suggestion — only to find that his "cleaner" operated a power lathe.

Once a piece of pewter has been brought up to its natural sheen by repeated home cleanings, it needs to be rubbed up only about twice a year. In this respect the metal differs most agreeably from either silver or brass.

In the chapter on the eight-inch-plate men I made constant reference to a table of comparative rarities, to one or the other of whose four grades I assigned each of the pewterers of that period. The table is here appended. But it should, I think, be prefixed by a few words of explanation.

It is, of course, quite impossible for a student-collector to assemble, through a series of years, a sufficiently large, varied, and representative collection for a pioneer study such as this to be based upon it, without finding more or less definite convictions growing up in his mind as to the comparative rarity and desirability of the various forms assignable to the various makers represented.

Some of these convictions he could state with the utmost definiteness and defend with ease. Others he would find it difficult wholly to account for, even to himself. Which brings him (as author) up against a problem. For, manifestly, the essence of his slowly crystallized opinions, formulated under experience, would be of some value to collectors who follow him. And yet, in order to be of value, this essence must be purged of the personal equation and shown to conform to some criterion at once simple and valid.

I have, therefore, attempted to strain out the dogmatism of personal bias by the "softened focus" of four grades of approximately equal rarity. And I have chosen as the one available criterion of comparison the eight-inch plate — the one form that almost all of the makers concerned put out. In other words, I have imagined myself, or another, starting out to make a collection of the eight-inch plates made in America. And I have rated the makers of the eight-inch-plate period roughly by the difficulty that such a collector would encounter in each case — these difficulties being estimated by the number of such plates by each maker that I have come across in the past fourteen years.

In the first grade of comparative rarity I have listed those men by whom I have seen but a single such plate. In the second grade I have included the names of those makers by whom I have seen two or three such plates. In the third grade I have placed those makers by whom I have seen not to exceed ten or twelve such plates. And the rest have gone onto grade four.

The result is by no means a micrometer measurement. On the other hand, the information that it conveys is as little likely to suffer from what the time-tables call "change without notice" as may be. In two or three cases, where makers like Henry Will, Stephen Barns, and G. Lightner are already represented by nine-inch plates, but not as yet by the more usual eight-inch size, I have based their rating on what we know they made.

Here, then, is the list itself, with the alphabetical order adopted within the class limits, and with the transition workers listed separately on a *purely eight-inch plate basis:*

TABLE OF COMPARATIVE RARITIES AMONG THE EIGHT-INCH-PLATE MEN

First Grade of Rarity

Francis Bassett
——n Brigh——
Edward Danforth   D. Curtiss
C. &. J. Hera   Late I. Curtis
Richard Lee   J. Danforth
Henry Will
William Will

Second Grade of Rarity

Austin (Mass. Arms)
Stephen Barns
Frederick Bassett
Joseph Belcher
William Billings
Parks Boyd
Joseph Danforth
Will Danforth
Harbeson
Gershom Jones
S. Kilbourn

Late Boardman (Lion)
William Calder

G. Lightner
R. Palethorp, Jr.
Samuel Pierce
"Semper Eadem"
S. Stafford

Third Grade of Rarity

Nathaniel Austin
Richard Austin
Thos. D. Boardman
Samuel Danforth
Thomas Danforth (1)
Thomas Danforth (3)

Fourth Grade of Rarity

B. Barns
Thomas Badger
A. Griswold
D. Melvil

It may be interesting to state that this table is based upon a total of one hundred ninety-one eight-inch plates by thirty-five makers. Moreover, while it would be scarcely worth while to try to draw up a rating, for such makers as made them, based upon the other than eight-inch sizes of plates, both of the flat and the deep types, it may well prove interesting to students of comparative scarcity to set down here the numbers of the various sized plates by all makers that are on my lists. Here, then, is this tabulation:

Size of Plate	Total Number	Total Number Shallow Type	Total Number Deep Type	Total Number of Makers
Six-inch	6	5	1	4
Nine-inch	44	39	5	17
Ten-inch	5	3	2	3
Eleven-inch	28	4	24	14
Twelve-inch	10	10	0	9
Thirteen-inch	38	19	19	18
Fourteen-inch	1	1	0	1
Fifteen-inch	12	10	2	6

The general check list, showing all makers as yet known and all types as yet found bearing their marks, with which this chapter concludes, is so devised that it tabulates for the benefit of the student all the information of these kinds that could be gotten from this volume. It has, moreover, been so set up that new makers' names, as these are discovered, may be entered in the list by any owner of the volume. And it is both intended and hoped that each collector who is really interested in the subject of the output of the American makers will keep his copy of the list checked up to date; recording thereon not only unlisted pieces that come into his own possession, but such pieces seen by him in other collections. It is suggested also that this list may be used for a double purpose — that of a general check list, showing all known forms by all makers proved to have made them; and that of a check list of the owner's own collection. In this case the general check list might be kept up to date in black ink, while the personal list could be checked up in red. There are, naturally, many types of American pewter marked by makers to whom these types have not been credited on this list as printed. It is checked off to an overwhelming extent from my own collection alone. There are, probably, about a dozen entries that I owe to seeing in some other collection the article here checked, or to report made to me by collectors of whose accuracy I have absolute knowledge. I have, unfortunately, been too busy studying my own collection and hunting information about the makers there shown, to make as many visits as I should have liked to such collections of American pewter as exist. This check list, therefore, ought to be easily made considerably fuller. And I need scarcely say that I should greatly appreciate it if collectors who are able to add to the data here set down would share their knowledge with me and thus enable me to keep my own check list as fully informative as possible.

The list, as a glance will disclose, is so arranged that a full list of American makers as now known is made to read across a full list of American-made types as now known by me. A horizontal reading along any line will show what pieces are known, marked by the maker whose name is at the left. A perpendicular reading will show what makers are known to have made the type of piece shown at the head of the column.

The list follows. Note that in the first nine columns of this list, the letter F used as a check mark indicates a flat plate and the letter D a deep plate. In all succeeding columns, the letters used as check marks indicate the type of article to which the column is devoted.

Item	Anthony Allaire	Austin	Nathaniel Austin	Richard Austin	Babbitt, Crossman & Co.	Thomas Badger	O. & A. Bailey	Bailey & Putnam	C. Bancks	B. Barns	Stephen Barns	Francis Bassett	Frederick Bassett	S. Bast	Joseph Belcher	William Billings	James Bird	Boardman (Lion)	Henry S. Boardman	J. D. Boardman	L. Boardman	Sherman Boardman	Thomas D. Boardman	T. D. & S. Boardman	Timothy Boardman & Co.	Boardman & Co.	Boardman & Hall	Boardman & Hart
Warming pan																												
Ice pail																												
Commode form													C															
Bed pan																												
Cuspidor																												
Inkwell																			I									
Lamp							L																					L
Candlestick																												
Ladle																							L					
Spoon																												
Slop bowl																										B	B	B
Creamer																												
Sugar bowl																										S		
Tea-pot																			T				T	T		T		
Coffee-pot					P		P												P	P						P		P
Coffee-urn																											U	
Open pitcher																												O
Covered pitcher																			P	P						P	P	P
Baptismal bowl																												
Chalice																												
Flagon																			F				F	F		F		
2-in. beaker																												
3-in. beaker																								B				
4-in. beaker																			B					B	B			
Half pint mug																												
Pint mug										M	M																	M
Quart mug										M														M				
Pint tankard																												
Quart tankard										T																		
5-in. porringer															P	P						P	P	P		P		
4-in. porringer															P							P	P	P				
3-in. porringer																							P	P				
2-in. porringer																												
12-in. basin																												
10-in. basin																										B		
9-in. basin										B	B																	
8-in. basin			B	B		B				B					B								B					
7-in. basin																												
6-in. basin																						B						
15-in. plate			F	F		F							F															
14-in. plate						F	F																					
13-in. plate			F	F		F				D	D		F	F									F	D				
12-in. plate			F			F							F	F									D	F	F			
11-in. plate										D	D					D							D	F		D	F	
10-in. plate																							D			F	D	D
9-in. plate			F	F						F	F		F			D			D							F	F	D
8-in. plate		F	F	F		F				F		F	F		F	F		F	D				F			F	F	F
6-in. plate																										F	F	D

	6-in. plate	8-in. plate	9-in. plate	10-in. plate	11-in. plate	12-in. plate	13-in. plate	14-in. plate	15-in. plate	6-in. basin	7-in. basin	8-in. basin	9-in. basin	10-in. basin	12-in. basin	2-in. porringer	3-in. porringer	4-in. porringer	5-in. porringer	Quart tankard	Pint tankard	Quart mug	Pint mug	Half pint mug	4-in. beaker	3-in. beaker	2-in. beaker	Flagon	Chalice	Baptismal bowl	Covered pitcher	Open pitcher	Coffee-urn	Coffee-pot	Tea-pot	Sugar bowl	Creamer	Slop bowl	Spoon	Ladle	Candlestick	Lamp	Inkwell	Cuspidor	Bed pan	Commode form	Ice pail	Warming pan
Parks Boyd	F	F			D																		M																									
Robert Boyle	F																						M																									
Cornelius Bradford																																																
William Bradford		F																																														
——n Brigh—																																										L						
Brook Farm																																																
David S. Brooks																																																
Thomas Bumsteed																																																
William Calder	F	F		F								B		B				P	P			M	M					F														L						
Capen & Molineux																		P	P			M																				L						
Thomas Clarke																																																
Cleveland & Bros.																																																
George Coldwell																																								L								
John Comer																																							S									
Thomas Connell																																																
Crossman, West & Leonard																																O				S		B										
D. Curtis	F	F			D							B																																				
I. Curtis	F	F																																														
Curtis & Co.																																																
Edward Danforth	F	F	F	D	D																																											
J. Danforth		F	F		D																																											
Joseph Danforth	F F	F F					F																																									
Samuel Danforth	F	F	F		D	F	D			B		B										M				B								P	T					L								
Thomas Danforth (1)	F						F																																									
Thomas Danforth (2)	F	F	F		D	F							B					P				M																										
Thomas Danforth (3)	F F	F F	F F		D		D					B										M																										
Will Danforth	F F		F F		D		D							B	B																																	
T. S. Derby																																																
John Dolbear																																		P	T									C				

	R. Dunham	R. Dunham & Sons	Eastman & Co.	Simon Edgell	William L. Elsworth	Edm. Endicott	Endicott & Sumner	James Everett	Fenn	Philip Fields	Fuller & Smith	Lewis Ganty	Gerhardt & Co.	Roswell Gleason	Samuel Grame	Henry Graves	J. B. & H. Graves	Richard Graves	Andrew Green	Samuel Green	Thomas Green	Henry Grilley	Ashbil Griswold	John Halden	Franklin Hall	Hall & Boardman	Hall & Cotton	Samuel Hamlin	William Hamlin
Warming pan																													
Ice pail																													
Commode form																													
Bed pan																													
Cuspidor														C															
Inkwell									I														I						
Lamp	L				L									L													L		
Candlestick	C				C									C			C												
Ladle																													
Spoon																													
Slop bowl																													
Creamer																													
Sugar bowl																													
Tea-pot		T												T															
Coffee-pot																P							P						
Coffee-urn														U															
Open pitcher	O																												
Covered pitcher														P															
Baptismal bowl														B															
Chalice																													
Flagon	F													F															
2-in. beaker																													
3-in. beaker																							B						
4-in. beaker																													
Half pint mug																													
Pint mug										M				M															
Quart mug																												M	M
Pint tankard														T															
Quart tankard																													
5-in. porringer																													
4-in. porringer																												P	P
3-in. porringer																													
2-in. porringer																													
12-in. basin																													
10-in. basin																													
9-in. basin																													
8-in. basin																													B
7-in. basin																												B	B
6-in. basin																												D	B
15-in. plate																												D	B
14-in. plate																													
13-in. plate																				F								F	
12-in. plate											F												D					D	
11-in. plate																												D	
10-in. plate																													
9-in. plate											F									F			D						
8-in. plate																													
6-in. plate																													

	Warming pan	Ice pail	Commode form	Bed pan	Cuspidor	Inkwell	Lamp	Candlestick	Ladle	Spoon	Slop bowl	Creamer	Sugar bowl	Tea-pot	Coffee-pot	Coffee-urn	Open pitcher	Covered pitcher	Baptismal bowl	Chalice	Flagon	2-in. beaker	3-in. beaker	4-in. beaker	Half pint mug	Pint mug	Quart mug	Pint tankard	Quart tankard	5-in. porringer	4-in. porringer	3-in. porringer	2-in. porringer	12-in. basin	10-in. basin	9-in. basin	8-in. basin	7-in. basin	6-in. basin	15-in. plate	14-in. plate	13-in. plate	12-in. plate	11-in. plate	10-in. plate	9-in. plate	8-in. plate	6-in. plate
Harbeson																																												D		F	F	F
Lucius Hart																																														F	F	F
Christian Hera																																																
C. & J. Hera																																																
Christian & John Hera																																														F		
John Hera																																																
Charlotte Hero																																																
Christian Hero																																																
Christopher Hero																																																
Christiana Herroe																																																
Holmes & Sons							L								P																																	
Homans & Co		I																																														
Henry Hopper							L	C									O																															
William Horsewell																																																
Houghton & Wallace							L																																									
Edwin House																																																
M. Hyde							L																																									
Mary Jackson																																																
Daniel H. Jagger																																																
James H. Jagger																																																
Walter W. Jagger																																																
Gershom Jones																														P										D							F	
Keen																																																
Samuel Kilbourn																																			B									D			F	
Kilbourn & Porter																																										D						
William Kirby																																																

The table below lists pewterers (columns, read at the bottom) against the forms they produced (rows, read at the left). Only cells bearing a mark are shown; all other intersections are blank.

Maker	Ice pail	Lamp	Ladle	Tea-pot	Coffee-pot	Open pitcher	Covered pitcher	Chalice	Flagon	2-in. porringer	3-in. porringer	4-in. porringer	5-in. porringer	8-in. basin	8-in. plate	9-in. plate	11-in. plate	12-in. plate	13-in. plate	14-in. plate
W. W. Knight	'																			
Knowles & Ladd																				
L. Kruger			L																	
Moses Lafetra																				
Lafetra & Allaire																				
James Leddel			L											B	F					
Richard Lee (1)										P	P	P								
Richard Lee (2)																				
Leonard, Reed & Barton								C	F									F		
George Lightner														B		F				
John Lightner																	D		D	
J. D. Locke				T																
Locke & Carter																				
Bartholomew Longstreet																				
Malcolm McEwen																				
Malcolm & Duncan McEwen																				
Malcolm McEwen & Son																				
William McQuilkin				T	P	O	P													
Thaddeus Manning													P							
Marston		L																		
Marcus Maton																				
D. Melvil														B	F					F
Joshua Metzger																				
Andre Michel																				
S. Moore																				
Morey & Ober		L																		
Morey, Ober & Co.																				
Morey & Smith		L																		

	6-in. plate	8-in. plate	9-in. plate	10-in. plate	11-in. plate	12-in. plate	13-in. plate	14-in. plate	15-in. plate	6-in. basin	7-in. basin	8-in. basin	9-in. basin	10-in. basin	12-in. basin	2-in. porringer	3-in. porringer	4-in. porringer	5-in. porringer	Quart tankard	Pint tankard	Quart mug	Pint mug	Half pint mug	4-in. beaker	3-in. beaker	2-in. beaker	Flagon	Chalice	Baptismal bowl	Covered pitcher	Open pitcher	Coffee-urn	Coffee-pot	Tea-pot	Sugar bowl	Creamer	Slop bowl	Spoon	Ladle	Candlestick	Lamp	Inkwell	Cuspidor	Bed pan	Commode form	Ice pail	Warming pan
J. Munson																																		P														
Ostrander & Norris																																										L						
J. H. Palethorp																							M			B								P						L								
J. H. & Robt. Palethorp		F	F				F													T			M		B																							
Robert Palethorp, Jr.			F																																													
Palethorp & Connell																																																
C. Parker & Co.		F																																														
Robert Pearse																																							S									
Samuel Pierce							D					B										M													T													
A. Porter																																										L						
Edmund Porter (1)																																																
Edmund Porter (2)																																O																
F. Porter																																		P							C	L						
James Porter																																																
Lincoln Porter																																																
Samuel Porter																																																
Putnam																																		P								L	•					
Reed & Barton																																																
Paul Revere																													C																			
G. Richardson																															C	O		P	T	S												
George Richardson																																																
Thomas Rigden																																																
Leonard M. Rust																																																
John & Samuel Rust																																																
Samuel Rust																																										L						
Sage & Beebe																																		P	T													
Savage																																		P														
Savage & Graham																																		P														

The following table records the forms made by each manufacturer, using letter symbols entered in the grid. Items (columns) with no recorded marks are omitted.

Manufacturer	Lamp	Candlestick	Slop bowl	Tea-pot	Coffee-pot	Chalice	Flagon	3-in. beaker	4-in. beaker	13-in. plate	12-in. plate	8-in. plate
Sellew & Co.	L											F
"Semper Eadem"											F	F
Sheldon & Feltman					P		F					
Henry Shrimpton												
Samuel Simpson				T	P							
Simpson & Benham												
John Skinner												F
E. Smith	L			T	P		F					
Smith & Co.	L	C		T								
Smith & Feltman							F					
S. Stafford										D		F
William H. Starr												
S. Stedman												
Jireh Strange												
Joseph Strange												
Taunton Britannia Mfg. Co.	L	C	B			C	F		B			
Israel Trask	L				P		F					
John Trask												
Oliver Trask												
Vose & Co.												
Lester Wadsworth												
R. Wallace												
H. B. Ward & Co.					P							
James Ward												
J. Weekes		L						B				
Weekes & Co.	L	C										

Form	E. Whitehouse	George & William Wild	Thomas Wildes	George Wills	Henry Will	William Will	Lorenzo L. Williams	Richard Williams	J. B. Woodbury	Woodbury & Colton	Woodman, Cook & Co.	Charles Yale	H. Yale & Co.	W. & S. Yale	William Yale	Yale & Curtis	George Youle	George Youle & Co.	Thomas Youle	Thomas Youle & Co.	Widow Youle (of Thomas)
Warming pan						W															
Ice pail																					
Commode form																					
Bed pan																					
Cuspidor																					
Inkwell																					
Lamp		L	L							L						L					
Candlestick									C	L											
Ladle		L																			
Spoon					S																
Slop bowl													B								
Creamer							C														
Sugar bowl							S														
Tea-pot										T			T								
Coffee-pot							P			P											
Coffee-urn																					
Open pitcher																					
Covered pitcher																					
Baptismal bowl																					
Chalice																					
Flagon																					
2-in. beaker																					
3-in. beaker																					
4-in. beaker																					
Half pint mug																					
Pint mug																					
Quart mug																					
Pint tankard																					
Quart tankard					L																
5-in. porringer																					
4-in. porringer																					
3-in. porringer																					
2-in. porringer																					
12-in. basin																					
10-in. basin																					
9-in. basin																					
8-in. basin																					
7-in. basin														B								
6-in. basin				B	B																
15-in. plate																					
14-in. plate																					
13-in. plate																					
12-in. plate																					
11-in. plate												D									
10-in. plate																					
9-in. plate				F																	
8-in. plate					F																
6-in. plate																					

INDEX

oil, 187, 210; with two burners, 187; whale-oil, nowhere made but in America, 191, 192, 208; Roman, 208; "Betty," 208; whale-oil, 208-13, *see* whale-oil lamps; ship's, 211, 212; dealers in, 213.

Lathe-finishing, 195.

Lawshe, W. R., 52.

Lead in pewter, 15, 16, 99.

Lee, Richard, of Taunton, listed as pewterer, 35, 58; porringers by, 45, 83; other work of, 83; his touch, 83, 198, 203; in table of comparative rarities, 217.

Lee, Richard, of Providence, 58, 83.

Leonard, Gustavus, of the firm of Leonard, Reed & Barton, 152, 166.

Leonard, Reed & Barton, listed as pewterers, 58; the firm, 152, 166.

"Leopard's Head," heraldic emblem in marks, 190.

Lewellyn & Co., sometimes listed as pewterers, 61.

Ley men, 38, 188.

Ley metal, 16, 17, 38; marking of, early required, 188.

Liddell, James, pewterer, 35.

Lightner, George, listed as pewterer, 58; his work, 113; in table of comparative rarities, 218.

Limoges pewterers, 17.

Lion mark, 74, 75, 77, 82 *n.*, 94, 109, 110; with fleur-de-lys decorations, 76, 77; with dots, 76; with crowned rose, 77, 80, 92; Rhode Island coat of arms in, 81, 82, 90; suspended sheep in, 81, 90, 100.

"Lion Passant," heraldic emblem in marks, 190.

"Lion's Head Erased," heraldic emblem in marks, 190.

Lists: American pewterers who spanned the Revolution, 35; general list of American pewterers, 54-61; names sometimes appearing in lists of American pewterers, 61; American pewterers providing no statistical information, 62; list showing distribution of American pewterers at successive periods, 63-67; summary by cities, 63; summary by states, 70; summary by eras, 70; American pewterers of eight-inch-plate period specimens of whose work are known, 73; American pewterers of the coffee-pot period specimens of whose work are known, 151, 152; American pewterers using English style of mark, 198; lamp-makers, 209, 210; check list, 221-28. *See* Table.

Locke, J. D., listed as pewterer, 58; his name in New York City Directory, 167.

London Guild of Pewterers, 11; methods of, 80.

Machine-made and hand-wrought, 15.

Mallenson, Joseph, agent of John Caxy, 24.

Man, as a collecting animal, 1.

Manning, E. B., sometimes listed as pewterer, 61.

Mark (or Marks), of Thomas Danforth (1), 74, 75, 110, 111, 198, 202; of Thomas Danforth (2), 74, 202; lion, *see* Lion mark; of Joseph Danforth, 75, 198, 202; of Francis and Frederick Bassett, 76-79, 196, 198; of Henry Will, 80, 196, 198; of Gershom Jones, 81, 82, 94, 198, 202; of Austin, Boston, 82, 84; of Richard Lee, 83; "King's Inn," 84; of Austin, Boston, 84; of Nathaniel Austin, 86, 123, 198, 202; of William Will, 89, 124; of Daniel Melvil, 82, 90, 198, 202; of Joseph Belcher, 91; "Semper Eadem," 92, 93, 196; of Thomas Badger, 93; of Edward Danforth, 94, 202; of Samuel Pierce, 96; of William Billings, 97, 198; of George Coldwell, 98; of the Harbesons, 99; of Richard Austin, 100, 101, 196, 199; of Park Boyd, 103, 200, 201; of B. Barns, 103, 200; of Thomas Danforth (3), 103, 108-11, 123, 200; of William Danforth, 104; of C. & J. Hera, 107; of Thomas Danforth (2) and of Thomas Danforth (3), 108-11, 123; of George Lightner, 113; of Samuel Danforth, 111, 112, 123, 200, 202, 204; of B. Barnes, 115, 123; of Samuel Kilbourn, 116; of Robert Palethorp, Jr., 117, 118, 200; of Samuel Hamlin, 118, 119, 198, 199; of S. Stafford, 120; of Stephen Barns, 121; of Boardman brothers, 128, 145; of Thomas D. Boardman, 129, 204; the "X," 129, 183, 191, 204; of D. Curtiss, 132; of the more prolific makers, choice if rare, 134; of Boardman firms, 138-45, 200, 201, 204; "T.D. & S.B." 139, 145; of Roswell Gleason, 148, 200; of L. Boardman, 154; of Capen & Molineux, 156; of R. Dunham, 158; of Endicott & Sumner, 159; earliest instance of incised type, 165; of William McQuilkin, 168; of J. Munson, 169; of J. H. Palethorp, 170; of F. Porter, 172; of George Richardson, 173, 200; of Samuel Rust, 174; of Sage & Beebe, 175; of Taunton Britannia Manufacturing Company, 181; of Weekes & Co. (J. Weekes), 182; incised, of Lo-

renzo L. Williams, 184; of J. B. Woodbury, 185, 200; official and individual, 188-90; early forms of, allowed, 188, 189; on touch plates, 189; information conveyed by, 189, 190; before 1697, 190; between 1697 and 1720, 190; after 1784, 190; official heraldic emblems, 190; Continental, 190, 191; of American pewter, 191, 196-207; familiarity with, important for the collector, 195; three changes in types of, used by eight-inch-plate men, 196, 197; eagles as, 197, 199, 200; American pewterers using English style of, 198; indications of coming plain-name-plate fashion, 200, 201; the placing of dots in, 203, 204; the use of initials on porringers, 205; the counterfeiting of, 206, 207.

Marking of pewterware, origin of custom, 188; made obligatory in 1503, 188, 193; in England, 188-91, *see* Mark; on the Continent, 190, 191; in America, 191, 196-207.

Marshes & Shepherd, sometimes listed as pewterers, 61.

Massachusetts, arms of, in touch of Austin of Boston, 84, 90.

Massée, H. J. L. J., a sub-committee of one, 4; his treatise on Pewter Plate," 4; exhibition of pewter arranged by, 4; on formulæ for pewter, 16, 17; on "Sawcers," 26; his "The Pewter Collector," 96; on marking of pewter, 188; on specializing in pewter at country fairs, 194.

Massey, Robert, pewter bequeathed by, 23.

McDaniel, John S., 181.

McQuilkin, William, listed as pewterer, 58; his output, 168.

Meacham, Miss M. I., 98.

Measures, graded, in invoice of 1693, 28.

Melvil, Daniel, listed as pewterer, 35, 58; porringer by, 45; mark of, 82, 90, 198, 202; plates of, 85; date of, 90; work of, 90; in table of comparative rarities, 218.

Molineux, George, member of firm of Capen & Molineux, 156.

Montpelier pewterers, 17.

Moore, N. Hudson, her "Old Pewter, Brass, Copper, and Sheffield Plate," 52, 53, 76.

Morey, David B., of firm of Morey & Ober, 169.

Morey & Ober, listed as pewterers, 59; specialized in lamps, 169, 210.

Morey, Ober & Co., listed as pewterers, 59; specialized in lamps, 169.

Morey & Smith, listed as pewterers, 59; specialized in lamps, 169, 210.